When we, The Care Collective, published The Care Manifesto *one of our intentions was to challenge people into thinking more 'promiscuously' about the ways that they cared. By 'promiscuous' we did not mean meaningless and fleeting but instead multiplying and experimenting with caring practices beyond the shriveled forms that prevail today.* Promiscuous Infrastructures *has accepted this challenge and runs with it. Beginning its life as the activities of an interdisciplinary study group at the Willem de Kooning Academy, this project takes seriously the urgent need to imagine diverse infrastructures of care at every scale of planetary existence. Intersectional, trans-national and post-human, this book is promiscuous at the levels of both form (epistolary exchange, collage, recipes) and content (education, queer intimacies, soil). As such,* Promiscuous Infrastructures *is an impressive and significant intervention into that key political struggle that has come to define our age—the struggle for care.*

—The Care Collective, author of *The Care Manifesto*

How can we practice infrastructural care otherwise? How can we learn to resist and dismantle the institutionalization of infrastructural injustice? With care-filled precision the Promiscuous Care Study Group renders visible that the presumption of infrastructure's neutrality is a form of deep violence. Insisting that infrastructure does not only act on bodies, but that bodies act with and through infrastructure, this collection's lively thinking provides new words and new pedagogies for radically re-imagining the making and the use of infrastructures.

—Dr. Elke Krasny, author of *Living with an Infected Planet: Covid-19, Feminism, and the Global Frontline of Care*

Promiscuous Infrastructures

Edited by Michelle Teran, Marc Herbst, Vivian Sky Rehberg, Renée Turner and The Promiscuous Care Study Group

practicing care

"We were invited to bring food, tea, concerns, our bodies, our fatigue and our pains, our needs, anger, joy, refusal and differences as well as our thoughts, research and references to our meetings. [...] This acknowledgement became, in practice, a method for relating to one another: 'check ins,' where each person in the group talked about pressing thoughts or feelings, while initially a way to introduce the sessions, gradually took over and became the ground from which our conversation grew."

—Kari Robertson, from her essay *Gravity, Immunity and Soil*, p. 96

Table of Contents

Extending Conversations

How are you?

Let's have a listening round, do you want to begin?

Forward

I imagine that this *Promiscuous Infrastructures* book is like the texts from Rotterdam's Willem de Kooning Academy's holiday party where most of its authors work; or maybe it's a record from a circle of complaining colleagues, or perhaps it's the crib notes from a planned minor insurrection. Let us embrace this third possibility, though the other social scenarios are also relevant, and say that this is a book written by insiders to articulate their vision for change... to each other and to you, the promiscuously related reader.

As this book's outside editor, I say it's about "structuring care within uncaring institutions." Not living in the Netherlands and beyond the other contributors' entangled relationships, three recognitions helped me approach this book; this book was conceived and partially written through the portal of Covid, at the book's core was the collective's very social navigation of their relationships around and to their shared academic work, and this book is all about breath. This book yawns—in a particular way towards particular ends.

According to the London-based The Care Collective, "Promiscuous care means caring more and in ways that remain experimental and extensive by current standards. [...] To encourage promiscuous care means building institutions that are both capacious and agile enough to recognize and resource wider forms of care at the level of kinship." It was this experimenting with caring relations between one another and their wider situation that gives the writers their sense of purpose. And it was both the impact of Covid and the navigation of their shared institution that gave focus to the work. A gift of Covid, for those lucky enough to appreciate it, was that it helped us recognize how little time we take for ourselves and our chosen families. It highlighted how precariously we organize our work lives even if you have a solid job, and how tenuous our caring networks are. It asked us to care better. Thus, the shadow of the transformative possibilities that Covid cast are throughout this book. Possibilities that relate to the portal that so many real challenges open up for us; climate change, facism... And it demonstrates how being within and besides institutions not set up for caring can be suggestive of other ways to socially and professionally be together. Navigating these tensions highlighted by this process called for breath; for individuals to take their time, and for the collective to give each other time to pause, breathe, be with it and move through it—whatever "it" was.

Inserting printed mentions for pauses and respites, finding ways to design space for breaks, giving teachers time to teach and students time to learn towards the multiple ends that breath allows; there were at least four times our editorial conversations revolved around how to give spaces for pause within the book. So, ultimately, what this book is, is that vision, a representation of a progressive and human fabulation of an institution concretized through the breath that Covid gave its authors. The absolute radicality of a culture that allows itself (that is, for everyone, the janitors, secretaries, students, teachers, artists) the space to be human should not be underappreciated. The absolute radicality of a culture that allows itself to complain and listen when the boss, colleague, teacher or manager says otherwise, should not be underappreciated. The absolute radicality for a culture that puts care first within learning and living should not be underappreciated.

How am I doing?

I'm kind of in a liminal state.

Preface

Promiscuous Infrastructures is a reader comprising essays, visual schematics and scores, personal letters, recipes and conversations around practices of caring infrastructures and promiscuous care. It brings together more than 20 art and social practitioners, researchers and educators who, in their individual and collective practices, explore the relations between the individual, social and institutional bodies and infrastructures. This interdisciplinary publication emerges from the work of the Promiscuous Care Study Group, situated around the Willem de Kooning Academy in Rotterdam. Made up of students, teachers and researchers working within an academy of art and design, the group formed around shared sensibilities, practices and approaches that reach through and beyond our institutional roles and individual work as artists, designers, writers and educators.

The academy that hosts the group created the conditions that require it, through its felt absence of caring infrastructure. The study group operates as an interruption of institutional pacing and alienation. It is a space held for slowness, for nourishment, grief, uncertainty, for attentiveness to bodies, relations and needs. Against the dominant Dutch consensus model, the study group offers a moment where we invite different understanding to co-exist, and where consensus is not sought or desired. The design and table of contents of *Promiscuous Infrastructures* reflect this.

This reader is structured around a series of texts produced by members of the group. They are diverse in approach and subject matter, touching themes ranging from institutional change, communal responsibility and accountability practices, reparative reading, hospitality and hosting, soil and contamination, counter-histories, and collective grief. Bodies are central to many of these texts. Shared thematics manifest in a focus on reproductive labor; of cooking, gardening, stitching and weaving. Undervalued or under-represented histories and counter-histories are dug, dredged, reclaimed and examined with care. The precarious, invisible, and the peripheral are explored through witnessing bodies, intimate pedagogies and testimonial forms.

Threaded through these texts are conversations excerpts had and recorded during the Promiscuous Care Study Group sessions. Additionally, selected contributions, practices based on process, are entwined and enmeshed throughout the reader. These texts and approaches offer insights into not only the content of the sessions but the relational form we developed over many months.

The reader includes an *extending conversations* section where invited practitioners offer their insights and deepen conversations unfolding within our study group; around soil politics, mental health and collective care, generative conflict, intergenerational learning, joy and visibility, and the poetics of imagining otherwise.

Promiscuous Infrastructures bears witness to an ongoing process of care and coalition building, and offers its readers insight into questions of accountability and practices of human resistance to the demands of uncaring institutions. It situates care within a genealogy of artistic and general social practice and demonstrates how the authors actively smuggled sustained and cumulative practices of care into institutional frameworks. *Promiscuous Infrastructures* includes proposals to facilitate hosting, that acknowledge the invisible and material structures that facilitate working together, and that cultivate a different kind of being together than what institutional expediency desires.

I'm struggling with a lot of feelings at the moment about work. The place I work. Out of work.

A Non-Intro Introduction

This non-intro introduction is an interweaving of several conversations on promiscuous care infrastructure by members of the Promiscuous Care Study Group. Most of the text is comprised of minutes taken during a meeting by our study group on October 12, 2022, where those present discussed ideas for the title of this book. Not everybody was present during that meeting; there were perhaps seven present. I don't know exactly. Non-obligatory attendance was one of the group agreements established by the study group, so nobody took attendance during this particular meeting. Within this text I added snippets of conversations and other reflections from several members of the group since this October 12th meeting took place. Inspired by a suggestive provocation by cultural theorist Fred Moten,[1] I have added question marks at the end of some sentences to show that they are more tentative than declarative, imperfect and inquisitive rather than aggressively argumentative. I have used this convention to try to emulate conversations amongst the group that follow a line of generative and generous inquiry in order to bring the exchange to another level of emergent complexity. Everybody in our group had a chance to review and suggest edits to this text.

Michelle Teran, January 2024

October 12, 2022

So, let's talk about titles.

I'll begin. How about *Caring Infrastructures*? Mentally, visually, what that does for me. It really relates to how people try to build infrastructures, infrastructures emphasizing care.

I like caring infrastructures as an overarching theme and title for the book. I'm seeing these skeleton buildings that intertwine and overlap.

I don't know how to prioritize any more urgencies.

1. Jared Ware, "'A Dam Against the Motion of History—Fred Moten on Palestine & the Nation-State of Israel," Millenials Are Killing Capitalism (podcast), November 2023, https://millennialsarekilling-capitalism.libsyn.com/a-dam-against-the-motion-of-history-fred-moten-on-palestine-the-nation-state-of-israel.

I haven't let go of "promiscuity" though, a word that keeps popping up in our conversations. I don't know if I am building infrastructure? I don't know if that is the main goal in my work. I'm more into connecting and moving. I don't want to forget about movement and connections, so I wonder if we can hold on to both infrastructure and movement. I don't want to lose that. I wonder if we can hold both?

[while listening, scribbles down some words on a piece of paper]

Look here. I just wrote down the words "caring infrastructures" and "promiscuous care" alongside each other. Promiscuous care and caring infrastructures: these terms unfold in terms of practices, in the different ways that they spatially relate, the different threads and networks they suggest based on and built from practices of care.

And are we also rethinking what infrastructures are?

I don't relate so much to the word promiscuous or promiscuity. I like infrastructures more. Promiscuity for me links to...

[a second voice interrupts the first voice]

... which is exactly why I like the word. It has a very specific connotation attached to it. Promiscuity has a history of being attached to sexual behavior and sexuality.

Reclaiming and using that word as a transgressive boundary word. In my own practice, I purposely like to use erotic or sexual innuendos a lot. I think this is why I'm drawn to it.

Did you just say "transgressive boundary word?"

Yes, a boundary word, a word that provides an opportunity to transgress its normative meaning and the assumed behavior attached to it.

I also like the transgressive kind of—reclaiming the term—promiscuous, that usually has a negative misogynistic connotation to the word.

Hold on, let me look up the word promiscuous in the dictionary. I found something quite interesting. The first definition revolves around having casual sexual encounters. The second definition involves lacking standards of selection, acting without judgment, or acting indiscriminately.

That second definition is really interesting while thinking about care. Acting with care without judgment?

I was also thinking about something like a promiscuous infrastructure. What would that architecture be like? It has something to do with supporting the possibility for relation in a multifarious non-judgmental way, which I find really exciting. This I feel is like the way that we've been working together, in the study group and now in this book.

I'm just a bit afraid of our reader. Who are we talking to, and what kind of language should we use? How accessible is our language?

I relate a lot to infrastructures. And also to this second thing you said—about promiscuity, this second meaning. I really agree with you that the first thing that comes to mind is a lot of sexual relationships. I would be really confused if I would go to a bookshop or something, and find a book on promiscuous infrastructures that does not have anything to do with sex parties or dance clubs.

At the same time, I can't help but wonder what is triggered and catalyzed by bringing or placing these two words together. How does that juxtaposition generate tension? Create a transgression? Does it? Or could it potentially reanimate very oppressive systemic forces that discriminate against certain bodies within a patriarchal, capitalist, and colonial structure? Meaning, a structure that separates, alienates, disenfranchises, exploits and perpetuates othering. It could go both ways.

Yet, promising nonetheless? By taking ownership of the word promiscuous and putting it alongside the word infrastructure, this meeting can generate new meanings, and even destabilize assumptions of what is infrastructure and what is care.

So it could be very generative, this meeting of promiscuous infrastructure.

I need to meditate on the word infrastructure. It feels cold to me. I guess that if we're talking about transgression and recontextualizing words, then maybe that's good?

Cold. Infrastructure can also be evident. It can be boring. Policy, rules, steps, protocols, structure. At

I feel terrified about how people have come back to 'usual.' There is no transition.

2. Judith Butler, *What World is This?* (New York: Columbia University Press, 2022), 62.

the same time, infrastructure could come across as a very human-designed, systematic way of thinking?

IMHO, infrastructure is crucial. It's not boring at all. Cold? It's piping hot! Consider, for example, when a civic infrastructure of one set of people living under systematized forms of oppression is restricted, controlled, or outright destroyed by another. It's about controlling resources. Electrical grids go down, fuel supplies dry up, food supply chains are disrupted, borders close, military checkpoints arise, and there is limited access to basic life-supporting needs: medical aid, decent living conditions, clean water supply, daily food intake or the ability to move freely and get out of harm's way. Horrific.

It can also directly mean that care infrastructure is an infrastructure that facilitates hosting. It can suggest the invisible structures that actually facilitate working together, and for our purposes a different kind of being together?

What you just said makes me think that to live in ways, as Judith Butler offers, "for a life to be livable,"[2] what is required are mutual care structures that come down to fundamental needs of feeling supported, sheltered, even finding sanctuary in the midst of a violent, uncaring world.

But then what are infrastructures for us?

I have been thinking that if you don't have caring infrastructures in place in a work environment, a place to care besides the thought and research that we do as educators or academics, or if you are expected to care within a system that is tenuous, precarious and unsupporting, then the actually existing infrastructure will inevitably become exploitative. A toxic infrastructure even?

We speak to the institution that brought us together and its toxic infrastructure. The institution is an uncaring one. It's inhospitable in what it does to bodies, our and other bodies, whose only value is whatever can be squeezed out of them before their contracts expire, or they burn themselves out. Whichever comes first.

Sad but true. These uncaring infrastructures, which we are all entangled in, take a toll on mental and physical health, our bodies, and our energy. It reinforces competitiveness, scarcity, fragmentation, and in general, feelings of stress and being stretched to the limit. In our way of coming together, we try to develop, nourish, and foster infrastructures of care, some directly referring to the spaces of higher education and some to other institutional bodies.

There's also this kind of multi-species gesturing in the words "promiscuous" and "infrastructures", like talking about the promiscuity of molecules, promiscuity of bacteria.

Or even the promiscuity of our gardens and green spaces from where we learn and act.

Can we agree that care infrastructures are life-affirming infrastructures? That they are responses to a demand to keep and sustain life and to not fall under some abysmal necropolitical chokehold? A promiscuous infrastructure takes on this life-affirming premise that multiplies and expands to a radical interdependence that is already here, though neither acknowledged nor considered relevant by the business as usual.

Cue in the richest 1% of humanity responsible for more carbon emissions than the poorest 66%.[3]

Ideally, a collective infrastructure is a collective responsibility.

Also it builds the capacity to hold space for grief. And it serves to locate the critical and embodied tools and practices for working through and with our collective pain.

I want to offer that by collectively creating this book, we are creating a care infrastructure. Meaning that we are allowing ourselves a space to speak about sensitive issues, real situations we experienced, situations we've seen. And that we are not afraid to talk about mental health, our doubts and insecurities. As a concrete example, we could speak about our practice of checking in with each other? That checking in has become an integral part of our working together. It is because of the structures happening around us within the academy that we developed this practice as a way of carving out a space and searching for the potential cracks of instituting otherwise.

Yeah, once you start this research you realize what is missing.

How might we begin to check in with the reader? Our meetings have always been interrupted by our bodies and our bodily needs. It would be nice to replicate that somehow, to bring in that physicality into the book. Our breathing. Our breath.

3. Jonathan Watts, "Richest 1% account for more carbon emissions than poorest 66%, report says," *The Guardian*, (November 2023), December 19, 2023, https://www.theguardian.com/environment/2023/nov/20/richest-1-account-for-more-carbon-emissions-than-poorest-66-report-says.

This feeling of vulnerability, of not being in control really, but what does it mean to be in control.

So is the book a breathing document?

So are we all in agreement of the title then, *Promiscuous Infrastructures*?

Yes? If so, I would suggest that we move onto housekeeping and other agenda points.

[meeting continues for another 10 minutes]

Group Agreements

In setting up a structure of working, all 12 members of the study group have agreed to:

check in with each other

share and go deep into each other's practices

connect personal experiences to broader topics

allow space for intimate themes and discussions

make space for hormones, children, and other things

speak about mental health

bring together ideas, generate other relations

allow for emergent pedagogical forms

listen to a guest, not with the aim of mastering but rather expanding on the "subject"

And yeah, there are a range of emotions.

appreciate knowledge that you cannot access in books

use writing and transcribing as a form of listening

agree to what gets documented, what is written in
and out of any document produced by the project

be sensitive to people's energy and time

allow conflict and utilize conflict rules

try to meet in person rather than online

meet every two weeks in the afternoons

non-obligatory attendance

bring food and enjoy it

devote the last 15 minutes of each meeting to housekeeping.

Why

care?

Thread
ing
Con
versa
tions

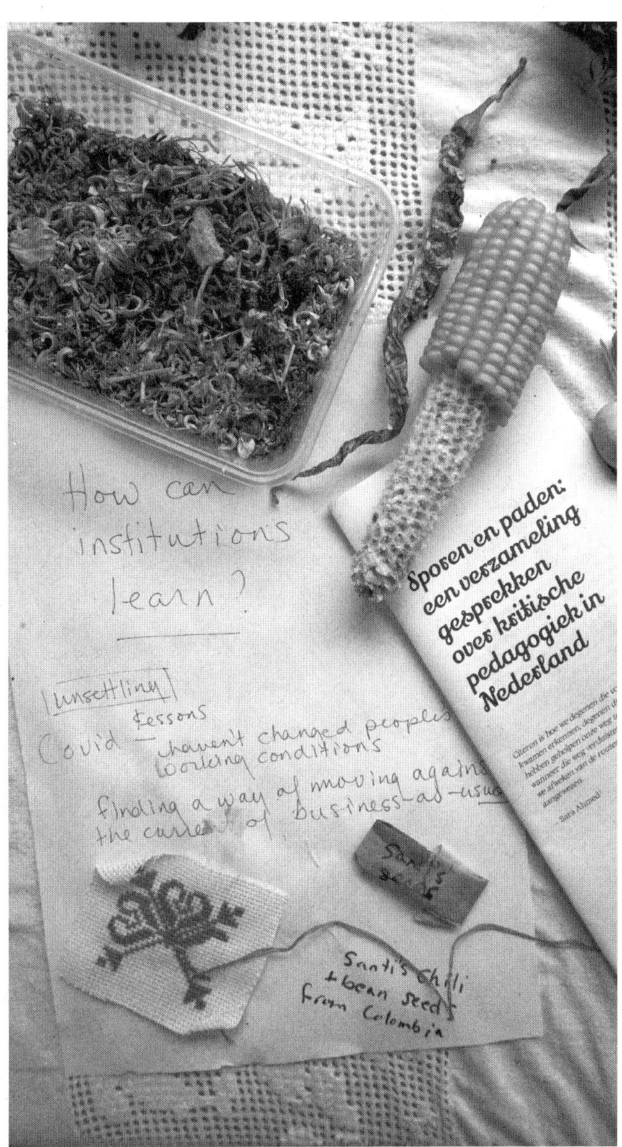

How can institutions learn? Table detail, De Zandweg allotment garden, Rotterdam South. Photographed by Michelle Teran.

Against Alienation:

promiscuous (adj.)

c. 1600, of people or things, "mingled confusedly or indiscriminately, consisting of parts or individuals grouped together without order, consisting of a disorderly mix," from Latin *promiscuus* "mixed, indiscriminate, in common, without distinction, to which all are admitted without distinction," from *pro* (see **pro-**) + *miscere* "to mix" (from PIE root ***meik-** "to mix").

Meaning "indiscriminate in sexual relations" is recorded by 1857, from **promiscuity** in the related sense, the meaning then shading into "not restricted to one individual." The Latin adjective also was used sexually, with *conubia* (of sexual union between patricians and plebeians). Related: *Promiscuously; promiscuousness.*

care (v.)

Old English carian, cearian "be anxious or solicitous; grieve; feel concern or interest," from Proto-Germanic **karo-* "lament," hence "grief, care" (source also of Old Saxon karon "to lament, to care, to sorrow, complain," Old High German *charon* "complain, lament," Gothic karon "be anxious"), said to be from PIE root **gar-* "cry out, call, scream" (source also of Irish *gairm* "shout, cry, call;" see **garrulous**).

If so, the prehistoric sense development is from "cry" to "lamentation" to "grief." A different sense evolution is represented in related Dutch *karig* "scanty, frugal," German *karg* "stingy, scanty." It is not considered to be related to Latin *cura*. Positive senses, such as "have an inclination" (1550s); "have fondness for" (1520s) seem to have developed later as mirrors to the earlier negative ones.

care (n.)

Old English *caru, cearu* "sorrow, anxiety, grief," also "burdens of mind; serious mental attention," in late Old English also "concern, anxiety caused by apprehension of evil or the weight of many burdens," from Proto-Germanic **karō* "lament; grief, care" (source also of Old Saxon *kara* "sorrow;" Old High German *chara* "wail, lament;" Gothic *kara* "sorrow, trouble, care;" German *Karfreitag* "Good Friday;" see **care** (v.)).

How am I doing?
I just have a big knot in my stomach.

Academy / Asylum

infrastructure (n.)

1887, from French *infrastructure* (1875); see **infra- + structure** (n.). The installations that form the basis for any operation or system. Originally in a military sense.

What's in a name? What's in a title? What do we mean by "Promiscuous Care"? And what is "Promiscuous Care Infrastructure"? It seems to me that the "Promiscuous Care Study Group" has undertaken, since our very first conversation in October 2021, a critical linguistic project of reframing terms—care, study, infrastructure—that have been circulating within contemporary art and art education spheres for some time, and to such a recent extent that some of us felt hesitant to gather under their aegis.[1] Care, study, and infrastructure are inescapable concerns in our shared institutional context, a public sector art academy within a larger university, both of which are buffeted by transformations that privately and publicly expose vulnerabilities, demands, expectations, trials, and errors. The purposes and agendas that regulate educational institutions don't only promote learning, they emphasize larger scale social, economic, and political interests in expansion, impact, and solvency conceived in a neoliberal capitalist sense to mitigate vulnerabilities—so to take care, but in ways that rate measurable self-initiative and self-management, for example. Hence, educational institutions inevitably reflect and reproduce societal inequalities while holding themselves accountable to market-driven conceptions of the value of learning and of work in

1. Examples abound, compare these recent and ongoing initiatives: 84 Steps at Kunstinstituut Melly, Rotterdam, (https://www.kunstinstituutmelly.nl/en/experience/29-84-steps); iLiana Fokianaki's "Bureau of Care" (http://thebureauofcare.org/) based out of Athens and Rotterdam; Jacqueline Millner's "Care Project Network" (https://www.careprojectnetwork.com/) established in Australia. See also *freethought collective*'s work on infrastructure (http://freethought-collective.net/performative-platforms/the-infrastructure-summit.html and https://www.bakonline.org/long-term-project/spectral-infrastructure/). For influence, see *freethought* members Stefano Harney and Fred Moten's *The Undercommons: Fugitive Planning & Black Study* (Chico, CA: AK Press, 2013).

the society in which they play a vital role.[2]

The (economic, managerial, curricular, social) systems and structures in which we—administrative staff, managers, policymakers, researchers, teachers, and students—all try to work with care, herd us practically and rhetorically into a solution-oriented survival mode that yields a subjective and collective compartmentalization of energies and homogenization of agencies. These systems and structures are built to discipline us toward serving a productive ideal that clashes with realities involved in art and design production and distribution in and outside of education. Given this fundamental conflict, it's no wonder that throughout our widespread and diverse community there is no dearth of differently scaled initiatives and plans to redress acute institutional needs and calls for change; this publication is evidence of just one. Our challenges, perhaps especially in an art school with a creative mandate at its core, are to resist internalizing disciplining compartmentalization and homogenization. If we can keep learning how to operate in the zones of tension between purposes and agendas, and see the abundance in those zones, perhaps we can dream up alternatives that go beyond solving institutional problems just so we can show up to work in the most profitable manner.

According to The Care Collective, responsible for *The Care Manifesto* from which we've adapted the notion of promiscuous care, "it is only by proliferating our circles of care—in the first instance by expanding our notion of kinship—that we can achieve the psychic infrastructures necessary for building a caring society that has universal care as its foundation. Diverse forms of care between all human and non-human creatures need to be recognised and valued. This is what we call 'an ethics of promiscuous care'."[3] A promiscuous care infrastructure that would reflect this ethics and "recognize our mutual interdependence and the intrinsic value of all living creatures," as well as "account for the paradoxes, ambivalences, and contradictions inherent in care and caretaking," could provide fertile grounds for the flourishing of a climate of care in an institution such as ours.[4]

Despite the upheavals of the pandemic, the situation

2. For critiques of the neoliberal university consider: Kevin M. Gannon, *Radical Hope: A Teaching Manifesto* (Morgantown WV: West Virginia University Press, 2020); Paul Ashwin, *Transforming University Education: A Manifesto* (London: Bloomsbury Academic, 2020); Stephen Cowden and Gurnam Singh, *Acts of Knowing: Critical Pedagogy In, Against, and Beyond the University* (London: Bloomsbury Academic, 2013).

3. The Care Collective, "COVID-19 Pandemic: A Crisis of Care," Verso (blog) March 26, 2020, https://www.versobooks.com/en-gb/blogs/news/4617-covid-19-pandemic-a-crisis-of-care#_edn1.

4. The Care Collective (Andreas Chatzidakis, Jamie Hakim, Jo Littler, Catherine Rottenberg, and Lynne Segal), *The Care Manifesto: The Politics of Interdependence* (London: Verso, 2020), 21.

I have a lot of feelings which are transformed into rage.

in which we find ourselves is not unique, and it is not new. Contesting rampant managerial and market logics, psychoanalyst and philosopher Cynthia Fleury considers education and health care as the "primary sites of human construction and protection."[5] In these spheres, Fleury tethers care to D.W. Winnicott's concept of "imaginative elaboration" that obliges the caregiver (educator, health-care professional, patient, student) to reinvent norms and enter into a dynamic of subjective co-creation.[6] Her position resonates with that of The Care Collective, which writes: "All education and vocational training needs to emphasise care and caretaking practices, developing the capabilities of each person to hone their caring skills, while insisting that learning is about enhancing old as well as discovering new ways to nurture life and the world—whether in the sciences, humanities, carpentry or cooking."[7]

For quite some time, I've been preoccupied with thinking through possible connections between the organization of education and health care toward human and environmental construction and protection, toward climates of care, in the art academy and the psychiatric asylum, specifically. Our university's slogan is "Overtref Jezelf," or surpass yourself.[8] It's worth asking what conception of psychic infrastructure is operative here. What is the emotional register and sensibility of such a command? What are our responsibilities to each other when surpassing the self is the goal? For whom or for what purpose am I supposed to surpass myself, at this later stage in my professional life?

It puzzles me because this exhortation to maximize and optimize is completely at odds with my decades of experience working in the psycho-social milieus of art academies, where I've found myself sometimes literally, sometimes figuratively, in the vicinity of individual and institutional madness. In every professional educational role I've had, I've encountered (and sometimes identified with) students and colleagues in economic precarity, burdened with debts, scraping by, hungry, homeless, couch surfing, selling drugs, selling sex, undocumented, and uninsured. Students and colleagues grieving, who have lost friends and family to illness, suicide, crime, or estrangement. Students

5. Cythia Fleury, *Le soin est un humanisme* (Paris: Gallimard, 2019), 12. Cynthia Fleury is Chair of Humanities and Health at the Conservatoire National des Arts et Métiers in Paris. She has piloted continuing education and exchange between health care professionals and patients in the French hospital system through the establishment of internal Research Chairs in Philosophy and Patients' Universities. On designing for care, see also Cynthia Fleury and Antoine Fenoglio, *Ce qui ne peut être volé: Charte du Verstohlen* (Paris: Gallimard, 2022).

6. Fleury citing English pediatrician and psychoanalyst, D.W. Winnicott in Fleur (n 5) 12-13.

7. The Care Collective (n 4) 63.

8. Between the delivery and editing of this text, the slogan has been voted obsolete. Thanks to Renée Turner for reminding me that the slogan has been debated in the RUAS. According to these reports, even the outgoing head of the executive board, Ron Bormans, has never been enamored of it: https://profielen.hr.nl/2022/het-einde-van-overtref-jezelf/ and https://profielen.hr.nl/2022/het-panel-de-leus-overtref-jezelf-is-dringend-aan-vervanging-toe/.

and colleagues who have been sexually assaulted, who undergo constant discrimination, who have survived and are surviving wars. Protesting students and colleagues, those with diagnosed and undiagnosed medical conditions. Addicted students and colleagues, those in physical pain and psychological anguish. Students and colleagues displaced from their homes and families, students and colleagues in recovery. I've witnessed and been subject to the deliberate flouting of rules, thefts, physical and emotional abuse, break-ins, sexual transgressions, burnouts, breakdowns, bullying, subtle and unsubtle power plays. And though I am using the subject pronoun "I" here, I am aware that I am not alone, that I am referring to a "we." Given the collective nature of education, such experiences and encounters are shared, and commonplace. They have made me doubt at times whether the academy (by which I mean higher education at large) is in need of care, or a cure.

cure (v.)

late 14c., "to restore to health or a sound state," from Old French *curer* and directly from Latin *curare* "take care of," hence, in medical language, "treat medically, cure" (see **cure** (n.1)). In reference to fish, pork, etc., "prepare for preservation by drying, salting, etc.," attested by 1743. Related: *Cured; curing*.

Most words for "cure, heal" in European languages originally applied to the person being treated but now can be used with reference to the disease. Relatively few show an ancient connection to words for "physician"; typically they are connected instead to words for "make whole" or "tend to" or even "conjurer." French guérir (with Italian guarir, Old Spanish guarir) is from a Germanic verb stem also found in in Gothic warjan, Old English wearian "ward off, prevent, defend."

cure (n.1)

c. 1300, "care, heed," from Latin *cura* "care, concern, trouble," with many figurative extensions over time such as "study; administration; office of a parish priest; a mistress," and also "means of healing, successful remedial treatment of a disease" (late 14c.), from Old Latin *coira-*, a noun of unknown origin. Meaning "medical care" is late 14c.

In February 2020, I organized a screening at the WdKA Research Station of Belgian filmmaker Jérôme le

Maire's documentary *Burning Out* (2016), which details the work pressures of employees in a surgical unit in a Parisian hospital and the managerial response of a corporate-style audit. I paired the film with the text "The Hospital is Ill," an interview with Jean Oury, a co-founder in the mid-20th century of the *Institutional Psychotherapy* reform movement so we could start to discuss, if not diagnose, some of our own institutional maladies. Oury, along with François Tosquelles, Frantz Fanon, and Félix Guattari, departed from the premise that the segregationist, carceral, and deadly psychiatric hospital model they inherited from the Second World War represented a microsociety in need of a cure, if there was any hope of caring for patients.[9] Politically informed and active, sometimes militantly so, these men associated with avant-garde artists, thinkers and writers, and mixed and mingled neurobiology, philosophy, sociology, psychoanalysis and psychology. From its very conception at Tosquelles' war-time psychiatric clinic in St Alban, Institutional Psychotherapy situated individual pathologies in the nexus of the social. The movement's goal was "disalienation." It sought to undo the social and psychic alienation denoted by the French word for an insane person: "l'aliéné." And so they invented radical clinical and infrastructural adjustments in psychiatric care in their clinics in France (St Alban, La Borde) and Algeria (Blida Psychiatric Hospital, later renamed after Frantz Fanon).

Oury saw psychiatry as an "art of sympathetic conviviality" among colleagues and patients, and one of its primary goals to improve patient experience and autonomy. Famously, at the Clinique de la Borde, Oury and his staff, including Guattari, promoted a community-managed non-hierarchical organization, interdisciplinary health care methods, modes of collective learning about psychopathologies, and a revision of the language used to describe and define them. La Borde fostered a redistribution of knowledge, skills, and power through decisions as seemingly simple as doing away with medical uniforms and devising a rotating system for completing tasks ranging from dispensing medicines to laundry. These turned out to be quite complex in practice.[10] Internal collective processes of mediation, negotiation and feedback were omnipresent in the therapeutic community. For Fanon,

9. An estimated 48,000 psychiatric patients died of starvation alone in Nazi occupied France. In parallel to Institutional Psychotherapy, Jean Oury's brother, Fernand Oury, launched an Institutional Pedagogy reform movement to address material and psycho-social needs in schools.

10. For a comprehensive introduction to the French Institutional Psychotherapy movement see Camille Robcis, *Disalienation: Politics, Philosophy, and Radical Psychiatry in Postwar France* (Chicago: University of Chicago Press, 2021).

crucially, working under French rule in Blida, Algeria at the onset of the Algerian war, in a hospital that segregated European and North African patients, the work of disalienation could not be separated from decolonization. For all involved, the work of disalienation meant foregrounding heterogeneity and differentiation against the bureaucratic uniformization of psychiatric medicine.

Oury pushed for a vigilant dissociation of a person's status, role, and function within the institution, for a revision of the sense of oneself and others, and how these senses operate in an institutional framework. I've often thought it possible to similarly claim that the art academy requires disalienation through a massive, caring and careful reform in how we conceive, organize and support education. I've wondered what imaginative elaborations such disalienation could unleash.[11] As a proof of my care for such a project, I'm keen to trace the critical historical foundations of my claim, to link Institutional Psychotherapy with interdisciplinary work in theory and in practice around critical pedagogies, for example, that's gone before ours. But it feels too risky, even irresponsible, to schematize this rich and important past and the work of revolutionary practitioners just to proceed by analogy and association rather than years of serious scholarship. I originally intended to speculate and argue for parallels between developments in critical art pedagogies and the reform of the asylum for this publication. I trained as an art historian specializing in French art and politics during and after World War II, so I'm very familiar with and still fascinated by the period in which Institutional Psychotherapy and its pendant, *Institutional Pedagogy*, emerged. I'm also invested as a French citizen in the potential they offer our fractured present. But I've worried that "just" researching and writing could be misconstrued as settling into an intellectual comfort zone and I've questioned the purposes for which I would spend time producing value in the form of research outcomes. Frankly, I asked myself: "Who cares?"

For Cynthia Fleury, "Care makes the individual capable and it must approach vulnerability from a position that doesn't see it as a deficit."[12] An individual made capable is aware of and in relation with others, as

11. cf. the work of Laurence Rassel at erg (école de recherche graphique) in Brussels. Rassel, a founding member of Constant, an interdisciplinary arts and media association, has been trained in Institutional Psychotherapy and has instituted a process of collective reform at the academy. Some of this work is outlined in *Ce que Laurence Rassel Nous Fait Faire* (Paris: Paraguay Press, 2020).

12. Cynthia Fleury, "Mot Clé," L'humanité (blog), https://www.humanite.fr/mot-cle/cynthia-fleury, March 2019.

I think we are all at the breaking point.

well as aware of and in relation with themself. For me, the practices of promiscuous care study, nestled in the pockets we've embroidered into our institutional lives, have offered indispensable, destabilizing, and affirming alternatives to the traditional outcome-driven educational modes of production that call on us to surpass ourselves. Simply checking in to share where we are in our bodies and minds as well as where we are in our work has been salutary. For here's the truth that is difficult to confess: I cannot surpass myself. While I still hold in my mind an ideal of the kind of scholarly research and writing I would like to be able to reproduce, I no longer feel capable of the undertaking. I sit uneasily with this ambivalence as I write this text. After lifelong struggles with mental health conditions, my executive cognitive functions are impaired, which in my case makes it difficult to plan and organize according to the standards of academic scholarship I learned and succeeded at, to significant cost, during graduate school. It's always been hard to modulate my feelings and manage frustrations, and it takes a lot more effort than it used to for me to focus and sustain motivation. My selective attention is affected, multi-processing or multi-tasking is draining. I am easily overstimulated to the point of total distraction. I can get so excited by my individual experiences of reading and writing and in the presence of art that I must immediately rest. I can't read a Miro board or produce an Excel spreadsheet, and I couldn't build a memory palace to save my life.

So despite my monogamous intellectual inclinations, what my disordered and disoriented mind implies for my commitment to research and writing is that I must embrace psycho-social promiscuity, in which concepts and feelings get mixed up and can lose distinction, in which the expenditures of research or spending time together might not lead to impactful outcomes or lasting connections. This is how I am capable of study. I'm still in love with the thinkers, artists, practices I encountered in my youth, still attached to ideas of social and political engagement and creative accomplishment I long to fulfill. But I've had to disentangle myself, slowly, painfully, from long-held normative ideas of myself and the loci of my professional value.

Promiscuity is tainted by its association with casual

sex, or let's be honest, with women having casual sex. But etymologically it refers to a random assortment of things, and in my second language French, *promiscuité* means the different things in this random assortment are situated in proximity to one another. Kenneth Cmiel and John Durham Peters criticize the promiscuous knowledge they see as a symptom of our digital age. They argue it "erodes firm boundaries between formally produced knowledge and that asserted by popular or outside forces," and hence it risks "mixing the serious and the fraudulent."[13] But who among us hasn't felt like a serious fraud? Undoubtedly, promiscuous knowledge undermines the authority of the traditional keepers and distributors of knowledge. But the word promiscuous is polysemous: it has multiple meanings one can adopt and employ. I choose the meaning that shares a positive connotation with heterogeneity, with the congenial co-presence of difference.

This connotation is the one that fits best with infrastructure, a singular noun whose meaning denotes a plurality of differentiated elements. It's true those elements are conceived to support a larger, or greater project, but there's no definitional reason that an infrastructural project cannot involve an ethics of promiscuous care. In my post-pandemic (primarily remote) return to institutional life, it's been necessary to enter the existing infrastructure anew, promiscuously, and with care, also for my mind's sake. From my home office, I've had to "think knowledge away from assurance" and "infrastructure away from delivery."[14] These are the words of Irit Rogoff, on behalf of the *freethought* collective, which advocates we should reconfigure educational infrastructure so we can employ everything at our disposal. We should inhabit the relations and knowledges we have access to within institutions while simultaneously activating the relations and knowledges we engage with outside of them. Doesn't this seem inevitable? And like common sense? Whether I am in or outside Rotterdam, our evolving promiscuous care infrastructure has helped me start figuring out afresh how to work, how to shift my devotions, away from existing categories and practices, away from the logics of gaining and protecting expertise and more toward the vulnerabilities involved in losing and sharing. I'm enjoying trespassing as I leave surpassing behind. And while I

13. Kenneth Cmiel and John Durham Peters, *Promiscuous Knowledge: Information, Image, and Other Truth Games in History* (Chicago: University of Chicago Press, 2020), 223-225.

14. Irit Rogoff, "Infrastructure," *Former West* keynote lecture, bak basis voor actuele kunst, March 20, 2013: https://formerwest.org/DocumentsConstellationsProspects/Contributions/Infrastructure.

do so, I'm mindful of this recollection by Jean Oury, looking back at his work at the Clinique de la Borde: "To reach the simple fact of being-here, the fact of saying 'hello', of performing a very simple diagnostic, we need to traverse an enormous complexity … to create a space is a difficult task that necessitates reconsideration of the whole apparatus—a task that is always collective, whether it is in a hospital, a 'district hospital' or a home."[15] Or in an art academy, I'd like to venture.

15. Jean Oury, Mauricio Novello and David Reggio, "Jean Oury: The Hospital is Ill," *Radical Philosophy* 143, (May/June 2007): 34, https://www.radicalphilosophy.com/interview/jean-oury-the-hospital-is-ill.

The School Where I Work Has Many Stairs

It is important for me to work collectively, both in my practice and personally.

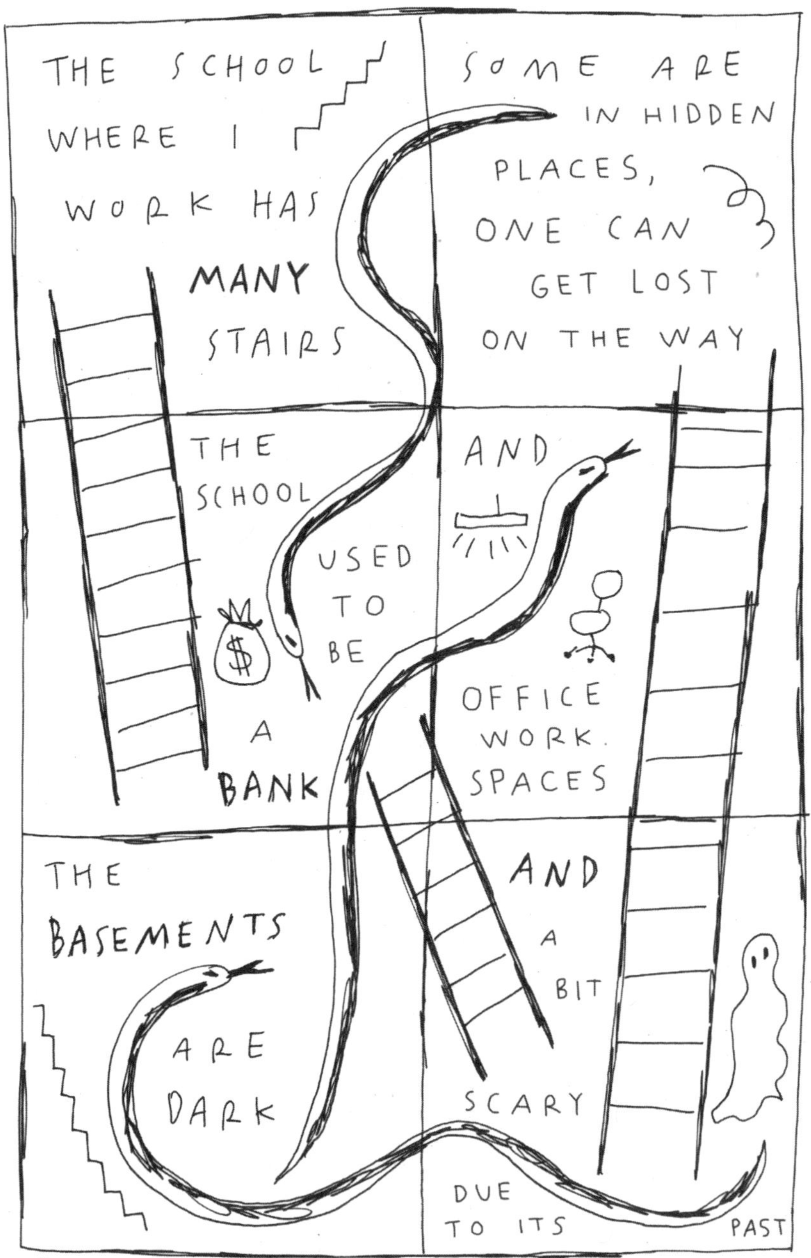
THE SCHOOL WHERE I WORK HAS
MANY STAIRS
SOME ARE IN HIDDEN PLACES,
ONE CAN GET LOST ON THE WAY
THE SCHOOL
USED TO BE
A BANK
AND
OFFICE WORK SPACES
THE BASEMENTS
ARE DARK
AND A BIT
SCARY
DUE TO ITS PAST
THE WALLS ARE NOT TO BE TOUCHED

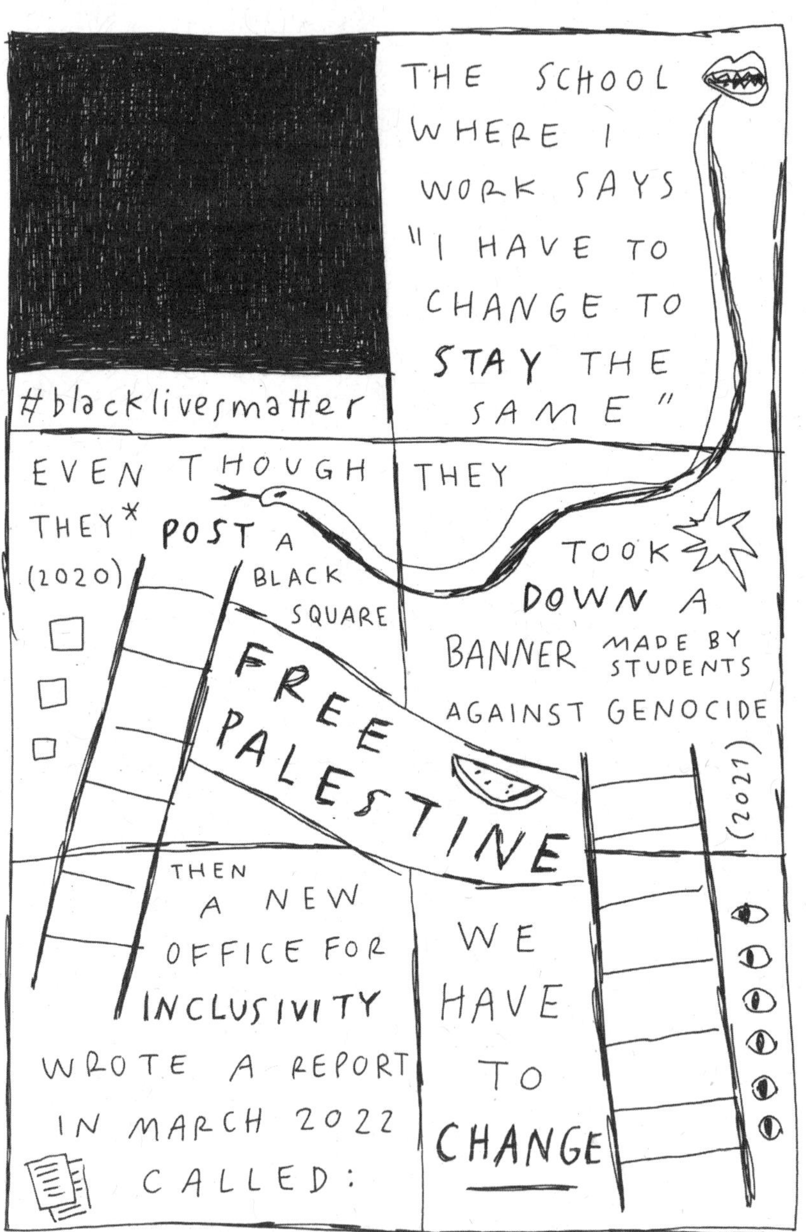

*THEY = DEAN & MANAGERS

I am finding it increasingly hard to focus on being in this pandemic moment.

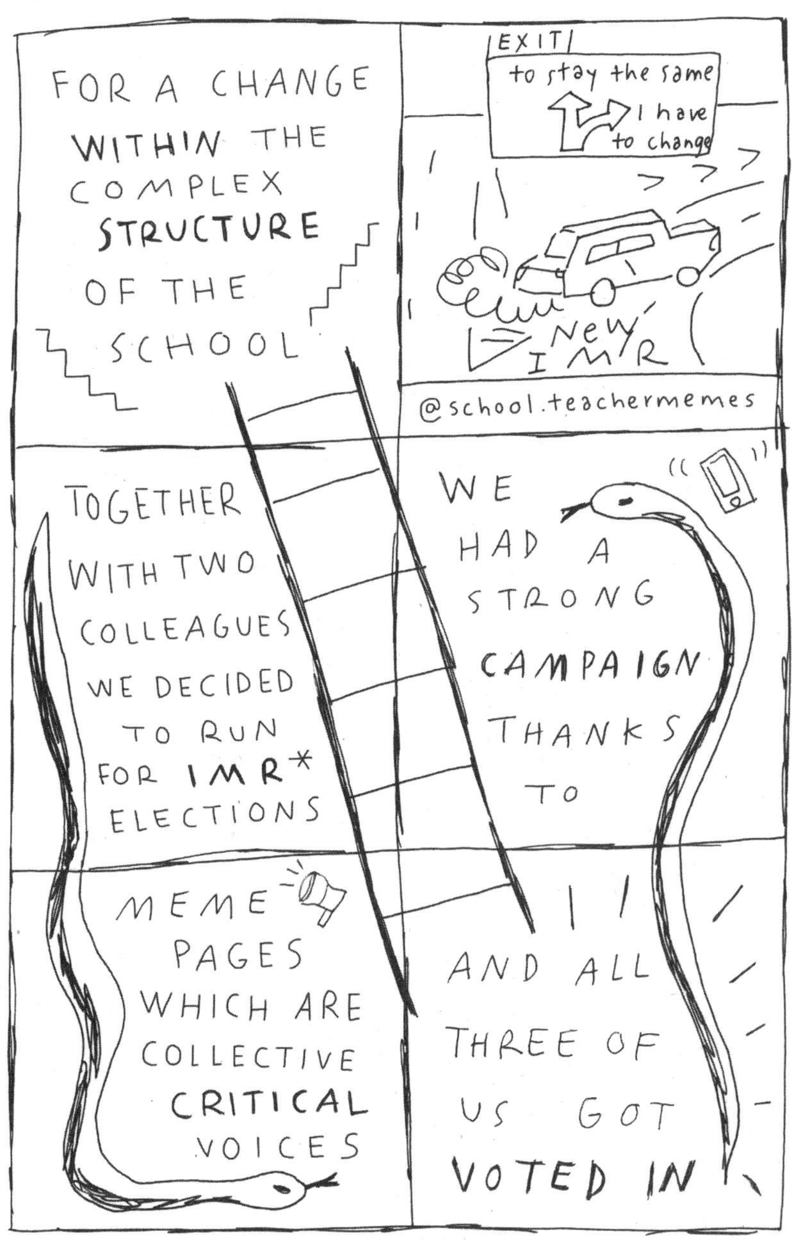

* IMR = INSTITUTE PARTICIPATION COUNCIL

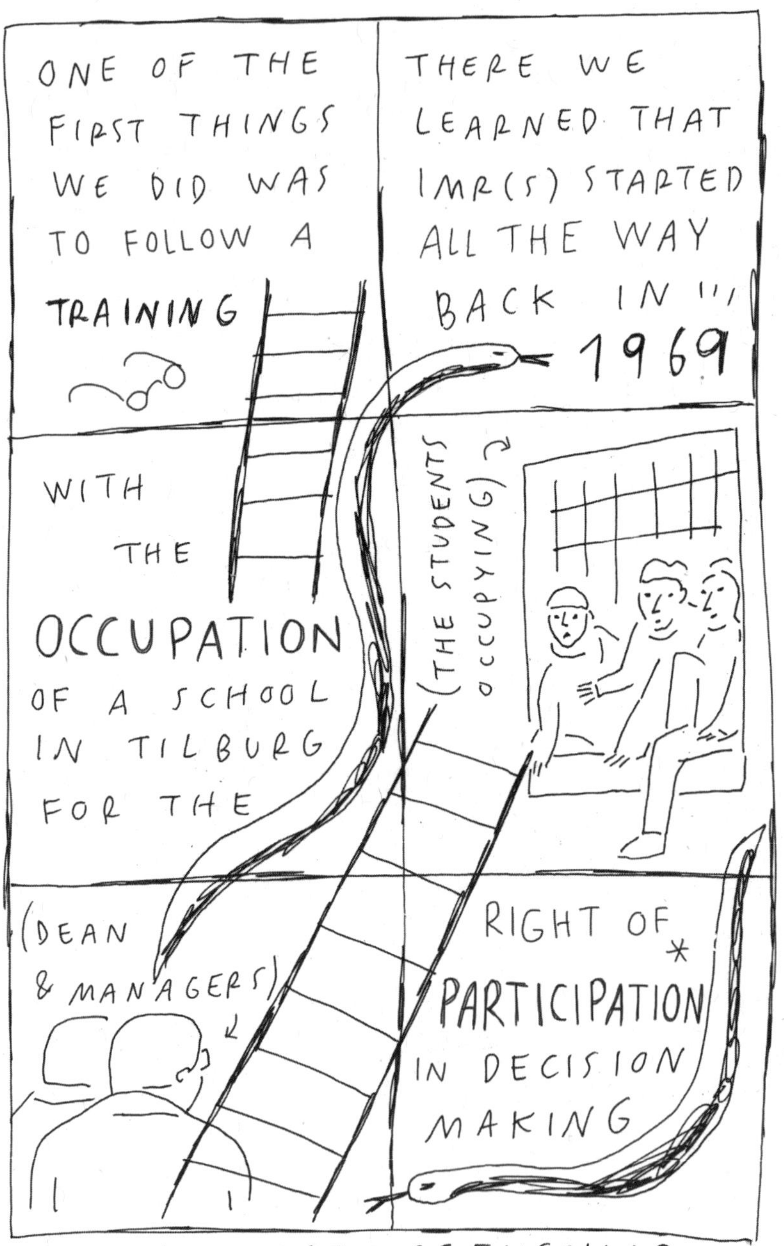

* IN NL = MEDEZEGGENSCHAP

It is hard not to be consumed by thinking about care in fractures and distant times where people seem to not care.

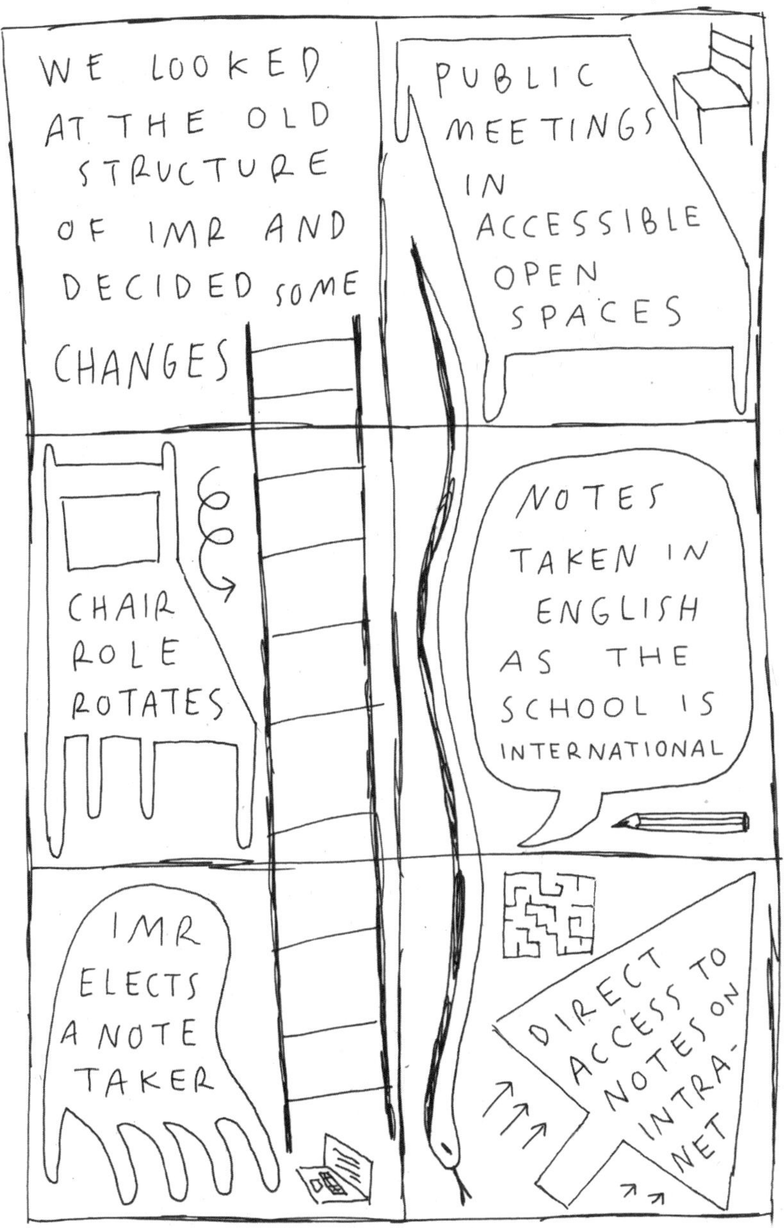
WE LOOKED AT THE OLD STRUCTURE OF IMR AND DECIDED SOME CHANGES
PUBLIC MEETINGS IN ACCESSIBLE OPEN SPACES
CHAIR ROLE ROTATES
NOTES TAKEN IN ENGLISH AS THE SCHOOL IS INTERNATIONAL
IMR ELECTS A NOTE TAKER
DIRECT ACCESS TO NOTES ON INTRA-NET

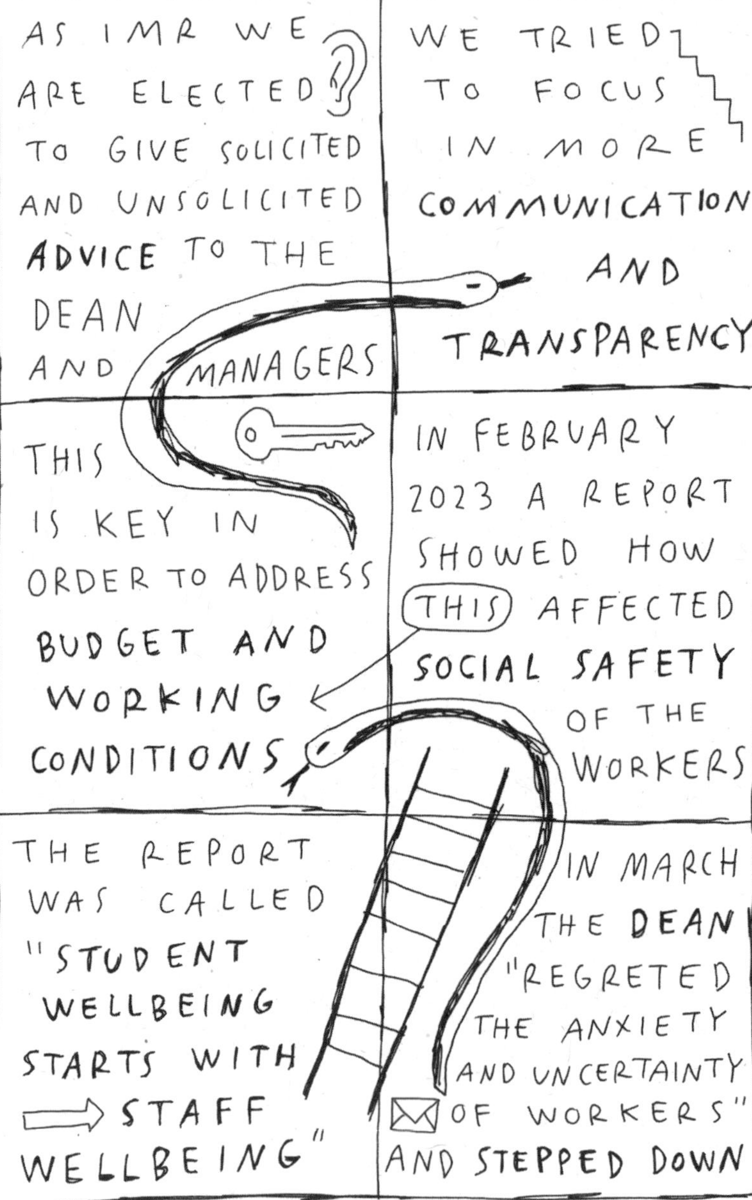
AS IMR WE ARE ELECTED TO GIVE SOLICITED AND UNSOLICITED ADVICE TO THE DEAN AND MANAGERS
WE TRIED TO FOCUS IN MORE COMMUNICATION AND TRANSPARENCY
THIS IS KEY IN ORDER TO ADDRESS BUDGET AND WORKING CONDITIONS
IN FEBRUARY 2023 A REPORT SHOWED HOW THIS AFFECTED SOCIAL SAFETY OF THE WORKERS
THE REPORT WAS CALLED "STUDENT WELLBEING STARTS WITH STAFF WELLBEING"
IN MARCH THE DEAN "REGRETED THE ANXIETY AND UNCERTAINTY OF WORKERS" AND STEPPED DOWN

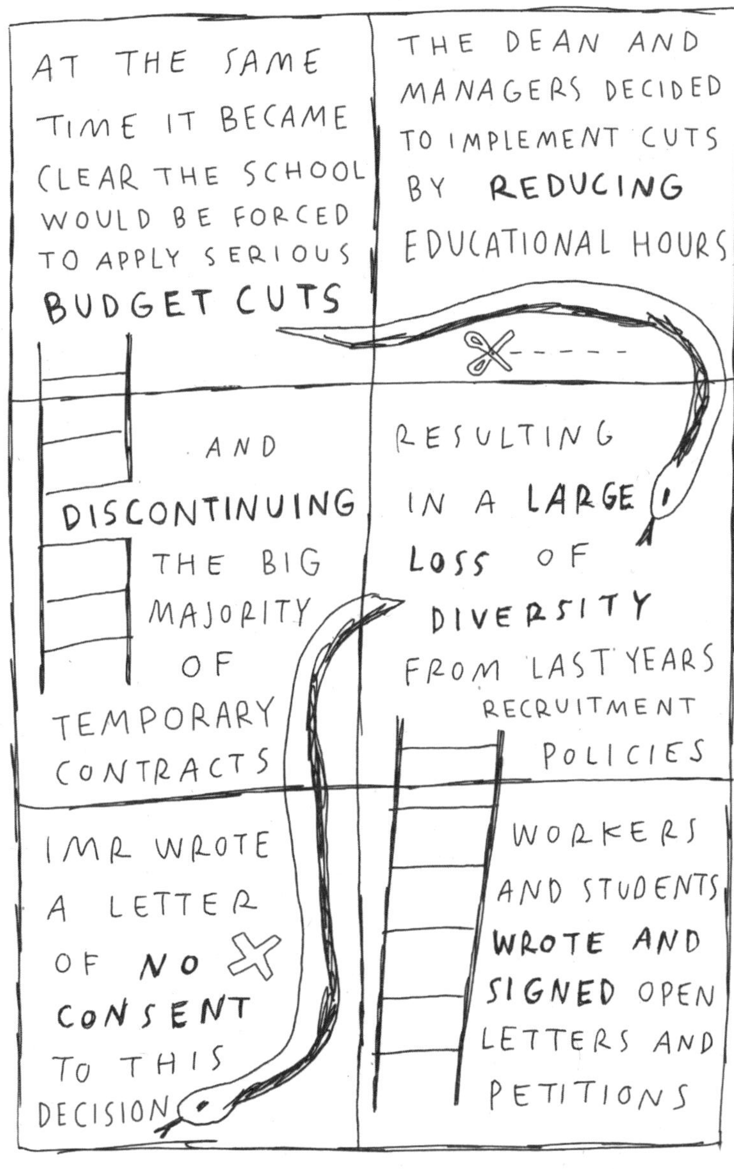
AT THE SAME TIME IT BECAME CLEAR THE SCHOOL WOULD BE FORCED TO APPLY SERIOUS BUDGET CUTS
THE DEAN AND MANAGERS DECIDED TO IMPLEMENT CUTS BY REDUCING EDUCATIONAL HOURS
AND DISCONTINUING THE BIG MAJORITY OF TEMPORARY CONTRACTS
RESULTING IN A LARGE LOSS OF DIVERSITY FROM LAST YEARS RECRUITMENT POLICIES
IMR WROTE A LETTER OF NO CONSENT TO THIS DECISION
WORKERS AND STUDENTS WROTE AND SIGNED OPEN LETTERS AND PETITIONS

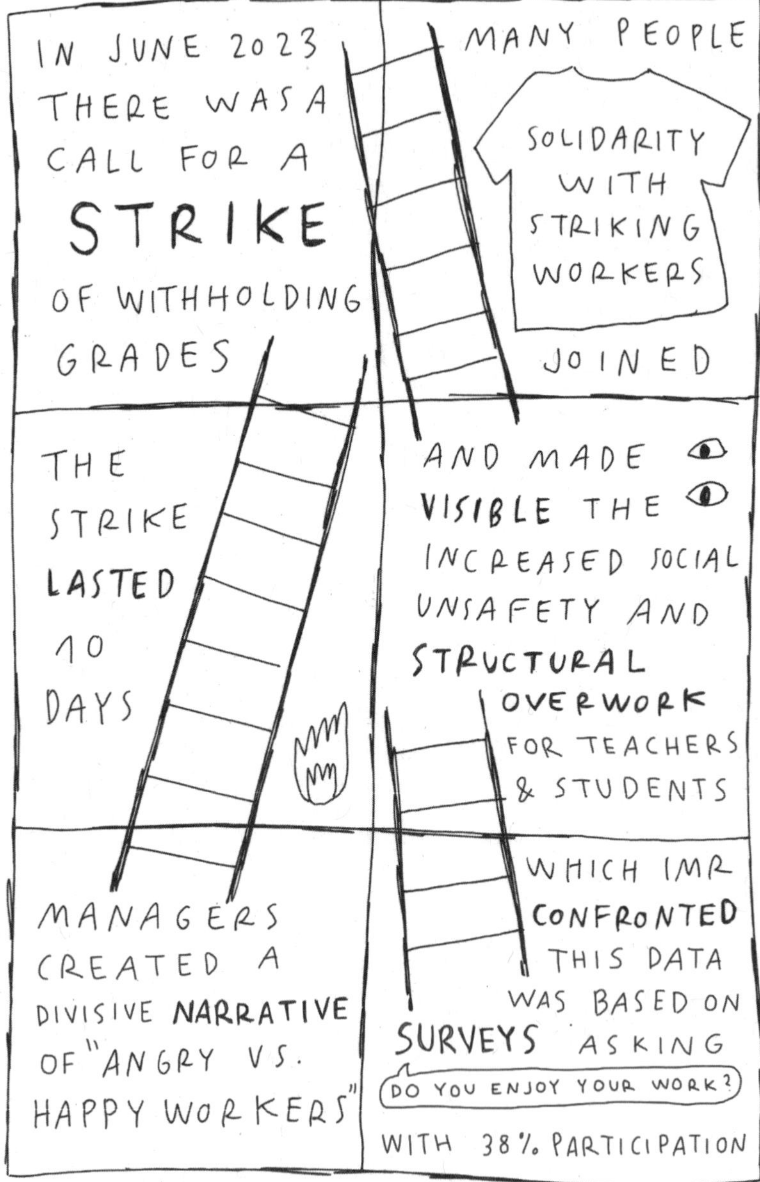
IN JUNE 2023
THERE WAS A
CALL FOR A
STRIKE
OF WITHHOLDING
GRADES
MANY PEOPLE
SOLIDARITY
WITH
STRIKING
WORKERS
JOINED
THE
STRIKE
LASTED
10
DAYS
AND MADE
VISIBLE THE
INCREASED SOCIAL
UNSAFETY AND
STRUCTURAL
OVERWORK
FOR TEACHERS
& STUDENTS
MANAGERS
CREATED A
DIVISIVE NARRATIVE
OF "ANGRY VS.
HAPPY WORKERS"
WHICH IMR
CONFRONTED
THIS DATA
WAS BASED ON
SURVEYS ASKING
DO YOU ENJOY YOUR WORK?
WITH 38% PARTICIPATION

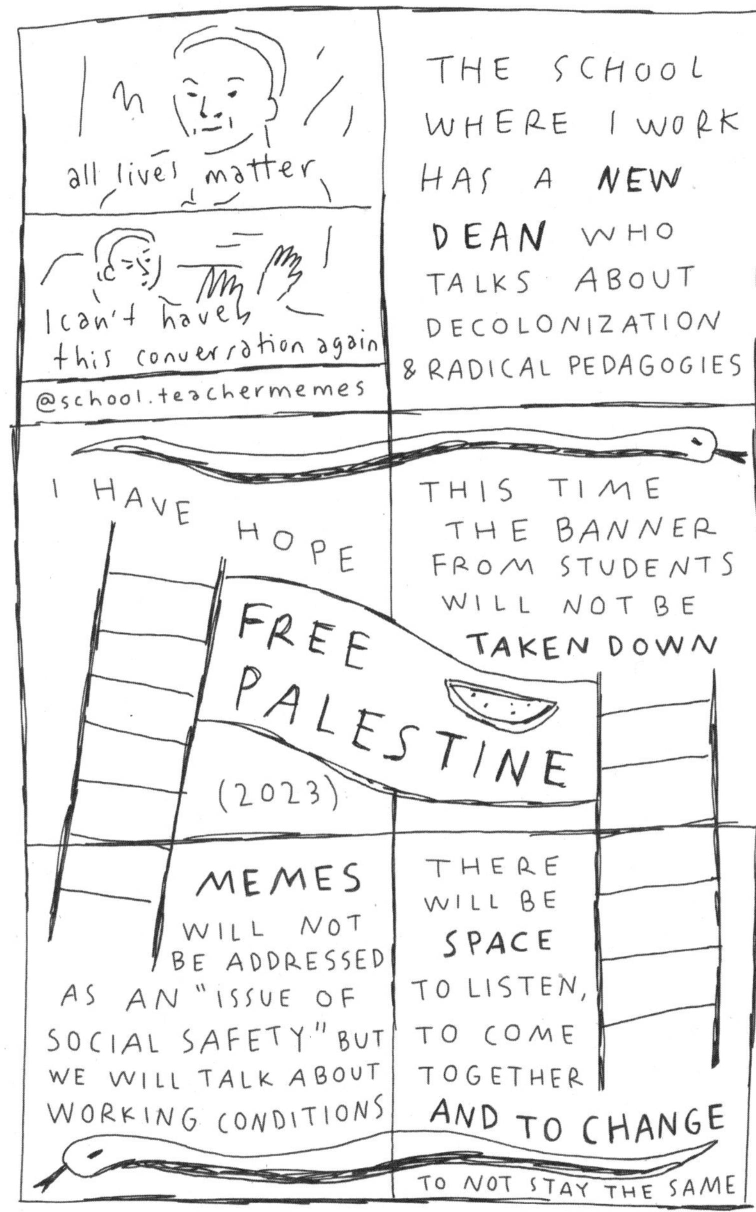
all lives matter
I can't have this conversation again
@school.teachermemes
THE SCHOOL WHERE I WORK HAS A NEW DEAN WHO TALKS ABOUT DECOLONIZATION & RADICAL PEDAGOGIES
I HAVE HOPE
THIS TIME THE BANNER FROM STUDENTS WILL NOT BE TAKEN DOWN
FREE PALESTINE
(2023)
MEMES WILL NOT BE ADDRESSED AS AN "ISSUE OF SOCIAL SAFETY" BUT WE WILL TALK ABOUT WORKING CONDITIONS
THERE WILL BE SPACE TO LISTEN, TO COME TOGETHER AND TO CHANGE
TO NOT STAY THE SAME

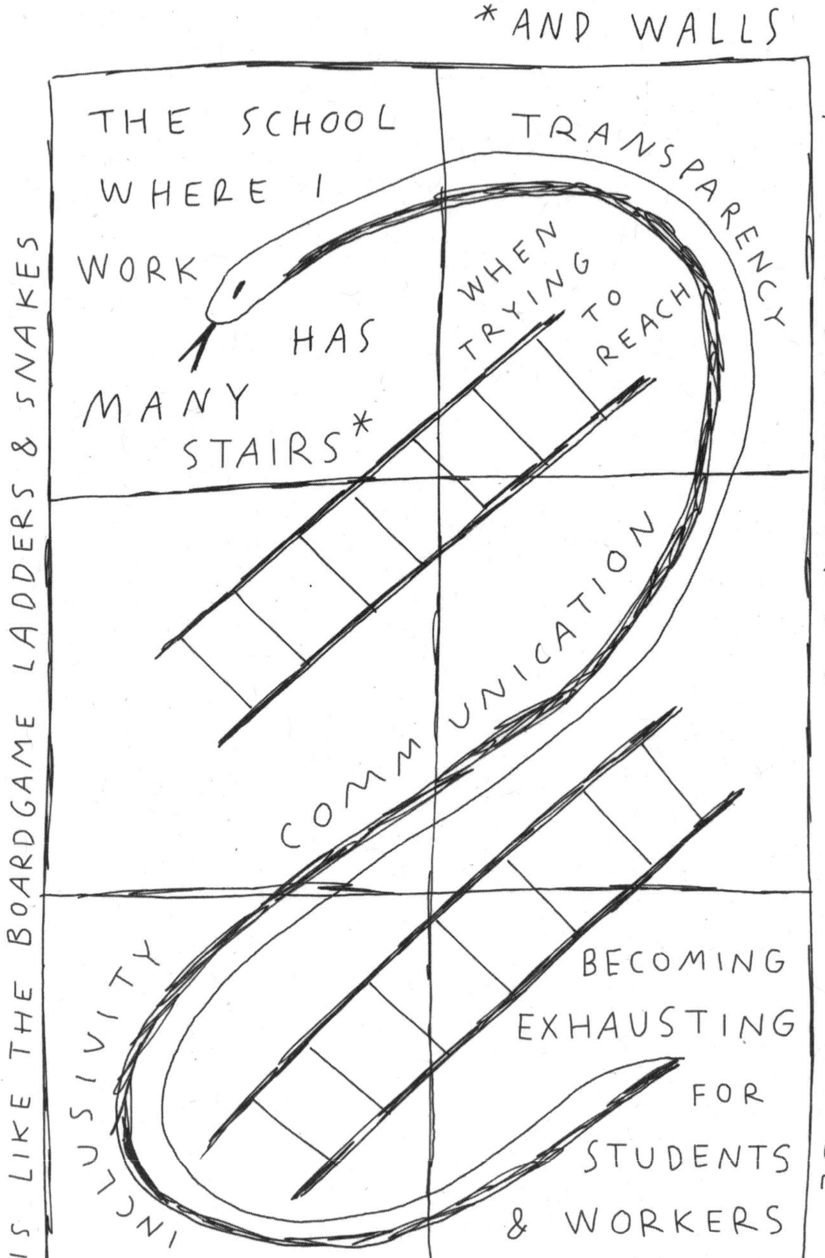

I have thought a lot about the role of rage in terms of being a constructive force.

AUTOARACHNOLOGY

INTRODUCTION: THREADS AND NODES OF FEELING, THOUGHT, AND ACTION

It matters what matters we use to think other matters with; it matters what stories we tell to tell other stories with; it matters what knots knot knots, what thoughts think thoughts, what descriptions describe descriptions, what ties tie ties. It matters what stories make worlds, what worlds make stories.

Donna Haraway, *Staying with the Trouble*[1]

During my journey as a student in a Dutch art academy, I became increasingly dissatisfied with the outlook of producing objects for an art market. The more I learned about "the artworld" and all its hypocrisies, the more I realized I didn't want to be another artist producing commodities for a privy elite and dropping them into an artworld that in the end maintains the status quo. Even though art institutions desire to be perceived as progressive and politically engaged, criticism and political perspectives are mostly concerned with representation, and institutions are seldomly willing to change the actual infrastructures.

Gradually, my interest shifted towards artistic or cultural practices that focus on building small-scale bottom-up infrastructures, learning together in horizontal ways, and employing creative strategies for political activism. I became involved in collectives, initiatives, and research groups, mostly based in and around the Willem de Kooning Academy in Rotterdam. There, we have been creating a student-led curriculum, organizing peer-to-peer feedback, reading groups, and get-togethers. The intention behind these efforts was to foster a sense of community and mutual support. The art academy is a heterogeneous place, composed of different interest groups with their own agendas and modes of doing things. Power resides in different places and is used

1. Donna Haraway, *Staying with the Trouble: Making Kin in the Chthulucene* (Durham: Duke University Press, 2016).

2. iLiana Fokianaki and Laura Raicovich, "The Role of Ideology in Institutions: iLiana Fokianaki and Laura Raicovich," E-flux podcast (podcast), February 2020, https://www.e-flux.com/podcasts/407862/the-role-of-ideology-in-institutions-iliana-fokianaki-and-laura-raicovich.pf0E4SCnY1N?si=68f14e8a5acb40a6.

3. I learned this from Michelle Teran.

The care of my family is a boundary.

to different ends. iLiana Fokianaki proposes cultural institutions as "formations of state power" that mimic the violence of the state.[2] This is made apparent for instance through the institution's actions of policing, gatekeeping, enforcing grind culture, and maintaining precarious working conditions, as well as being a key factor in organizing a cultural hegemony. In this sense, from many frustrating experiences and through accounts of others, working in this environment has taught me a lot about the workings of institutional power and its strategies. The most important lesson I learned is the relevance of finding allies across the spectrum. To not gloss over conflict but to stick with it and acknowledge difference.[3] To foster collaboration and mutual support rather than competition.

I came to understand the different projects, activities, groups, initiatives, and concrete instances as nodes in a complex, messy spider/web.[4] Tracing threads of feeling, thought, and action that interconnect these nodes, I noticed that in their own way, these projects create community in a non-oppositional fashion and smuggle[5] ways of doing things into the academy that don't fully align with what it desires. At the core of these projects is the urgency to learn from, with, and through each other, and to do so in a bottom-up way. Staying attentive and flexible to the consequences of our actions, we learn through trial and error with the knowledges present within us. Despite backlash, working this way generates a feeling of agency, joy, and de-alienation from each other, our environment, and ourselves. Trust and solidarity are important prerequisites for a feeling of collective agency and the courage to oppose unjust systems. Through these initiatives, we attempted to embody the change we wished for the academy, become each other's teachers and students, and engage in creative modes of learning that the academy doesn't otherwise provide.

The concept of autoarachnology emerged as a tool for thinking and a model for situating myself within all these entangled practices. Autoarachnology is the study of the self as a spider in a web of interrelated concerns, interests, activities, and urgencies. This self is not confined to this body, and certainly not to this mind. It emerges along the lines of an intersubjective web, through encounters with others, human, and

4. The term spider/web was coined by the studio of artist and researcher Tomás Saraceno: "According to numerous studies that have argued that the web is an extension of the spider's sensory and also cognitive systems—our approach is not to consider the web as separate to the web-building spider, but a living material assemblage we think of in terms of the conjunctive neologism: the spider/web."

Tomás Saraceno, "3-Dimensional Digital Archive of Spider/Webs," Arachnophilia (artist website), https://arachnophilia.net/scanning-the-web/.

5. Irit Rogoff, "Smuggling'—An Embodied Criticality," European Institute for Progressive Cultural Policies (website), 2006, eipcp.net/dlfiles/rogoff-smuggling.

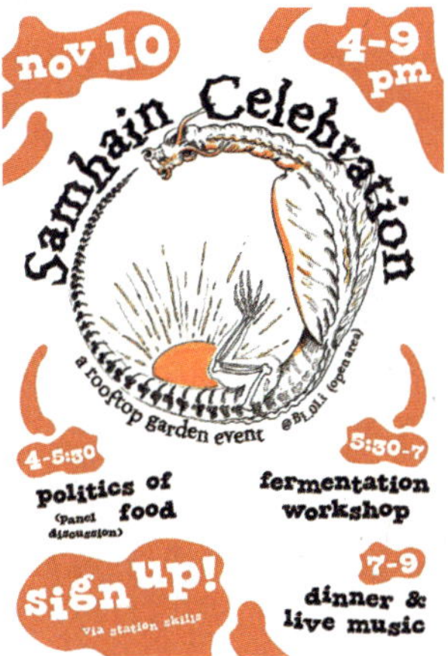

Poster designed by Juliette Douet with illustrations by Carla Arcos as part of SPIN collective, November 2022.

non-human. Autoarachnology is not about systematizing my practice, it is about embracing complexity and ambiguity. A web is not a fixed entity, it is continuously maintained and adapted. New connections are made, others severed. What works, depends on the context. After all, finding ways to navigate neoliberal infrastructures while searching for strategies of resistance and recipes for weaving, knitting, stitching, and knotting otherwise[6] webs based on solidarity, sustainability, and embeddedness in context is a process that involves experimentation.

AUTOARACHNOLOGY

> *The spider and her web are intrinsically linked. As part of her cognitive and sensory system, the web is at once the home and the extended body of the spider. Her way of sensing is a reciprocal one, along the silky strings of her web she sends out and receives vibration which traverses her body as seismic information. Spinning her silky threads, connecting, collecting pieces of information, situations, and people that stick, she weaves her interconnected habitat.*[7]

AUTO-

The Greek prefix auto- means "self."[8] In autoarachnology the auto refers to a self entangled in and constituted through its environments and experiences. Autoarachnology is not concerned with identity or the consolidated self. It understands the self as intrinsically linked to its context, constructed through its relations.[9] As carla bergman and Nick Montgomery put it "The self-enclosed individual is a fiction of Empire,[10] just like the State. 'I' am already a crowd, enmeshed in others."[11] It is also auto as in autotheory: an approach that mixes research and theory with narrative accounts of personal experience. Practicing through experience, theorizing through practice, autotheory focuses on situatedness in the world, in context. It puts emphasis on embodied experience and subjectivity and understands the dangers of pretending neutrality and objectivity.[12]

-ARACHNO-

Arachnids are mostly eight-legged invertebrate animals. Often the term refers to spiders, but the family also includes scorpions, ticks, and harvestmen.[13] The name

6. I borrowed my use of the term "otherwise" from Elizabeth Povinelli who employs it as follows: "The plane of existence is the given order of existents-as-arrangement. But every arrangement installs its own possible derangements and rearrangements. The otherwise is these immanent derangements and rearrangements." Zoénie Liwen Deng elaborates: '[...] I prefer 'otherwise' than 'alternative', since the latter already assumes the binary of "norm vs. the alternative."'
Elizabeth Povinelli, "Geontologies of the Otherwise," *Society for Cultural Anthropology* (January 13, 2014), https://culanth.org/fieldsights/geontologies-of-the-otherwise.
Zoénie Liwen Deng and Elaine W. Ho. "Strolling South: Reflecting on Our Institutionalisations & Otherwise Collectivity," in *Art for (and within) a Citizen Scene: A Look at Art Primarily Active in the Context of Daily Practices*, eds. Iris Ferrer, Emily Shin-Jie Lee, reinaart vanhoe, and Julia Wilhelm (Eindhoven: Onomatopee, 2022).

7. Text written by me (Julia Wilhelm) for the first iteration of Autoarachnology (January 2022).
Information on Spider/webs from: Tomás Saraceno (n 4).
Tomás Saraceno, "Vibrating with the Web," Arachnophilia (artist website), accessed May 28, 2022, https://arachnophilia.net/sonifying-the-web/.

8. "Auto" definition on Etymonline (website), accessed May 16, 2022, https://www.etymonline.com/search?q=auto-&ref=searchbar_searchhint.

can be traced back to Arachne, a mythological figure mentioned by the Roman poet Ovid. Arachne was famous for being extremely skilled at weaving. Disguised as an old woman, the goddess Athena visits her. When Arachne refuses to acknowledge she learned the skill of weaving from Athena herself, the goddess challenges her into a weaving contest. Athena's web depicts herself as a glorious heroïne and includes examples of how mortals who challenge the gods are punished, while Arachne represents scenes of mortals being harassed by gods. Athena reads Arachne's tapestry as an insult and is enraged by the skillfulness and quality of Arachne's weaving. The goddess punishes Arachne by destroying her work and beating her, which shames the mortal to the point of hanging herself. The goddess, feeling pity at this sight, decides to save Arachne's life by transforming her into a spider.[14]

In antiquity, weaving was a female-connotated activity and constituted one of the few means of artistic expression available to women.[15] It was also a common metaphor for writing and poetry. The word 'text' is derived from Latin 'texere' which means weaving.[16] Thoughts were understood as threads that the writer weaves.[17] The arts of entangling strings: weaving, knitting, crocheting, and embroidering, were considered female domestic duties in Europe long into the 20th century. Like most other tasks women performed in the house, these activities were not considered labor, thus not remunerated with a wage, which resulted in dependency on male family members. It formed part of the ongoing process of primitive accumulation: the theft of labor and land and the resulting wealth imbalance necessary to establish capitalist relations.[18] Along with the devaluation of women came the devaluation of their skills and knowledges, such as the textile crafts. But what if these strings and all the different techniques of looping and knotting them can become vehicles for thinking otherwise, for telling otherwise narratives? For weaving Donna Haraway's net bags that contain stories without masculinist heroes? Stories that focus on gathering and connecting, on allowing things to exist alongside each other, without imposing a hierarchy?

-LOGY

-logy is a Greek suffix that means "the study of." A relative of *logos* "word, speech, statement, discourse"

9. Haraway (n 1).

10. The term "Empire" is used by Michael Hardt and Antonio Negri in their book *Empire* (Cambridge: Harvard University Press, 2000) to describe postmodern Imperialism. In *Joyful Militancy* carla bergman and Nick Montgomery specify: "We use 'Empire' to name the organized destruction under which we live. Through its attempt to render everything profitable and controllable, Empire administers a war with other forms of life. [...] Prisons and cops lurk alongside discourses of inclusion and tolerance. Empire works to monopolize the whole field of life, crushing autonomy and inducing dependence." In carla bergman and Nick Montgomery, *Joyful Militancy: Building Thriving Resistance in Toxic Times* (Oakland: AK Press, 2017), 18.

11. Ibid 10.

12. Arianne Zwartjes, "Autotheory as Rebellion: On Research, Embodiment, and Imagination in Creative Nonfiction," *Michigan Quarterly Review* (July 2019), https://sites.lsa.umich.edu/mqr/2019/07/autotheory-as-rebellion-on-research-embodiment-and-imagination-in-creative-nonfiction/.

13. "Arachnid" definition on Wikipedia, Accessed May 16, 2022, https://en.wikipedia.org/wiki/Arachnid.

14. Ovid, *Metamorphoses: Book IV*, trans. A. S. Kline (Poetry in Translation, 2020).

it is specifically linked to spoken language. The word probably stems from PIE (Proto-Indo-European) leg-, which means "to gather, to collect."[19] Autoarachnology conceptualizes not only artistic or cultural practices, but also subjectivities as enmeshed, as leaking out of the boundaries of your/my/our skin, extending into an intersubjective web. Becoming a spider, following the threads, can help to understand and make explicit, while focusing on a specific aspect, and tracing its path through my experiences and influences, weaving them together into a tentative grasp.

ABOUT THE THREADS

Webs are built up of strings and threads: relations. It is the threads that make up the nodes, that keep the web afloat, that make sure the tension is right, so the web can serve as the spider's instrument. She stretches one of her long, hairy feet. Gently plucks the thread closest to her. Senses how the vibration traverses the thread, branches off into others, diverges into more. The spider stays alert, attunes her seismic sensibility to the signals traveling back to her. She gathers information about the length, weight, degree of entanglement, thickness, and flexibility of her threads. The threads are her context and sticky archive. Their adhesive surface holds traces of the genetic material of everything it ever touched. Vibratory signals always travel through this amalgamation of information; the intensities and rhythms of the present are perceived through the sediments of the past.[20]

Just like the spider's threads, her words have a history. They have their own baggage, contexts, and etymological specificities. They were spoken by many different tongues, in many different contexts, connoting and conjuring different concepts, situations, and affects. Some can be traced back to other writers and thinkers, all of them are composed somewhere along the lines of intersubjective knowledges, emerged in conversations, through activities; none are isolated. In her web, the spider describes, rather than defines, specific and situated meanings of these words. Through carefully interlacing threads, the spider asks: "Can art, at least to some extent, resist its commodification?" "Can it be a tool for political change?" Even though there are different, interlaced,

15. Latin 251 Class of Colby College 2022, "Weaving and Writing: Censorship in Arachne," in *Ovid and the Censored Voice*, ed. Kerill O'Neill (college classroom blog) 2022, https://web.colby.edu/ovid-censorship/censorship-in-ovids-myths/weaving-and-writing-censorship-in-arachne.

16. "Text (n.)" definition on Etymonline (website), accessed May 16, 2022, https://www.etymonline.com/word/text#etymonline_v_10699.

17. O'Neill (n 15).

18. Silvia Federici, *Caliban and the Witch: Women, the Body, and Primitive Accumulation* (London: Penguin Classics, 2021).

19. "-logy" definition on Etymonline (website), accessed May 16, 2022, https://www.etymonline.com/word/-logy#etymonline_v_12399.

20. Saraceno (n 4).

I guess this idea of safety which I feel lucky to have in my home.

and enmeshed art worlds which form the contexts for the spider's web, these are all, even if to varying degrees, shaped by flows of capital and prospects of influence, essentially mediated by funding bodies and art institutions. While many art institutions might represent themselves as critical, decolonial,[21] feminist sites of learning, they tend to resist actual decolonial practice and politics, made apparent for instance in top-down structures and the treatment of their workers.

Starting from the context of the art academy, where students with different backgrounds and urgencies are supposed to be prepared to navigate the art world(s), I am wondering if it is possible to build otherwise art infrastructures based on collectivity and solidarity? How flexible is the concept of art, and how much sense does it make to stretch it? Can activist strategies like unionizing, protesting, and organizing alternative education form part of artistic practices?

AMATEURISM

> *[...] we inhabit multiple roles, positions, and labels strategically. We become a translator, a friend, an artist, a writer, a cook, a gardener, a teacher, a student, or, perhaps, an eternal amateur. For me, the word "amateur" harnesses the affective side of doing things for collective pleasure/joy while resisting the dull practice of professionalism and business as usual. Being an amateur allows me to learn through the process, instead of assuming that I always know what I am doing or that I know everything about the people I work with.*

Brigitta Isabella to Rieneke de Vries, *Art for (and Within) a Citizen Scene*[22]

Being an amateur means focusing on the process, experimentation, learning, figuring things out (together). It means playing with skills and roles as activities rather than essentializing labels, while being open to failing, again and again. Embracing amateurism, the spider weaves new connections in order to gain an embodied understanding of what works in a specific context. A web is not just an abstract,

21. Eve Tuck and K. Wayne Yang, "Decolonization is not a Metaphor," *Decolonization: Indigeneity, Education & Society* 1, no. 1 (2012): 1-40, https://clas.osu.edu/sites/clas.osu.edu/files/Tuck%20and%20Yang%202012%20Decolonization%20is%20not%20a%20metaphor.pdf.

22. Brigitta Isabella and Rieneke de Vries, "We Sell Reality? Who Are 'We' and What Do We Mean by 'Reality'?" in *Art for (and within) a Citizen Scene: A Look at Art Primarily Active in the Context of Daily Practices*, eds. Iris Ferrer, Emily Shin-Jie Lee, reinaart vanhoe, and Julia Wilhelm (Eindhoven: Onomatopee, 2022), 125-145.

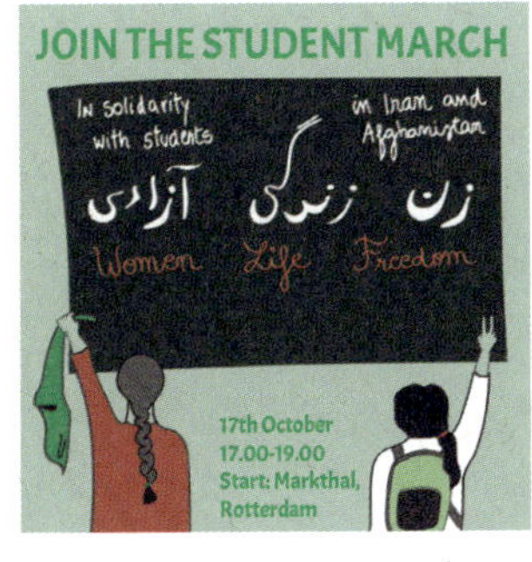

Poster designed and illustrated by Carla Arcos as part of SPIN collective, October 2022.

conceptual entity, but a set of skills, tools, and affects that stem from experience.

The word amateur originally comes from French "aimer,"—to love.[23] An amateur is passionate, but doesn't claim expertise, doesn't reaffirm the categories created by specialization and the alienation and separation that come along with it. The amateur steals from disciplines and the undisciplinary. This is what attracted me to art in the first place, the freedom of being able to play with knowledges from different contexts without having to adhere to professional confinements, to embody theory through practice and think practice through theory. This means recognizing that their separation is artificial, that the hierarchy implied between them is harmful and limiting. An amateur maintains joy and playfulness in learning and creating, which go hand in hand. The amateur refuses to settle with a fixed identity, to become graspable and marketable, as is usually expected from (young) artists. They embrace ambiguity.[24] They describe themselves with what they do rather than defining themselves with what they are.

JOY

> *When people find themselves genuinely supported and cared for, they are able to extend this to others in ways that seemed impossible or terrifying before. When people find their bellies filled and their minds sharpened among communal kitchens and libraries, hatred for capitalist ways of life grows amid belonging and connection. [...] When people begin to meet their everyday needs through neighbourhood assemblies and mutual aid, all of a sudden they are willing to fight the police and the fights deepens bonds of trust and solidarity. Joy can be contagious and dangerous.*

carla bergman and Nick Montgomery, *Joyful Militancy*[25]

Joy is not a feeling of bliss or happiness, but a feeling of collective agency, an ability to be affected by others, and to affect others in turn. bergman and Montgomery see mutual relationships of love, care, and trust, rather than abstract ideologies as prerequisites for joined struggle. Joy is about embodiment,

I get easily typecast as 'a mum' who has nothing more to offer and passed over which I also find very frustrating.

23. "Amateur" definition on Etymonline (website), accessed May 16, 2022, https://www.etymonline.com/word/amateur#etymonline_v_10949.

24. Emily Shin-Jie Lee and reinaart vanhoe, "A Warm Welcome," in *Art for (and within) a Citizen Scene: A Look at Art Primarily Active in the Context of Daily Practices*, eds. Iris Ferrer, Emily Shin-Jie Lee, reinaart vanhoe, and Julia Wilhelm (Eindhoven: Onomatopee, 2022), 5-9.

25. bergman and Montgomery (n 11).

about physically being part of something, about giving up control and critical distance.[26] Audre Lorde also emphasizes the importance of joy in organizing, "The sharing of joy, whether physical, emotional, psychic, or intellectual, forms a bridge between the sharers which can be the basis for understanding much of what is not shared between them, and lessens the threat of their difference."[27]

This joy entails moving away from conditioned pursuit of happiness and comfort.[28] Joy is the opposite of Mark Fisher's *depressive hedonia*, the constant search for superficial pleasures and excitements in the form of entertainment and consumption, accompanied by a feeling of resignation and powerlessness with regards to the injustices of our systems.[29] Similarly, Spinoza uses the term sadness to describe a state of passivity, a loss in capacity to be affected, to be set in movement by things, and to affect things in turn.[30]

The spider's threads are not only words, but sensations, experiences, and relationships that activate forces. The act of web-building is one of rediscovering agency, even if in tiny, silky pockets. The spider, working her way from thread to thread, knows that fighting for change at a local level is necessary for understanding how to affect change on a bigger scale.[31] And she weaves these silky threads of possibility together into a temporary architecture, a net bag for holding life.

CARE

The word "care" is very prevalent in the art world at the moment. One finds it in descriptions of workshops, festivals, exhibitions, and programs: climate care, community care, curation as care, etc. Is care just a trendy word that becomes increasingly shallow the more often it is repeated? Or does the popularity of the word attest to an urgency of our time?

"To care" describes a state of emotional affectability, of being touched, set in motion, by something or someone. Caring, in its non-institutionalised forms, means to refuse indifference. It means to refuse looking away. To refuse pretending like the

26. Ibid.

27. Audre Lorde, "Uses of the Erotic," in *When I Dare to Be Powerful: Women so Empowered are Dangerous* (London: Penguin Books, 2020).

28. Sara Ahmed, *The Promise of Happiness* (Durham: Duke University Press, 2010).

29. Mark Fisher, "Reflexive Impotence," *K-punk*, April 11, 2006. www.k-punk.abstractdynamics.org/archives/007656.html.

30. bergman and Montgomery (n 11).

31. adrienne maree brown, *Emergent Strategy* (Chico CA: AK Press, 2017).

Poster designed by Carla Arcos as part of SPIN collective, with illustrations by @samirakhorshidii, November 2022.

suffering of others has nothing to do with yourself. To refuse acting as if we do not hold any power over each other. Our lives are contingent, our actions don't exist in a vacuum, but in relation. Along the strings of these intersubjective webs we all hold power over each other's lives, and with this power comes responsibility. Caring means acknowledging this responsibility, or as Donna Haraway would say, response-ability for forming conditions in which human and non-human beings can thrive.[32]

Maybe the difference between care as a trendy catchphrase and 'real' care lies in the sustainability of care. Is care a continuous and sustained process that is reflected in the infrastructures, in how people interact and take responsibility for each other? Differing from the constant need for the new that the art world and capitalism thrive upon, care doesn't seek to innovate, but gives attention to and maintains that which is already there. Often delegated to the private, caring as a reproductive activity is essentially unpaid, not considered labor, and still mostly performed by women.[33] When it comes to institutionalized care, the jobs of care workers are often further complicated by laws and regulations that don't take the experience and needs of those working in the field into account.[34] As an alternative one might consider self-organized groups that provide support with getting abortions, advocate for mental health, defend the right to migration, distribute food, promote workers' rights, build community, construct infrastructures for education, and create spaces for being in caring relations.

Patriarchy compartmentalizes and individualizes care. It takes place either in highly regulated public social work or health care, or, in its unpaid form, is relegated to the home.[35] How can we care in a more collective way? iLiana Fokianaki raises this question in her text *Introductory Notes on the Care-less and Care-full*. She proposes to see care as the basis of everything that we do, not as an obligation but as part of collective joy as a "structural practice not only for others, but with others."[36] Maintaining the web means taking responsibility for the multiple beings entangled in it, and to make the web resilient and durable by resisting short-term thinking.

32. Haraway (n 1).

33. Nicole Cox and Sylvia Federici, *Counter-planning from the Kitchen: Wages for Housework, A Perspective on Capital and the Left* (New York: Wages for Housework Committee and Falling Wall Press, 1975).

34. Personal communication with care workers.

35. iLiana Fokianaki, "The Bureau of Care: Introductory Notes on the Care-less and Care-full," E-flux (blog), November 2020, https://www.e-flux.com/journal/113/359463/the-bureau-of-care-introductory-notes-on-the-care-less-and-care-full/.

36. Ibid.

The word of care and worrying is the same.

MAINTENANCE

> *Development: pure, individual creation; the new; change; progress, advance, excitement, flight or fleeting. Maintenance: keep the dust of the pure, individual creation; preserve the new; sustain the change; protect progress; defend and prolong the advance; renew the excitement; repeat the flight.*

Mierle Laderman Ukeles, *Manifesto for Maintenance Art*[37]

Durability requires maintenance. Maintenance requires commitment, and maybe a shift away from wanting to be the individual—the hero, the innovator, the main character. A shift towards the sidelines, out of visibility, to the tedious, boring, repetitious, repetitive. As Ursula K. le Guin describes in her *Carrier Bag Theory of Fiction*: those that used to nourish us in prehistoric times and still do so today, are the gatherers that collect food in baskets and bags, not the hunters that occasionally thrust spears into wild animals. But the stories we tell are too often centered around glorious heroes, around pioneers and innovators, told through linear, spear-shaped timelines. Le Guin proposes that a story can be shaped like a recipient instead, one that gathers a wide array of things next to each other, transporting them for nourishment and medicine.[38]

If we prioritize durability, we need to put maintenance and development on equal footing. We need to understand that there is no development without maintenance, that maintenance also requires creativity and knowledge.[39] The hardest part in cultivating different ways of being together, in building otherwise webs, is to not see them as a one-time experiment, but as a sustained process that needs to be cared for and tended to. This is made difficult through the short-term thinking that prevails in the artworld and the exhaustion we all experience. Like all infrastructures, the web is dependent on the constant maintenance of the spider. Without the spider's continuous commitment, it would slowly disintegrate.

37. Mierle Laderman Ukeles, *MANIFESTO FOR MAINTENANCE ART, 1969!* 1969, https://queensmuseum.org/wp-content/uploads/2016/04/Ukeles-Manifesto-for-Maintenance-Art-1969.pdf.

38. Ursula K. Le Guin, *The Carrier Bag Theory of Fiction*, 1986. Available online at the Anarchist Federation, https://www.anarchistfederation.net/ursula-k-le-guin-the-carrier-bag-theory-of-fiction/#/.

39. Yusser Salih, "Kom, behoor ook tot ons huishouden," *nY tijdschrift voor literatuur, kunst & kritiek*, studY, no. 47, March 2022.

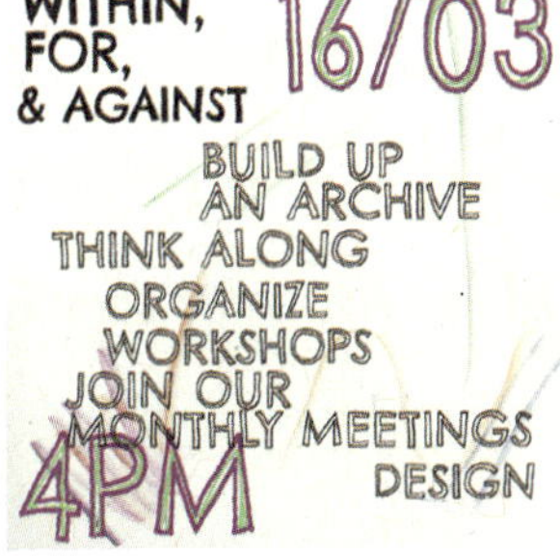

Poster designed by Runs Còdol for the archive of student initiatives Within, For, & Against, March 2023.

DIFFERENCE

Much of Western European history conditions us to see human differences in simplistic opposition to each other: dominant/subordinate, good/bad, up/down, superior/inferior. In a society where the good is defined in terms of profit rather than in terms of human need, there must always be some group of people who, through systematized oppression, can be made to feel surplus, to occupy the place of the dehumanized inferior.

Audre Lorde, *Age, Race, Class, and Sex: Women Redefining Difference*[40]

Audre Lorde speaks about the importance of recognizing and acknowledging difference, and being able to relate to each other as equals, not despite, but through difference. She sees the actual cause of political and social division, not in the differences between people, but in the failure to recognize them and deal with them.[41] Western thought constructs subjectivity in terms of sameness, in terms of accordance with a specific set of ideas or values; that are defined through being set in opposition against an Other. The Other in this sense, is necessary for constituting the normative subject. Rosi Braidotti argues for a positive conception of difference, for a subjectivity that does not rely on sameness. Her affirmative ethics promote an enlarged, interconnected sense of the self, where difference allows for a process of learning and transformation.[42]

NON-OPPOSITIONAL CRITICALITY

[...] possibilities for happiness today turn on the capacity to move beyond an "all or nothing" approach that subsumes everything under the dualism of capitalism and the revolutionary alternative to capitalism. [...] Non-binary resistance requires deconditioning oneself from what Mark Fisher has termed "depressive hedonia"—an inability to do anything else except pursue pleasure. Being happy is a way of life, not a goal that capitalism disseminates and promises to fulfil. Being happy is a practice of de-alienation and rehumanisation.

Zoénie Liwen Deng, *Be Water, My Friend*[43]

40. Audre Lorde, "Age, Race, Class, and Sex: Women Redefining Difference," in *When I Dare to Be Powerful: Women so Empowered are Dangerous* (London: Penguin Books, 2020).

41. Ibid.

42. Rosi Braidotti, "On Putting the Active Back into Activism," *New Formations: A Journal of Culture/Theory/Politics*, Special Issue: 'Deleuzian Politics?', no. 68, (2009): 42-57.

43. Zoénie Liwen Deng, "Be Water, My Friend: Non-Oppositional Criticalities of Socially Engaged Art in Urbanising China," Phd diss., (University of Amsterdam, 2020).

I am definitely worrying about various people in my life.

In her Phd thesis *Be Water, My Friend*, Zoénie Liwen Deng uses the term "non-oppositional criticality" to describe socially engaged artistic practices in China, which are critical of the status quo in a way that is not directly opposing the system, so as to evade censorship and repression. These practices often focus on organizing in ways that slightly deviate from the paradigm put forward by the authorities. Quoting Irit Rogoff who describes criticality in contrast to criticism and critique as "operating from an uncertain ground of actual embeddedness,"[44] Zoénie elaborates that this uncertainty emerges from defying the oppositional logic of either being "inside or outside a system, either working with or working against the authorities."[45]

44. Irit Rogoff, "From Criticism to Critique to Criticality," *Transversal Texts*, 2003, https://transversal.at/pdf/journal-text/1364/.

45. Liwen Deng (n 43).

The non-oppositional criticality Zoénie describes is a reaction to a very specific political context of censorship and repression, one that differs quite a lot from the strategies of appropriation in the western (art) context. But her plea for a non-binary approach might also hold valuable lessons here. Embracing a multiplicity of strategies, the spider builds webs in both the cracks of institutional concrete walls and in desolate forests. Hoping to carve transformative pockets from within institutional confines, the spider benefits from the infrastructure and from having access to resources for redistribution. All while being aware that institutions are tools of domination and will never truly enact the values of horizontality, transparency, and difference, which results in a necessity to build autonomous infrastructures that don't rely on institutional modes of operating.

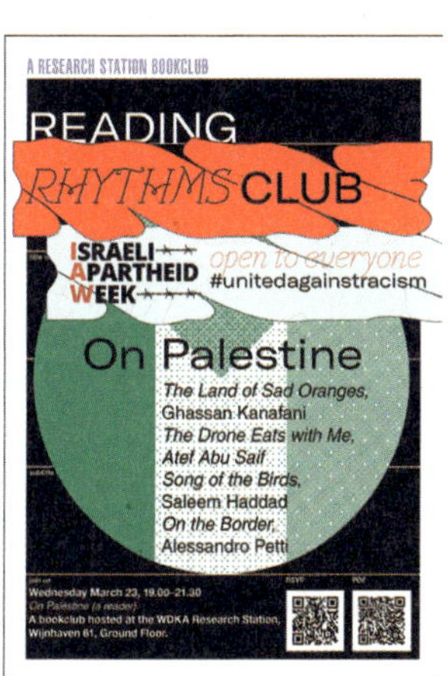

Poster designed by Senka Milutinović as part of Reading Rhythms Club, March 2022.

AFFIRMATIVE CRITICALITY

In some politically engaged circles, critique is often perceived as rejection or attack. How can it be understood as an invitation for growth and learning, for change instead? Rather than dismissing an idea, criticality can add nuance, complexity, and space for reconsideration. The book *Joyful Militancy* describes this phenomenon as rigid radicalism, and proposes to center the joy of doing things together, of becoming capable together instead.[46] How can critique open up possibilities, allow us to stay in movement, to not settle with the "right answers"?

Irit Rogoff proposes a shift from "criticism to critique to criticality—from finding fault, to examining the underlying assumptions that might allow something to appear as a convincing logic, to operating from an uncertain ground which [...] wants to inhabit culture in a relation other than one of critical analysis; other than one of illuminating flaws, locating elisions, allocating blames."[47] The criticality Rogoff describes is one that is embedded in the present, in experience, an active process, all while making use of the tools provided by critique.

I also want to emphasize Audre Lorde's writing on the erotic, on the sensorial, embodied experience that in Western thinking is mostly subdued to detached intellectual analysis. She describes the Erotic as a creative force, a being physically present, saying yes to life, as "physical, emotional, and psychic expressions of what is deepest and strongest and richest within each of us."[48] Oppression suppresses this source of energy, deriving the oppressed of the power necessary for real and profound change.

Affirmative criticality is about coming up with concrete, embodied perspectives for action and change, it is aimed at generating feelings of (collective) joy and agency. I believe in the importance of weaving webs that allows for an embodiment of other ways of relating to each other, putting the joy of being together to the forefront. This happens under the assumption that political consciousness can only arise in a context where a certain feeling of community, of belonging together, of collective responsibility is in place.

CHANGE

All that you touch
You Change.
All that you Change
Changes you.
The only lasting truth
is Change.
God
is Change.

Octavia E. Butler, *The Parable of the Sower*[49]

46. bergman and Montgomery (n 11).

47. Rogoff (n 44).

48. Lorde (n 27).

And then where's the safety net?

49. Octavia E. Butler, *Parable of the Sower* (New York: Grand Central Publishing, 1993).

50. brown (n 31) 56.

Autoarachnology is not about creating order out of chaos, rather, it asks for sticking with the chaos, staying with the trouble. Moving along lines rather than fixing points, autoarachnology embraces an ethics of movement. Web-building, figuring out ways to navigate the world we live in, is a process of experimentation towards other ends. This requires us to train adaptability and flexibility, as well as expanding our capacity for accepting uncertainty.[50]

Autoarachnology is devoted to change, to continue looping and flattening, knotting and solving, loosening and tightening, playing with the tension of the strings. It is not that the tension is never right, but that 'right' is a process, not a point. What works, depends on the context, is subject to change. Every account of the web is a snapshot, a moment frozen in time, while the web is already on the verge of becoming something else.

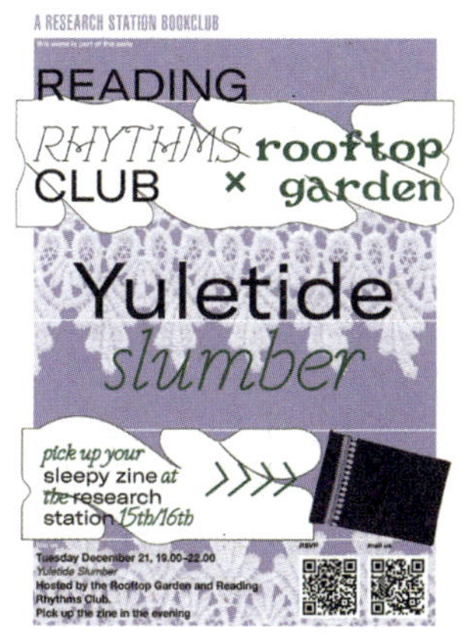

Poster designed by Juliette Douet and Senka Milutinović, December 2021.

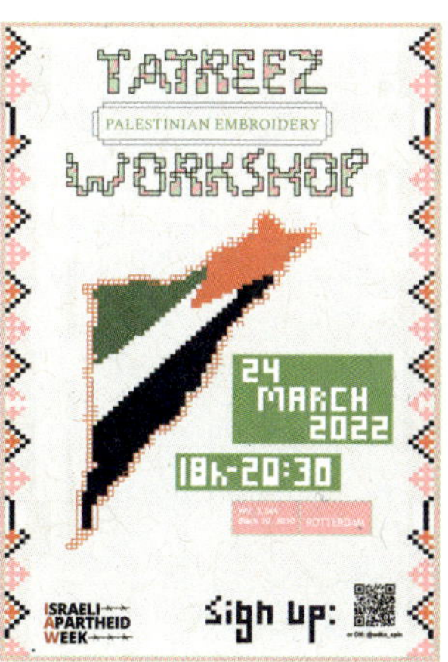

Poster designed by Carla Arcos as part of SPIN collective, March 2022.

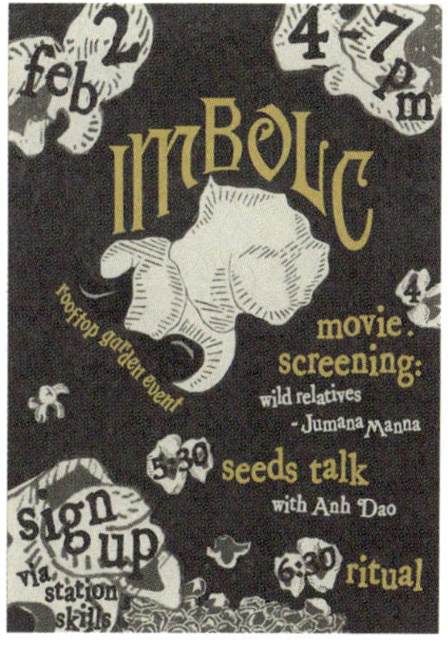

Poster designed by Juliette Douet with illustrations by Carla Arcos as part of SPIN collective, February 2022.

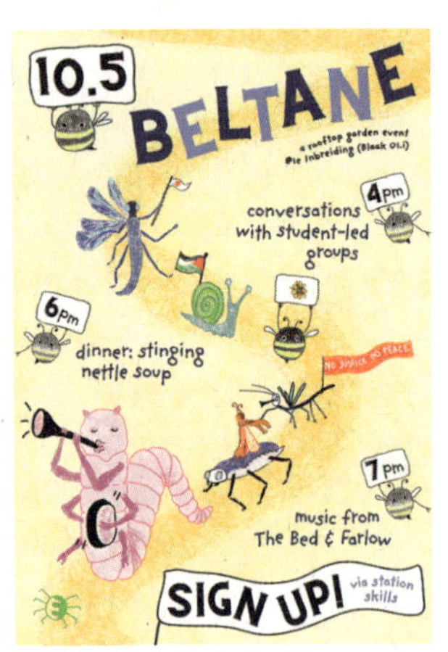

Poster designed by Juliette Douet with illustrations by Carla Arcos as part of SPIN collective, May 2022.

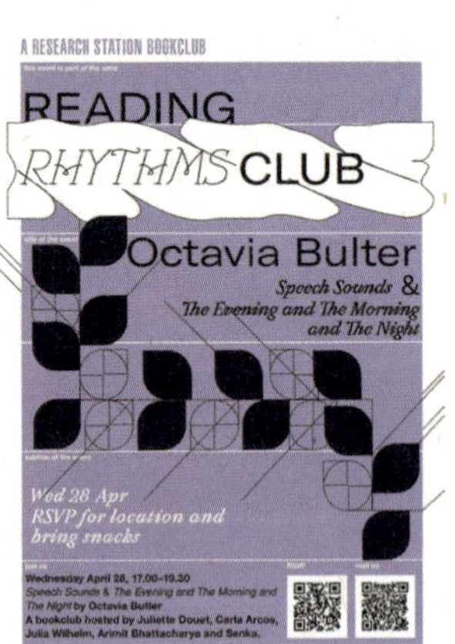

Poster designed by Senka Milutinović as part of Reading Rhythms Club, April 2021.

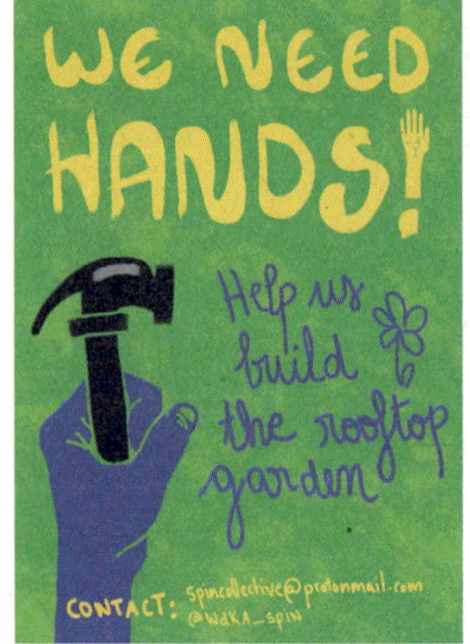

Poster designed and illustrated by Carla Arcos as part of SPIN collective, March 2022.

Cooking Something Up: A Cookbook

Cooking Something Up is a project centered around reproductive labor and care work. They want to politicize and make explicit these forms of labor. Intimacy is part of this process. Placing study within the realm of domestic work, how do you do that? How do you make connections explicit that study has always been within the domestic sphere? The collective organizes weekly dinners together, cooking for each other, and talking where they bring in their embodied and emotional experiences, and think about ways to do research in a way that acknowledges these things. They made a cookbook out of recipes inspired by dinners.

The complete cookbook is 124 pages, in the following selection you see pages: 1, 10, 12, 16, 19, 24, 29, 44, 47, 72-73, 81, 88, 104.

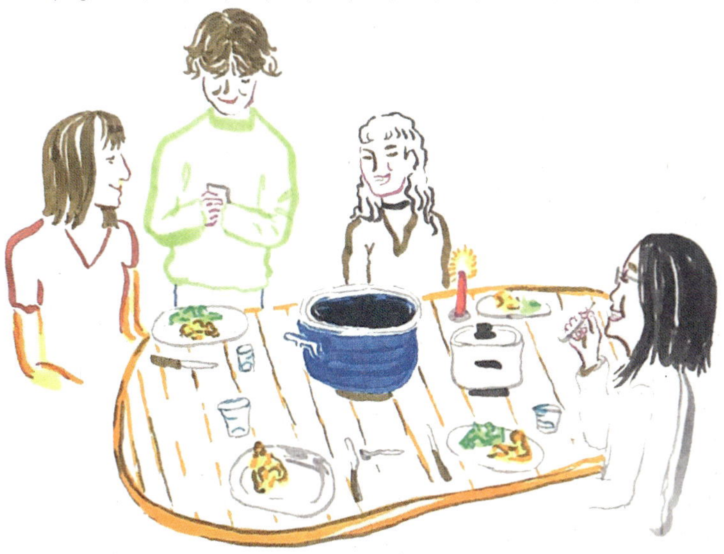

COOKING SOMETHING UP

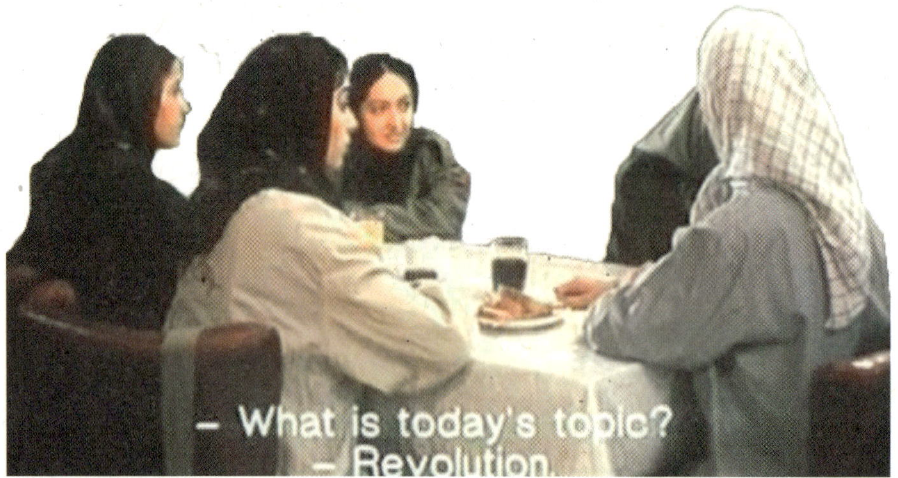

Utensil(s)

Sharing Dinners

First and foremost, sharing dinners is a tool to make friends, strengthen existing friendships and take care of each other. It makes people come together and enables a different kind of connection based on the joy and comfort that good food creates. Conversations that arise are situated within the sensual experience of tasting, smelling, sitting together. Sharing dinners with friends is also a way to share a part of yourself and introduce friends to what matters to you, be it food from your cultural background, food that you connect with specific memories or associations, or a new recipe you want to try out. Cooking is also part of the reproductive work associated with the private sphere of the kitchen. Opening up this private space to a collective, embodied experience, can offer ways to politicize and collectively handle reproductive work and personal experience and bring politics (back) into the kitchen. Silvia Federici writes: 'If the house is the oikos on which the economy is built, then it is women, historically the house workers and house prisoners, who must take the initiative to reclaim the house as a center of collective life, one traversed by multiple people and forms of cooperation, providing safety without isolation and fixation, allowing for the sharing and circulation of community possessions, and, above all, providing the foundation for collective forms of reproduction.'

Poetry

Poetry is a utensil that allows you to perceive, study, and embrace the world beyond what is deemed rational and objective. As a tool it gives space to feelings and hunches which cannot be expressed through a language that conveys meaning alone. Expressing oneself, alone or together, through poetry, is a way of palpating language, of playing with the possibilities it offers to find different ways of communication. Poetry embraces the personal and subjective, the tentative, the blurry. It helps to re-imagining what knowing can mean from a feminist point of view that takes into account and aims to dismantle the oppressive structures that generate the framework for knowledge-production. A framework which devalues intuition and emotional ways of knowing, traditionally attributed to women. Poetry as a tool allows to exceed this framework, to venture into, as Audre Lorde puts it, the 'dark, hidden places'.

Utensil(s)

The Undercommons

The undercommons is not a realm where we rebel and we create critique; it is not a place where we "take arms against a sea of troubles/and by opposing end them." The undercommons is a space and time which is always here. Our goal – and the "we" is always the right mode of address here – is not to end the troubles but to end the world that created those particular troubles as the ones that must be opposed.

The undercommons is a kind of comportment or ongoing experiment with and as the general antagonism, a kind of way of being with others, it's almost impossible that it could be matched up with particular institutional life. It would obviously be cut through in different kinds of ways and in different spaces and times.

In a way, the undercommons is a kind of break, between locating ourselves and dislocating ourselves. What's so enduring for us about the undercommons concept is that's what it continues to do when it is encountered in new circumstances. People always say, 'well, where the fuck is that.' Even if you do that clever Marxist thing like, 'oh it's not a place, it's a relation,' people are like, 'yeah, but where's the relation.' It has a continuing effect as a dislocation, and it always makes people feel a little uncomfortable about common.

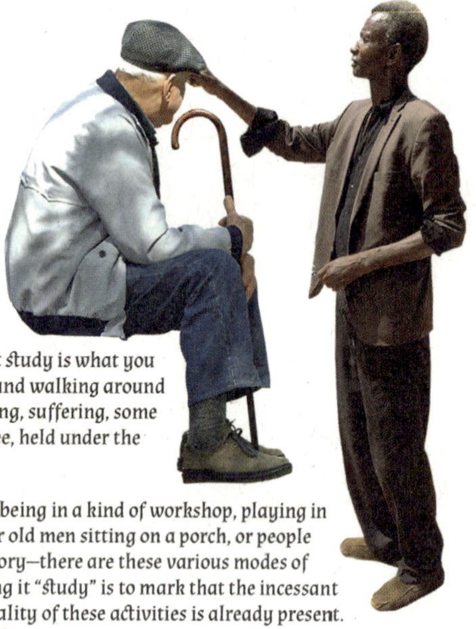

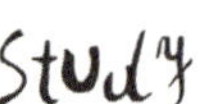

We are committed to the idea that study is what you do with other people. It's talking and walking around with other people, working, dancing, suffering, some irreducible convergence of all three, held under the name of speculative practice.

The notion of a rehearsal—being in a kind of workshop, playing in a band, in a jam session, or old men sitting on a porch, or people working together in a factory—there are these various modes of activity. The point of calling it "study" is to mark that the incessant and irreversible intellectuality of these activities is already present.

Study, a mode of thinking with others separate from the thinking that the institution requires of you, prepares us to be embedded in what Harney calls "the with and for" and allows you to spend less time antagonized and antagonizing

excerpts from "the undercommons" by Harney and Moten

It's always such a pleasure to see you. I'm happy that you are here.

Utensil(s)

Gossip

Gossip is a necessary utensil when it comes to study in order to validate different ways of sharing information and disinvest from narratives of authenticity and logic.

Access
This communicative tool is a form of making accessible, sharing and repurposing information especially for those who are excluded from media platforms, politics or educational systems.

Community building
Gossip stimulates social interactions, it allows for comparison, self-reflection through the examination of moral decisions. It is necessary for healing justice, firstly because gossip is a form of resistance, sometimes the only source of power left some communities have against their oppressors. It builds collectivity through sharing lifesaving information.

Speculation
This utensil is also a form of exploring narratives. Since gossiping is not about truths it can take the form of poetic intervention, imagining what could have been? How would this or that senario look like then? It is a tool to desorient narratives.

Self-empowerment
The #metoo movement shows the power gossip holds in the area of digital media serveing to hold accountable those who committed sexual harassment and rape. Gossip is cathartic, powerful and consciousness-raising.

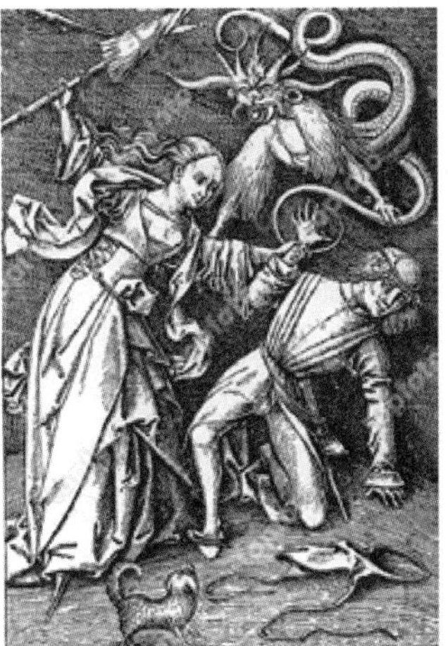

(Her)story
But why is Gossip nowadays used as a form of malicious talk, attention seeking or considered superficial ?
Let's look back to the etymology of the word:
Gossip stands for God + sibb (=a relative), the godsibb/gossip used to mean godparent. The word evolved into friend of the family, usually present at births, eventually gossip got generalized into meaning female friend. It is important to note that in the Europe of middle ages women were powerful, they were often represented standing up against their husbands. Women had very strong bonds with each other since their life and activities were mainly collective, supporting each other at birth, surrounding each other while sewing, washing their clothes etc... However, in the 16th century, as Silvia Federici describes in the "Witch....." women's position in society started to weaken by shaming men who were dominated by their wifes and by removing women from public life. Simultaneously, the meaning of gossip took a turn and started being used as backbiting talk, denigrating female solidarity. In 1567, Scotland, the first design of the repugnant 'gossip bridle' was made. Men were at war against women, they knew Gossip is a weaponized form of intimacy and responded with nasty, violent and humiliating tools of torture.

THE DINNERS

During the past months we came together every week to have dinner and cook with and for each other. Each week another group member hosted the dinner and decided on the meal we would have. By inviting each other into our homes, we were able to get to know each other in our personal, intimate spaces and experience each other's everyday surroundings.

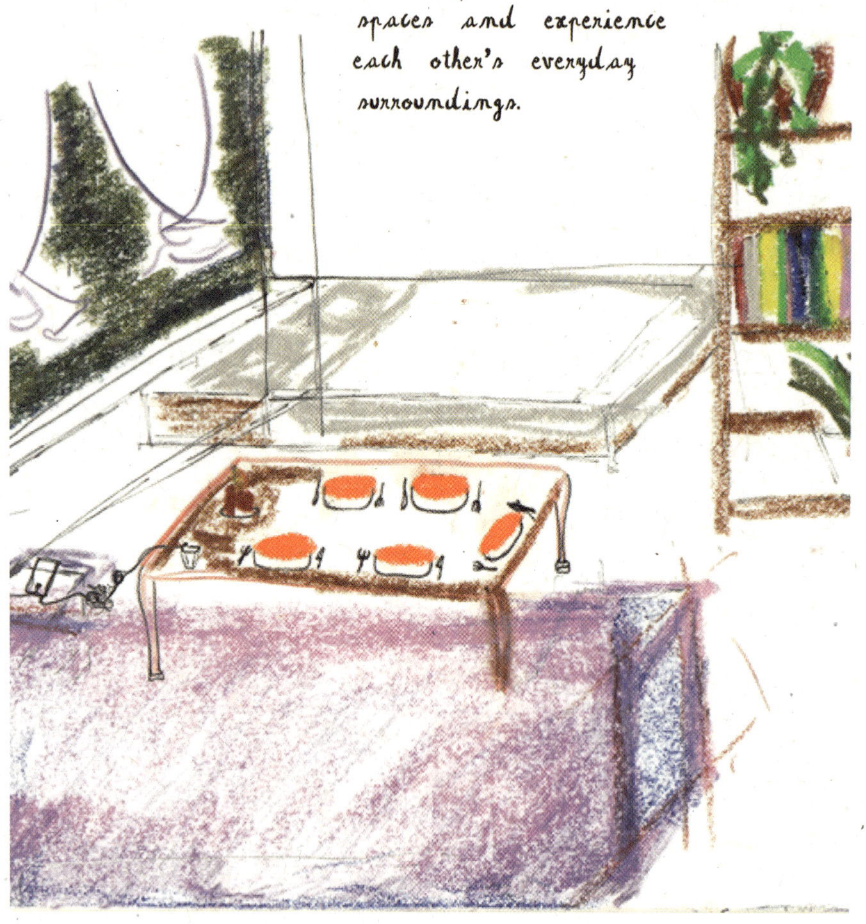

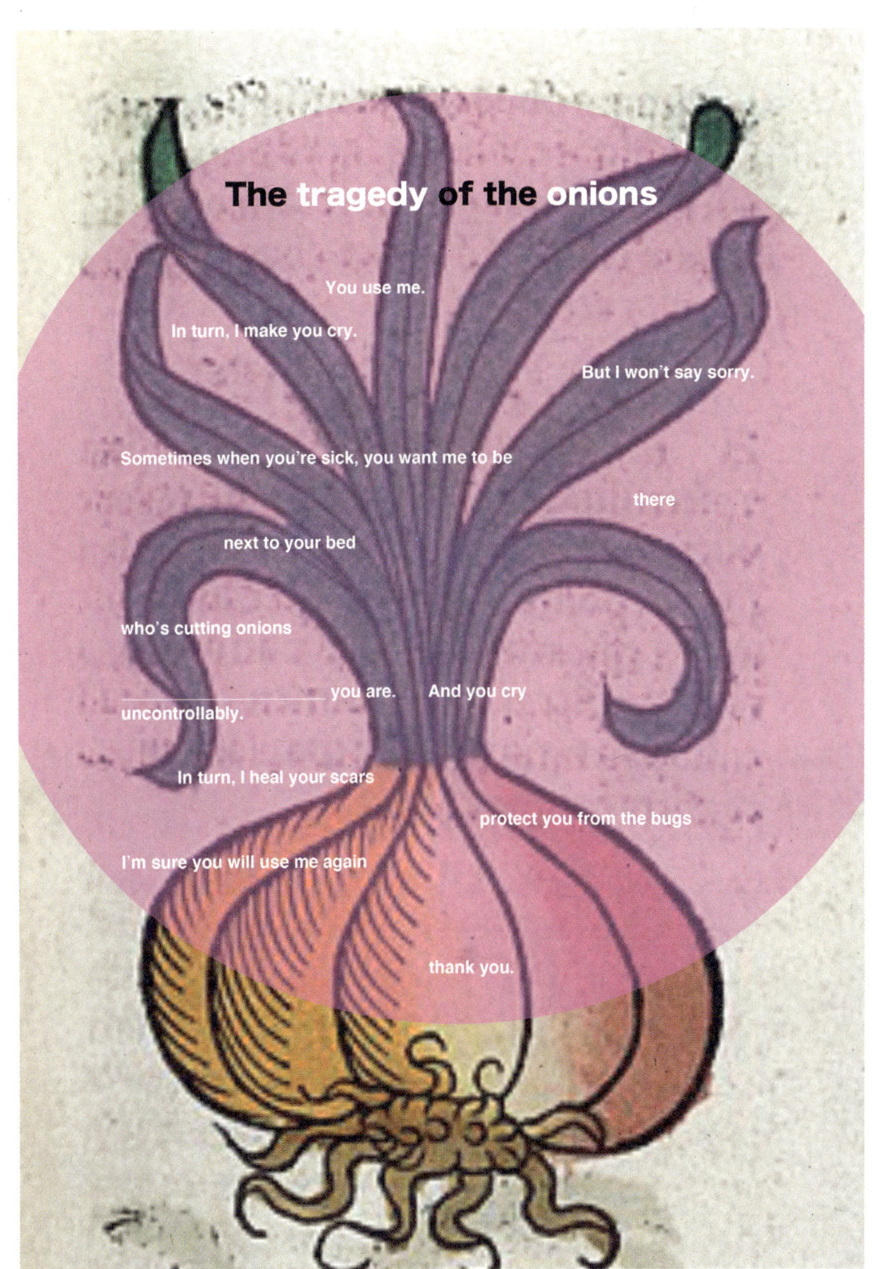
The tragedy of the onions
You use me.
In turn, I make you cry.
But I won't say sorry.
Sometimes when you're sick, you want me to be
there
next to your bed
who's cutting onions
__________ you are. And you cry
uncontrollably.
In turn, I heal your scars
protect you from the bugs
I'm sure you will use me again
thank you.

TUCKED IN KEBABIES

On the 12th of October, we had dinner at Yusser's home in Rotterdam Centrum. We had Tepsi Baytinijan, also often called Kabab Mgamot, meaning tucked in kabab. The dish left an aftertaste of parenting, which stayed in our mouths as we talked about our relationships with our parents, intergenerational trauma, and our part in carrying it with us. The atmosphere was vulnerable, caring and warm.

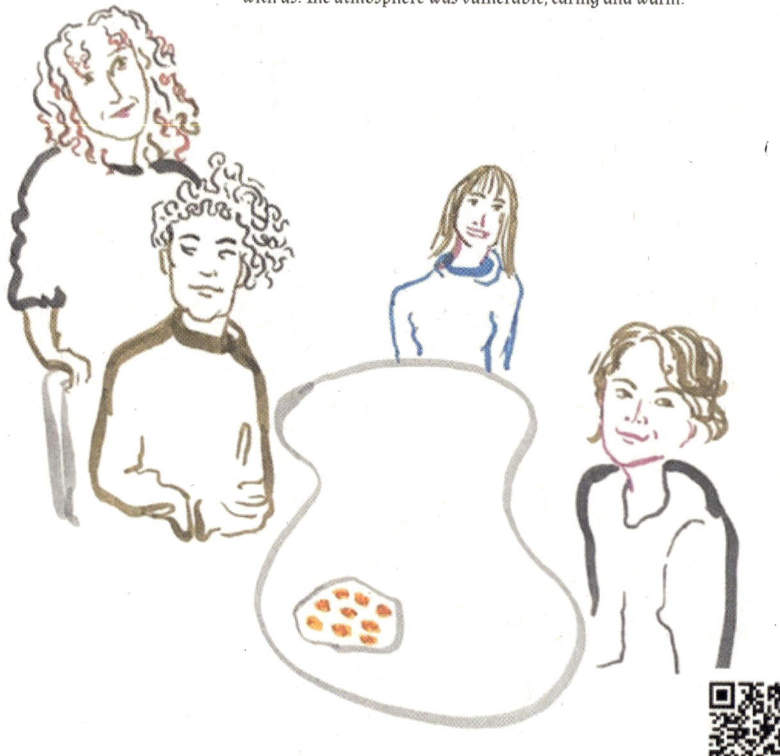

It's been intense. Fuck.

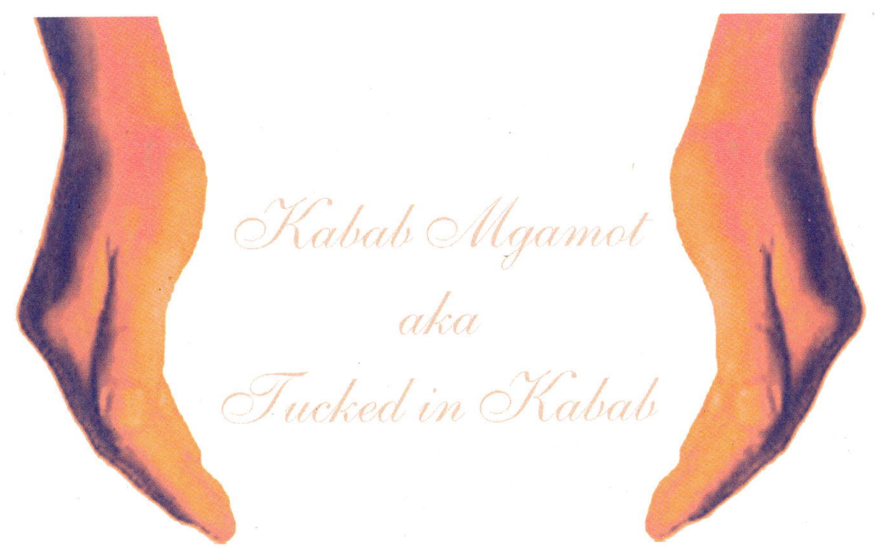

Kabab Mgamot aka Tucked in Kabab

Kabab mgamot literally means tucked in kabab, and this dish truly describes the setting we had created together. Our little meaty bodies tucked into a caring embrace. We discussed the family, our families, and the connections we longed to have had with our parents. As well as the realities, not glossing over how fucked up some of our upbringings had been, and how painful it is to acknowledge that. As the memories came up, the hurt did too, and we, like the kabab mgamot, scooched together, tucking each other in in our aubergine arms.

Making kabab mgamot takes a lot of steps.
Each ingredient demands your attention and care.
It's a bit like parenting, it seems easy but a lot of work actually goes in all these seemingly simple tasks.

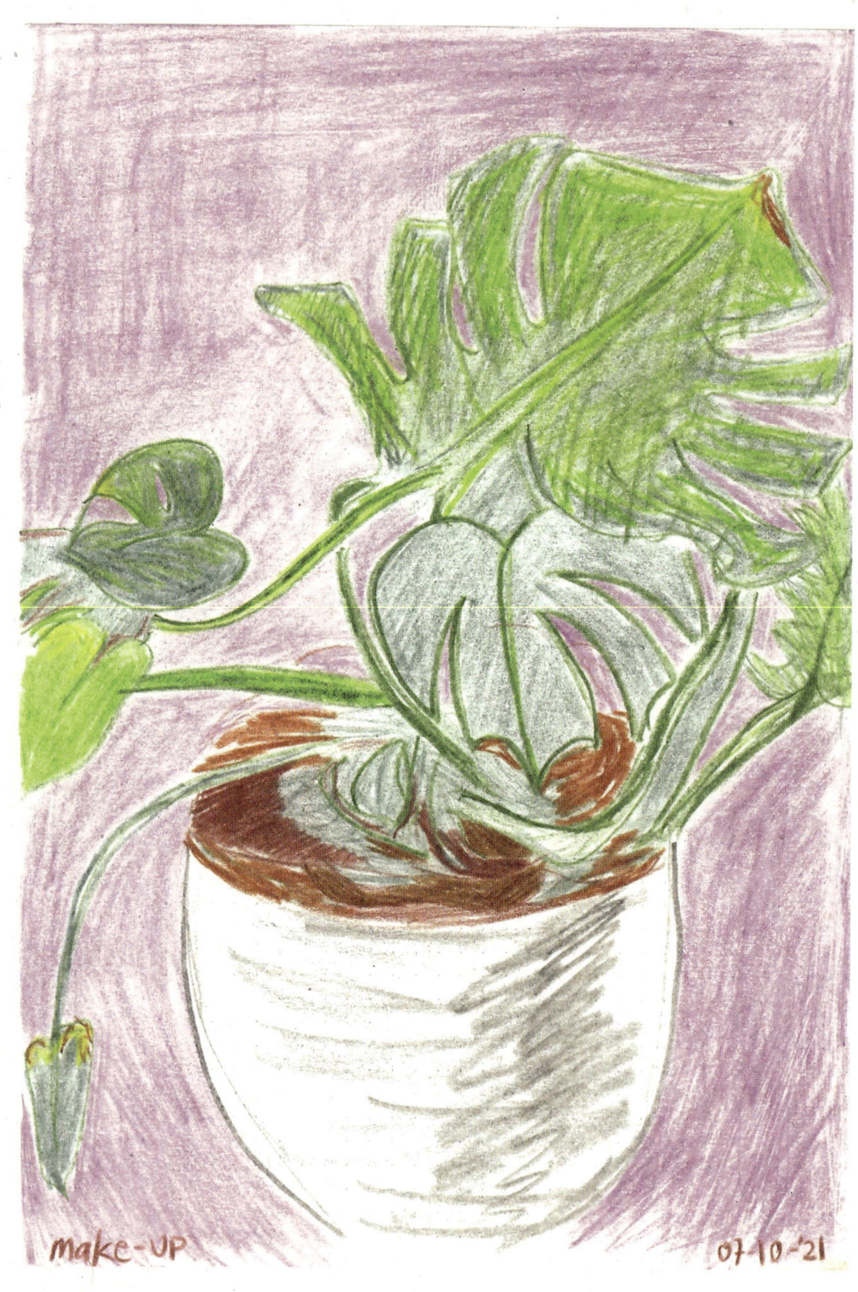

We always talk about the sinking ship and there are many holes.

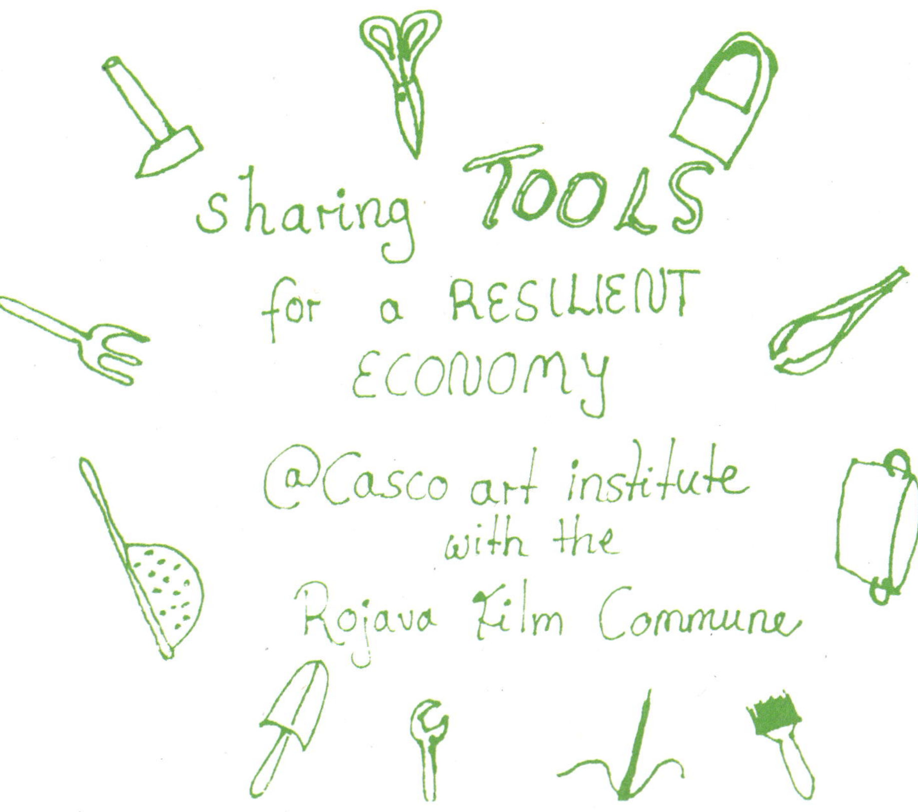

Do different societies need different tools to collectivize? Are tools context specific, dependent on culture and socio-economic structures?

- Rojava has a very community-based culture, so collectivizing and non-hierarchical organization are not difficult

- The contrary could be said for the western art system, which is based on success and achievements of the individual artist

Pouring water, mixing the water and rice with my hands and then pouring it out again. Rinse, repeat. Until the water runs almost clear.

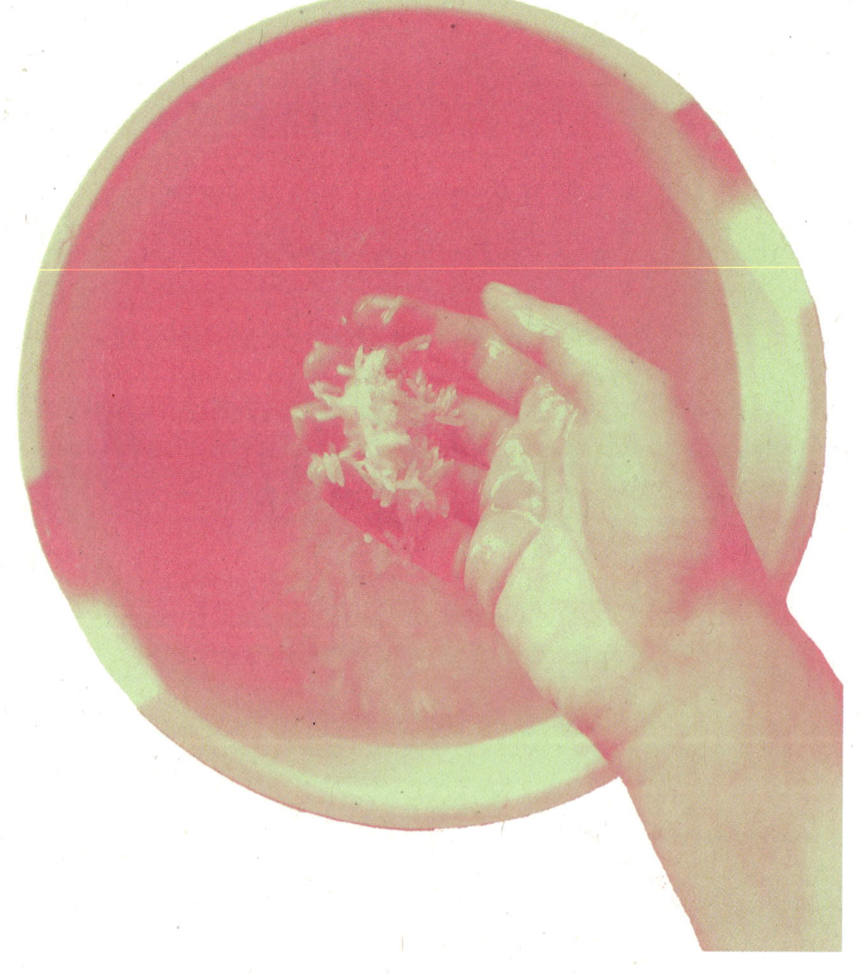

I think I am in an okay but confused state.

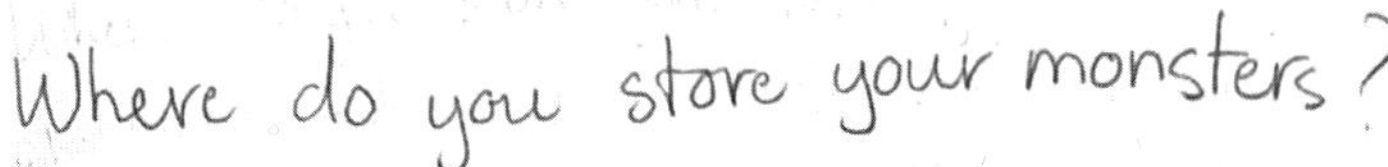

Sometimes I think about things that happened & bad, ugly thoughts would appear

NO! I have to hide them! Nobody can find out!

Double, Triple, Quadruple Locks!!!

Yet somehow they still escape

Pat Pat

We decided to work through things together now

It's not all good yet but at least they are not alone anymore

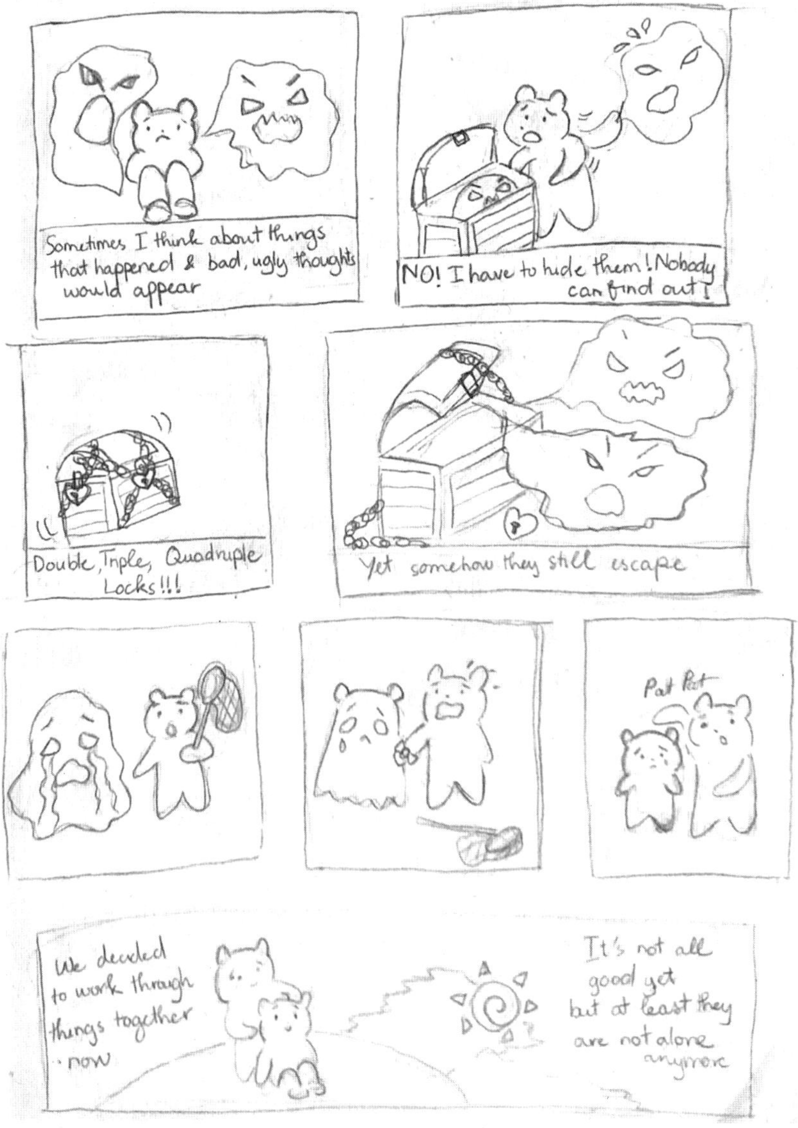

Recipe for an Autumn Equinox Celebration

[A recipe for attempting to create a community around a virtual garden

A recipe for attunement with cycles

A recipe for de-alienation (from ourselves, from the art academy environment, from each other, from the other-than human around us)]

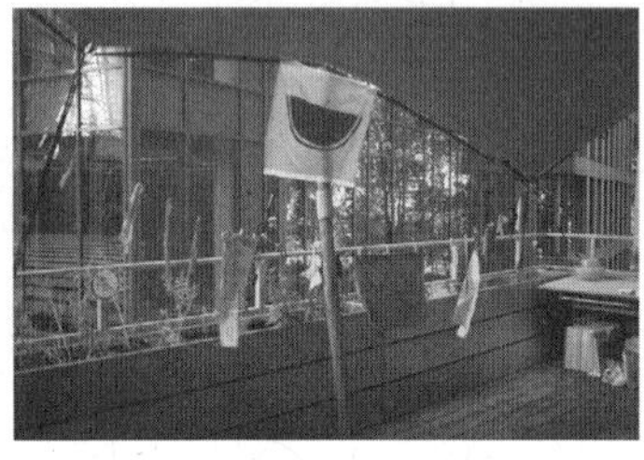

Ingredients:

- A small group of friends who are excited to organize things together
- A big network of friends of friends who are eager to help
- Some budget
- A not-quite yet rooftop garden
- An 'unpolitical' and 'neutral' art education institution
- A blend of uncomfortable power dynamics, bureaucracy, and concerns about SECCURITYYYY

(Note: We are not especially fond of this mixture, especially in combination these ingredients can cause intense nausea, still they are commonly found in every institutional pot, and we attempt to find ways to cook with them, to sweeten and spice up their bitter taste.)

- Lots of care
- Good posters for advertisement
- A choreographer who explores how bodies relate to architecture
- Some pieces of cloth
- Paper & pens
- Somebody to cook lots of soup with
- A cart full of spinach
- 12 loaves of bread
- Some homemade herb-infused water
- 2 singers, 1 DJ
- Sound Equipment such as a mixer, speakers, a microphone and plenty of extension cords
- Around 50 students, teachers, and friends

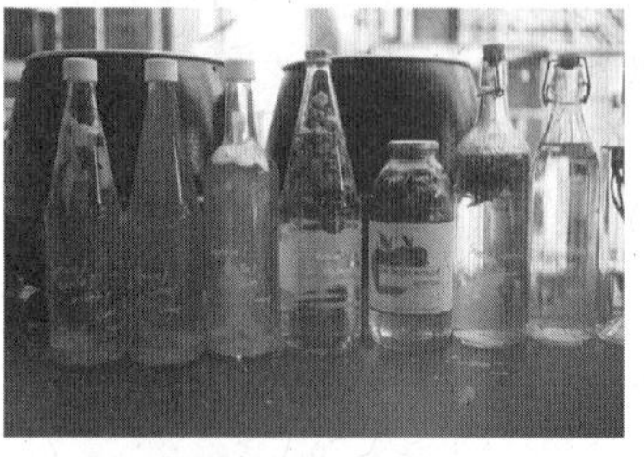

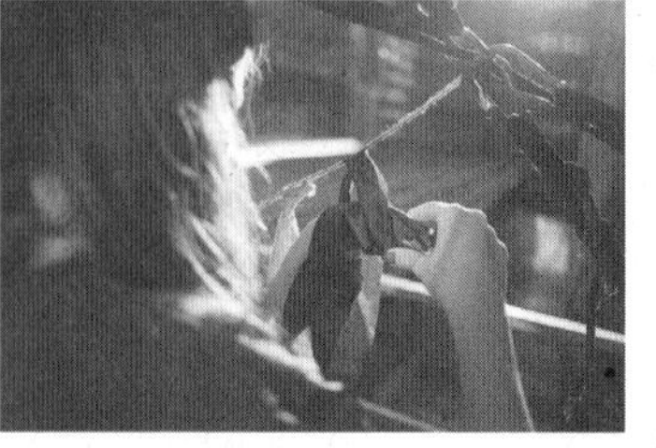

All the transitions that are happening at work, I can barely process it.

SEPTEMBER RECIPE:
A Forest Mix For Confronting Conflict

Ingredients:

- 1 or more poeple you are in conflict with
- 650g chestnuts
- a deap breath of honesty
- 315g mushrooms
- an open mind for listening
- 1 garlic clove
- 2 onions
- 75g butter
- parsley
-salt
- peper

It Doesn't Stop at Images

Introduction

Visual strata, physical layers of printed paper, vitrines, glass, boards, and thousands of photographs constituted visible constellations that excavated and uncovered references that had been invisible. These were the unseen references hidden within the normative structures of representation and visibility for gay identities, but they are still urgent images of love, care, affection, vulnerability, desire, admiration and community.

"It Doesn't Stop at Images" is a research-based project I developed with printed matter—magazines and daily publications—archived at the IHLIA (Internationaal Homo/Lesbisch Informatiecentrum en Archief) Heritage depot in Amsterdam.

Between 2020 and 2023, I tried to reposition my experience as a gay man within these publications and the imaginary reproduced in them throughout three decades—the 1970s, 1980s, and 1990s—that coincided with my childhood and adolescent years, which overlapped with the rise of the global AIDS pandemic.

"It Doesn't Stop at Images" is articulated around three chapters based on visual conversations between the materials of three chosen publications—Homologie (NL), The San Francisco Sentinel (US), and Lambda (ES)—and their consequent periodical issues expanding over three decades in relation to reflections on my experience of growing up gay.

The title of the project is borrowed from a passage written by David Wojnarowicz in his memoir, *Close to the Knives*. His original words used in the title operate as a trigger to avoid oblivion around the experience of men during the AIDS pandemic, and as a reminder to look further and beyond the photographs that reduce and fragment the visibility of these men's lives.

The text and the visual contribution for this publication are con-

sorry to jump into your check in.

Keywords:
images,
archive,
feel,
magazine,
thinking,
started,
called,
moment,
related,
publication,
gay,
connection,
barcelona,
day,
experience,
aids,
materials,
san francisco,
family,
completely

stituted by excerpts, transcriptions and constellations of words and images that emerged during the sharing sessions with the Promiscuous Care Study Group at the Willem de Kooning Academy. These sessions took place across the duration of my research at IHLIA Heritage and during the subsequent exhibition of "It Doesn't Stop at Images" at IHLIA in Amsterdam.

Conversational annotations, comments, visual reflections & revisions

Counter-narratives in response to lack of representation

[...] I landed here in IHLIA thinking, well, they're already a queer archive, I'm sure that they do an amazing work of representing the community. [...]

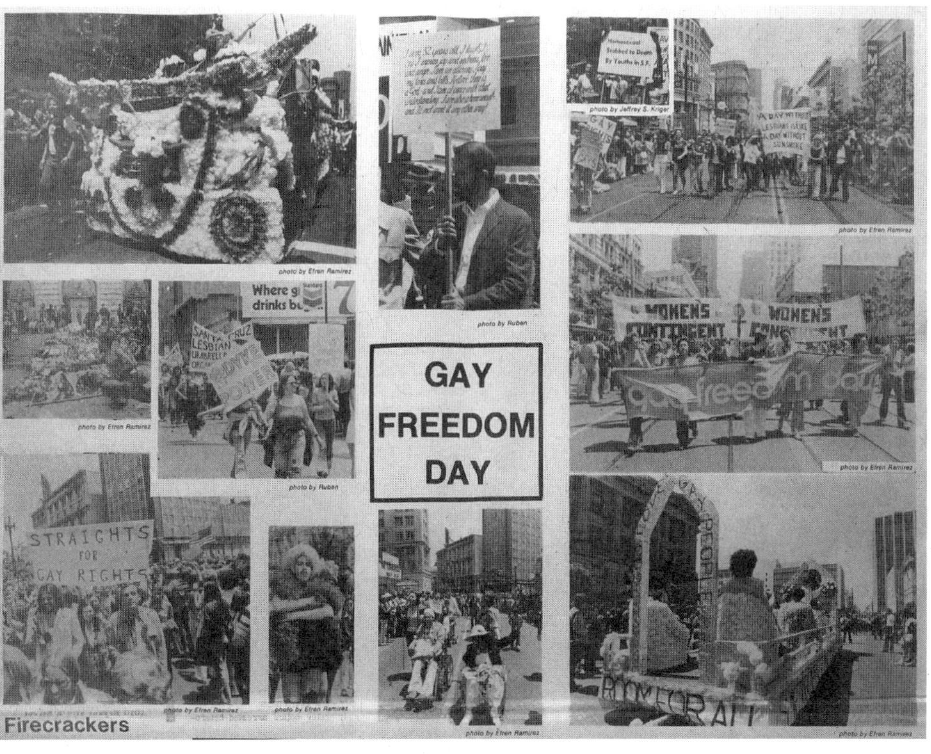

All images are sourced at the archives of *IHLIA LGBTI Heritage* from the publications *The San Francisco Sentinel* and *Homologie*.

How Do You Respond To Straight Men?

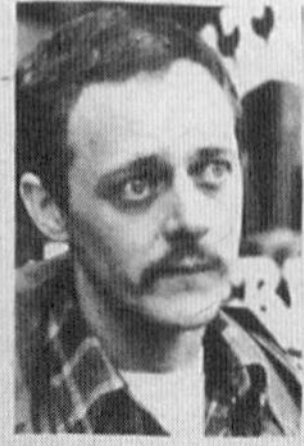

Paul Bratton, hairdresser: I like them. I love straight men as friends. They know I'm gay, they show a lot of affection for me.

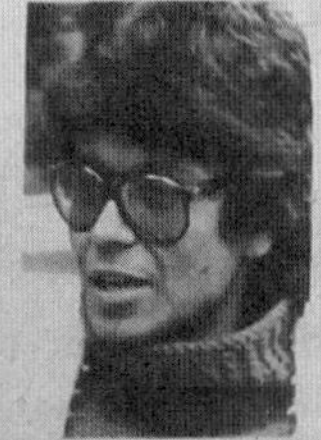

Michael Cortez, sales: Just like any other kind of man. I guess it depends on the kind of vibes I pick up. Nowadays I find it kind of hard to tell whether they are straight or gay. They show a lot of affection for men.

Tom Edwards, SPCA employee. Quite amicably, I work with them. My boss is straight. Most of my police advisors, with whom I work closely are straight. I find no difference. I was the first gay merchant on Castro and the climate we have now is thanks to the ability for us to work together. We started out as a minority and the proof of our compatability is Castro Village.

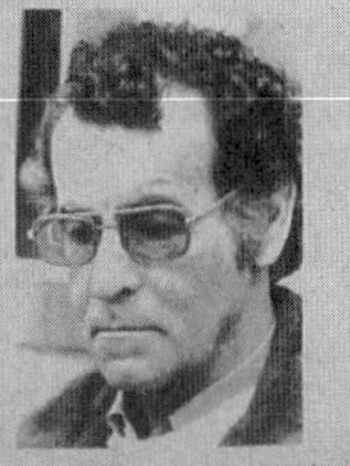

Mark, nursing student: I don't discriminate, especially in this city. It's important for us to let straight women and straight men know that we're supportive of them. Men that I've shared sexually with, who are totally in the closets, keep telling me that there is a lot more support for gay rights amongst young straight people in S.F. than we might suppose. I don't think we have as much support in the white middle class suburbs.

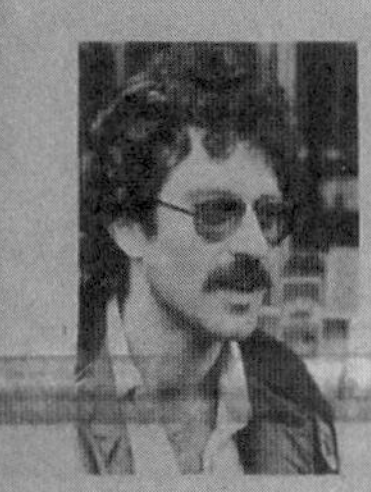

Warren Camsell, renovation and restoration: I get along with them just fine. I don't find any difficulty in relating to them at all. If I don't force my sexuality on them, they are not uptight.

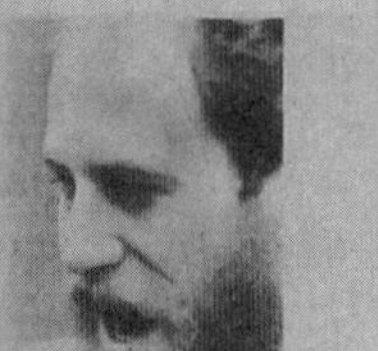

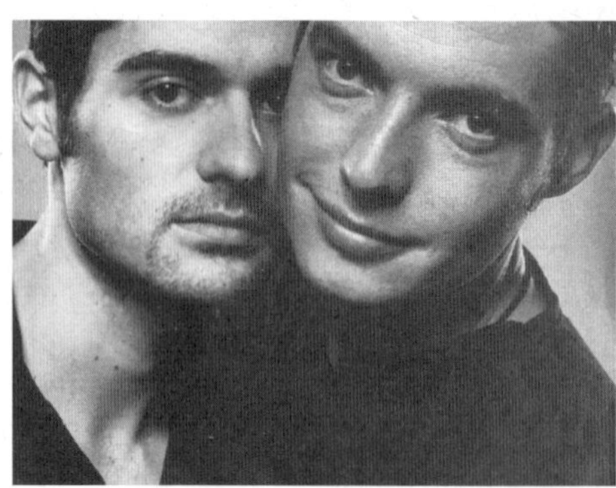

Expectations are thwarted due to the materials

[...] all of these materials that were very cliche, a stereotype and something that I've been fighting myself with, with my own identity, since I realized that I was gay. This idea that masculine values, queer masculine values, are related to promiscuity, sex, disease... standards of beauty. I always felt confronted by that. [...]

Even basic things like planning for the next day is a bit confusing.

Self-awareness and locating oneself in the archive

[...] I could recall this moment when I was a teenager. I think there is a picture here I can show... let me see if I can find it quickly... I'm looking for Barcelona. Yeah, here it is. So you can see this tiny image here, where you see a white building that looks like a church. This is a church and that one too. Those images are from a village outside of Barcelona. It's called Sitges, Sitges became for almost five decades, this beautiful place almost like a gay resort in the south of Europe. Kind of like Provincetown in the US or Fire Island. Where the LGBTQ community were gathering for decades, especially during the summer. A lot of people moved there and they lived throughout the entire year. I used to go there when I was a teenager with my parents. It's a very nice place to have dinner in the summer. So we went, the entire family, and it was kind of going to spend a day there.

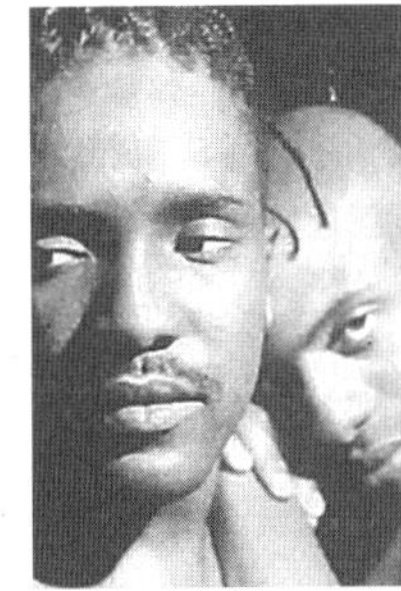

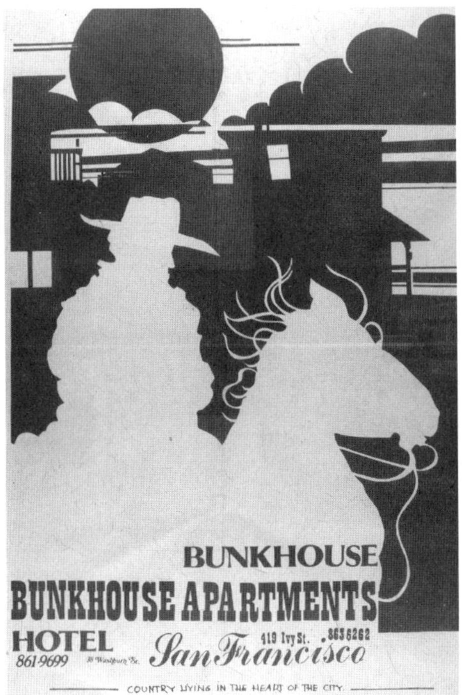

And I can recall walking on the board-walk in front of the sea, and seeing men, like this one here... but let me see if I can... yeah.... So I can recall seeing men. Like this one here. That Tom of Finland archetype. So someone wearing leather attire, very rough. And I remember seeing that when I was 12 or 13 and being amazed by the entire persona and thinking (inside my head) why they're wearing such a big amount of leather, in summer? It's summer, and so hot. Of course I didn't know anything but it was so flamboyant for me. And of course they were cruising. It was night, they were cruising with other guys. There were all of these sorts of sexual components.

Not only through the attire but also the attitude that they had. And for me, it was fascinating to see someone like them, but at the same time, I can recall the comments from my family, while we were walking along the boardwalk. And listening to them: Oh those are faggots, They're cruising. They want to have sex. Blah, blah, blah. [...]

[...] when I went to IHLIA. And I encountered all these images, again, all of these stereotypes. I can recall that moment. Suddenly I realized that I grew up with such a big amount of stereotypes towards the gay community. [...]

What Do You Do When You're Lonely?

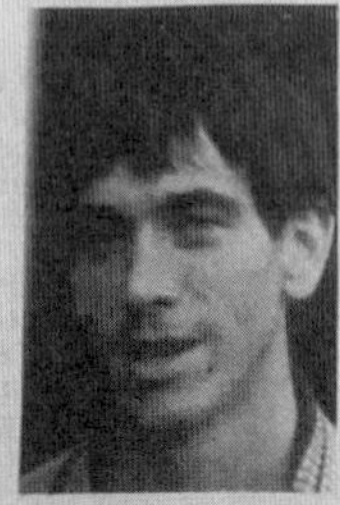

MICHAEL, Boxer: Look through the ads in the Advocate and I run on the beach.

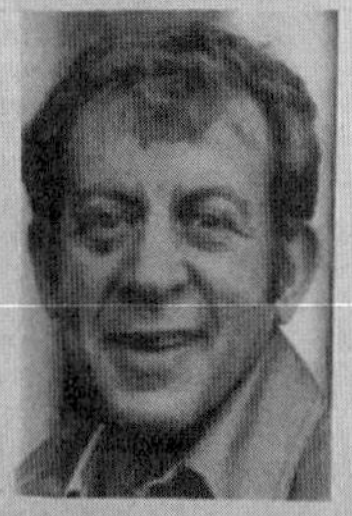

MIKE, Hairstylist: I reflect on all the good things in my life and try to think pleasant thoughts and if that don't work I go and have a drink!

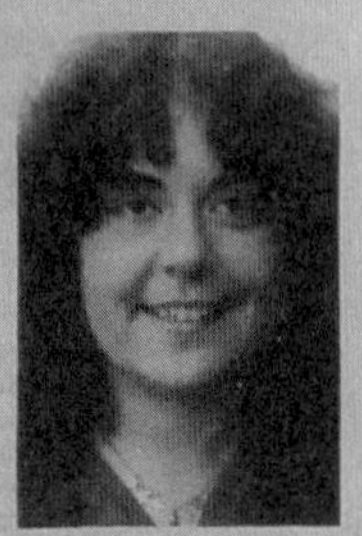

ARLA, Attorney: I don't think I ever am.

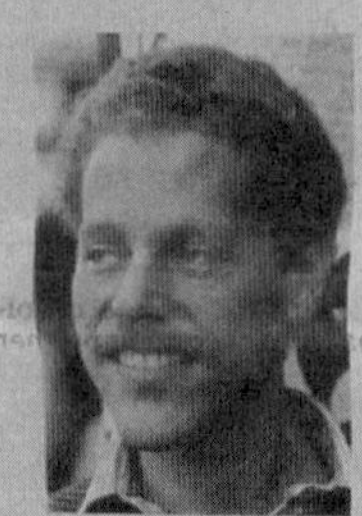

MARTIN, Attorney: I think about the state of lonliness; usually ends up being intellectualized into something else.

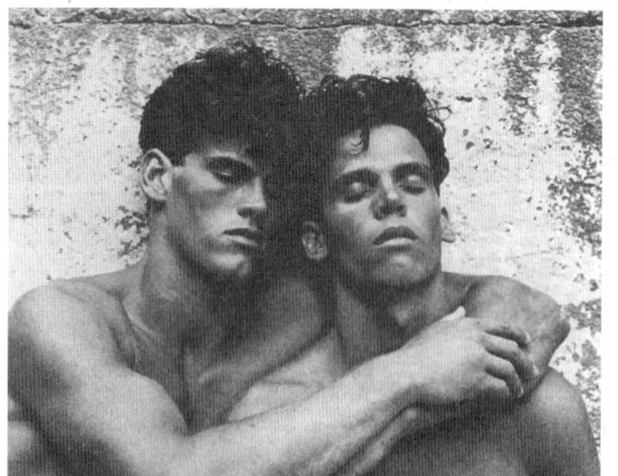

Where Do You Go On Special Occasions?

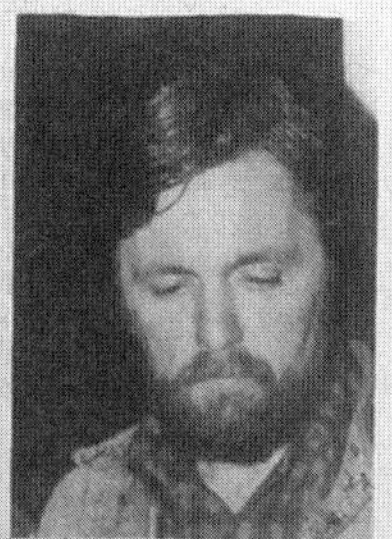

HARRY, Reservationist for a cruise line: Ruby's . . . good service, their food is exceptional and the prices are really reasonable and I feel really comfortable there.

GAIL, Msseuse and dancer: The lat place I took an out of town person was Calistoga, to the mud baths. It is pretty there.

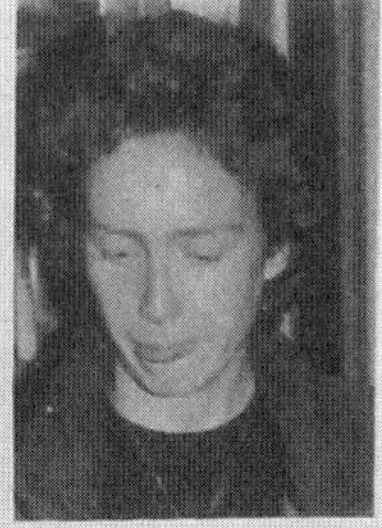

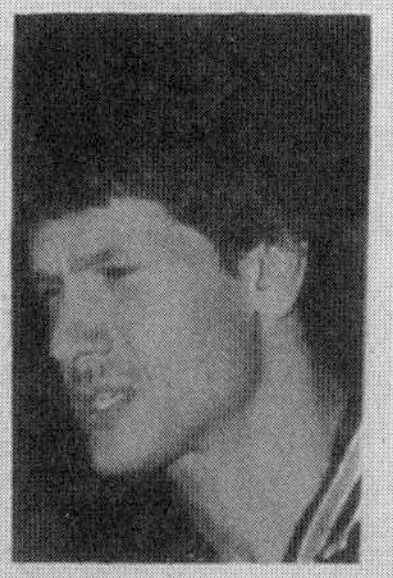

CRAIG, Former account manager: I go to the Japanese Tea Garden or to my bedroom and be by myself.

PAUL, Psychologist: Telegraph Hill and the Pump Room.

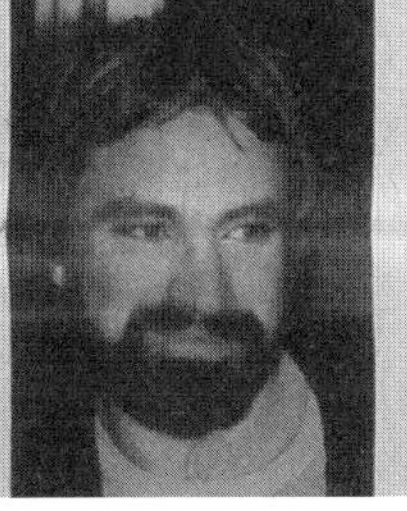

Demystification of stereotypes instead of counter-narrative in response to lack of representation

[...] I came across these three pages, an interview in a major newspaper, from the 70s in the Netherlands. And I saw a picture of a family, mom, dad and kids. I was intrigued about the text. So I asked Martha who was assisting me: Hey, can you help me to translate these quickly? I mean, we weren't going to be able to read the entire article. But basically the article was about these journalists asking this family, the mom and dad, how it was for them to raise a gay child. And definitely Wow moment... 70s, major newspaper, interview with pictures, three pages. There was something here that was already clicking with my experience. [...]

[...] And that's how I jumped into the magazine section because it's the biggest section of printed matter. And as I think about my experience, recalling this moment in Sitges and thinking about the different places where I've been living throughout my life, they were informing my experience and my relation with the LGBTQ community. [...]

Locus of desire

[...] It always becomes like a time loop when I'm working with archival materials that I want to activate. So I created the timeframe and then thought about locations that came really fast to me. I'm now living in the Netherlands, I've lived here for a couple of years. Before this, I lived in the US where my kids were born where I came out completely as a family. And before that I grew up in Spain. So how these three locations can help inform my experience. [...]

Importance of being grounded in own experience

[...] And through the process of just looking into every page of each magazine, there were already categories that were happening in my head. [...]

How Old Were You When You Realized You Were Interested in Someone of The Same Sex?

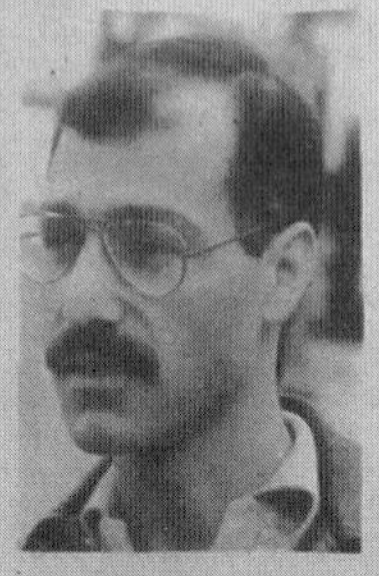

Charles Drew, haircutter: I was twenty years old but I wasn't able to have sexual fulfillment with another male til I was twenty-four, five. It's a wonderful feeling to finally have the type of sexual experience that I enjoy.

Taj, Human service consultant: Jeez! That's real, real hard. The hard part about it is sexually. Eighteen? My first attachments with men were more emotional. I was heterosexually oriented. I realize now I had strong attachments with men. I was twenty-two by the time it hit me I could want to be gay.

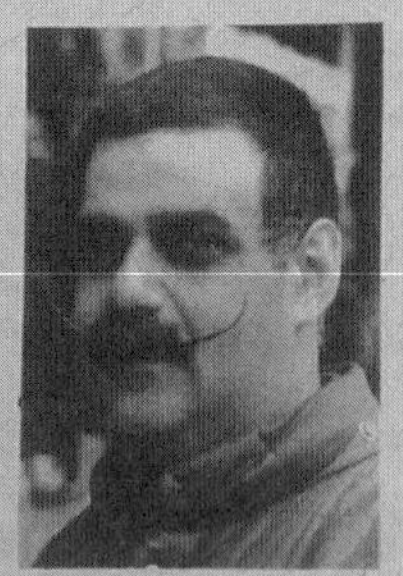

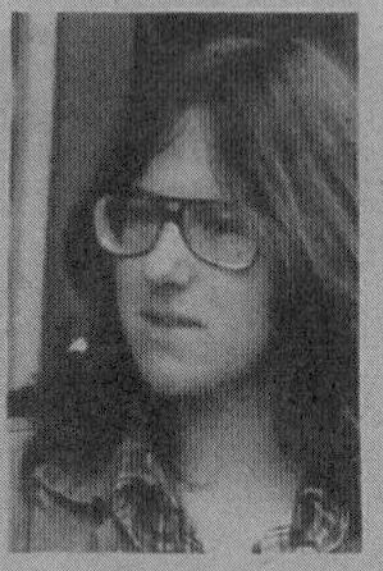

Bess, biology student: I'd say . . . fourteen. I had a lot of trouble in the beginning with men, and stuff . . . I had a female friend, we hit it off. One thing led to another. I was lucky. Life has been much better since we met.

Lloyd Parker, retired from the ships: I was one of the late closet ones. When I was ready to divorce; about—(I had just gotten out of the navy) 24, 25. That's pretty late, isn't it? Very likely I would never have known anything about it if I hadn't divorced. She was having a baby by another man.

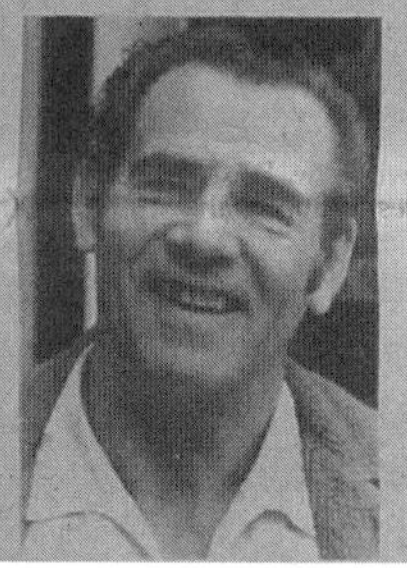

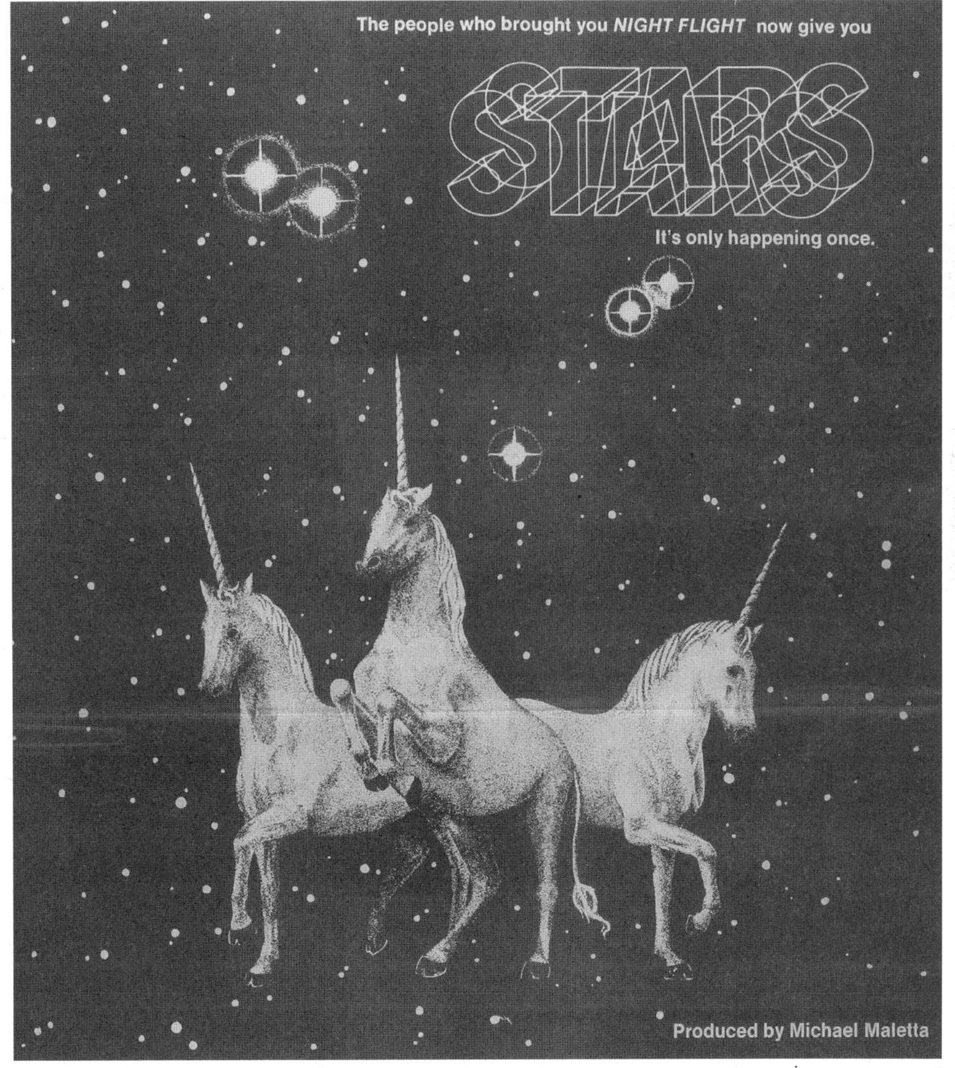
The people who brought you *NIGHT FLIGHT* now give you
STARS
It's only happening once.
Produced by Michael Maletta

How Do You Relate To Former Lovers?

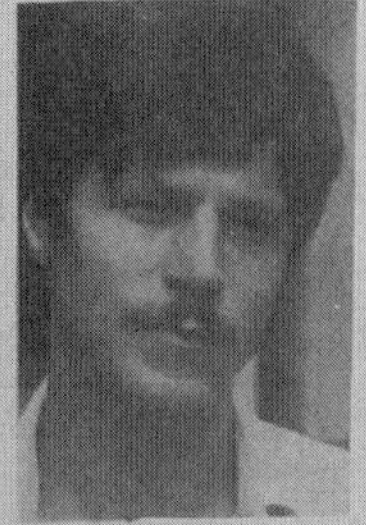

P. Herrera, furniture mover: Very well. In fact we're closer now than we ever were. I've only got one. It's like a family.

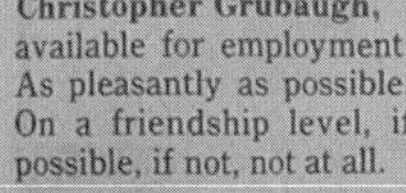

Christopher Grubaugh, available for employment: As pleasantly as possible. On a friendship level, if possible, if not, not at all.

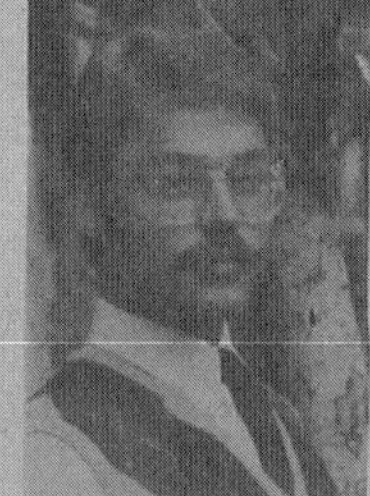

Bruce Monette, artist: Oh . . . as friends, usually, if possible. Also as learning experiences. I think everybody has something to give to each other, and just because the loving has ended doesn't mean the giving has to end.

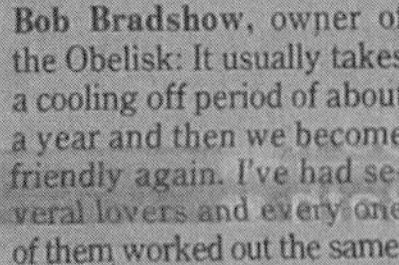

Bob Bradshow, owner of the Obelisk: It usually takes a cooling off period of about a year and then we become friendly again. I've had several lovers and every one of them worked out the same.

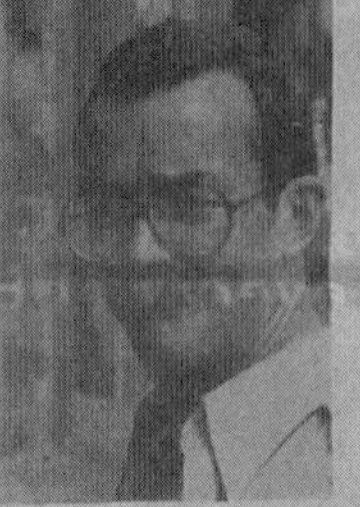

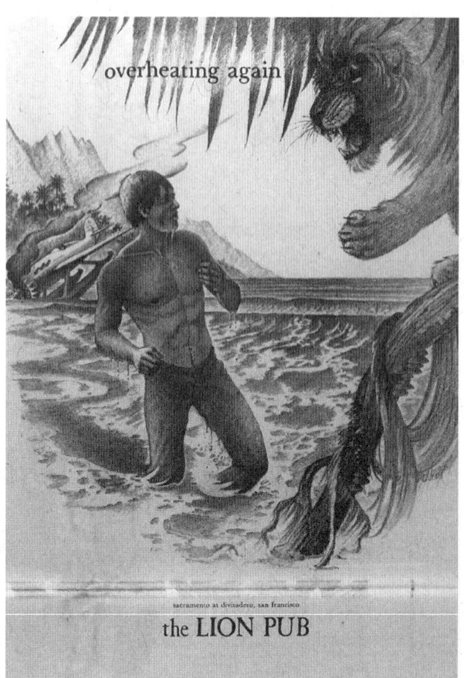

He was sick for like five days and then I got sick, and then someone got sick after.

Heaps and galaxies (different forms)

[...] *It Doesn't Stop at Images*. The title comes from the book *Close to the Knives* by David Wojnarowicz, who was an artist who died of AIDS in the 90s in New York. And in this chapter of *Close to the Knives*, he starts the paragraph saying it doesn't stop at images and continues the paragraph basically verbalizing the situation that the LGBTQ community and specifically the gay image in the US is having with the representation of AIDS in the media, and how they're completely targeting the gay community. And he wants to say that the LGBTQ community and the gay community is just not an image in the media. [...]

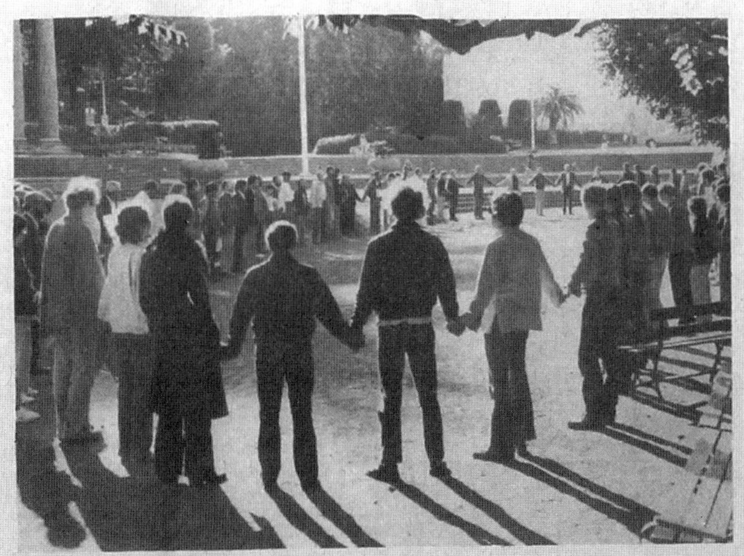

Citizens and politicians alike gathered in Golden Gate Park the day before the Gay Freedom Day Parade to plant a tree in memory of Robert Hillsborough, a gay gardener who worked in the park and was slain last year one week before Gay Freedom Day. ***(Savage Photography photo.)***

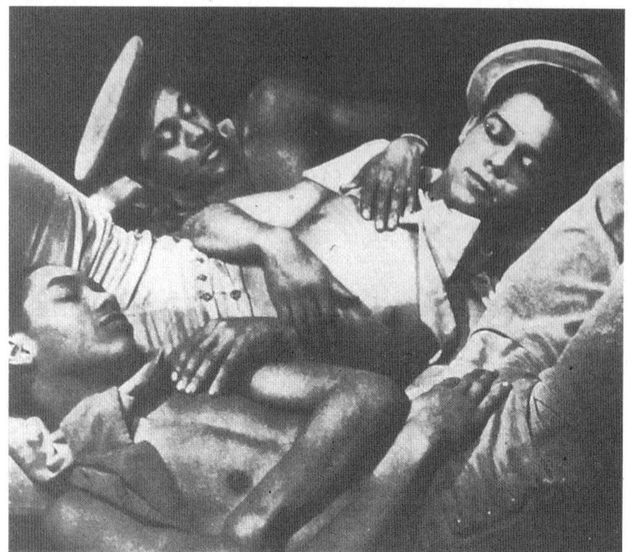

An intertwining (constellation) new archive? or re-reading an existing archive (does it matter?)

[...] You see connections through San Francisco, Barcelona, Netherlands, and they're all colliding and happening at the same time, in the same decades, but they are different places.

So, for me, it's beautiful how these collective things happen. And I'm able to align them. [...]

Kids of Gays Normal

The June 17 issue of *Science News* ran an article discussing the results of a study by a professor at the State University of New York at Stonybrook, which indicates that the children of gays and transsexuals are not adversely affected in the area of their sexual identity.

37 children, reared in families in which both parents are female or one of the parents have changed sex were studied by Richard Green who published the results for the American Journal of Psychiatry.

Thirty-six of the children are heterosexually oriented, meaning that those of adolescent age are attracted to members of the opposite sex and the younger members of the group show indications that they are developing "normally".

According to the article in *Science News*, Green's report "punches some holes in psychoanalytic theory." Before analyzing his results, Green reasoned that the stages of normal sexual development, like "penis envy, castration fear and the resolution of family romance" would be absent from these households and would in fact, reverse or adversely affect this development.

However, Green found out differently. Green observed that "What one can say at this time, based on the best indicators of emerging sexual identity, psychosexual development appears to be typical in at least 36 of the 37 children described in this paper."

Eighteen males and nineteen females ages 3-20 were studied for a period of two years. Twenty-one of these children were parented by homosexuals and sixteen were parented by transsexuals.

In fact, several of the children parented by transsexuals remember the parent in his pre-operative sexual state.

The report involved studying the younger children in toy and game choices and "peer group composition" which is usually same-sex for grade school ages. The younger children were also studied for their clothing preferences, vocational aspirations and "draw-a-person" tests. It is interesting to note that the male children normally drew males first and females second and vice versa for female children.

The adolescents were observed through their romantic crushes, sexual behavior and erotic fantasies.

Except for one of the children observed, none of the children displayed homosexual or transsexual behavior of fantasy activity. The vocational choices were standard and, *Science News* observed, "even somewhat chauvinistically flavored preferences, with boys designating positions such as doctors, engineers, firemen, scientists and policemen opting for nurses and teachers. Only two girls ever chose "housewife" or "mommy" and "one set her sights on 'popsicle lady.'"

Concluding the article, Green remarked that there are, of course, outside influences and role-models such as school, peer-groups and television.

Green's final comment was "At this stage I tentatively suggest that children being raised by transsexual and homosexual parents do not differ appreciably from children raised in more conventional family settings."

What Especially Turns You On About Other People

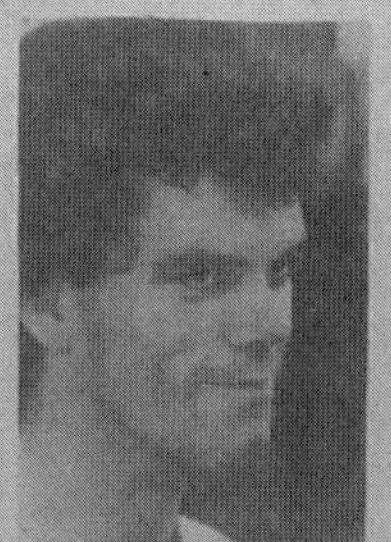

Scott Neail, person-having-a-good-time: Personalities mainly, above everything else. Outgoing, sincere, basically honest people that feel good about themselves and don't play games. I need to relate on a personal basis, as far as what makes them tick, before I can relate physically.

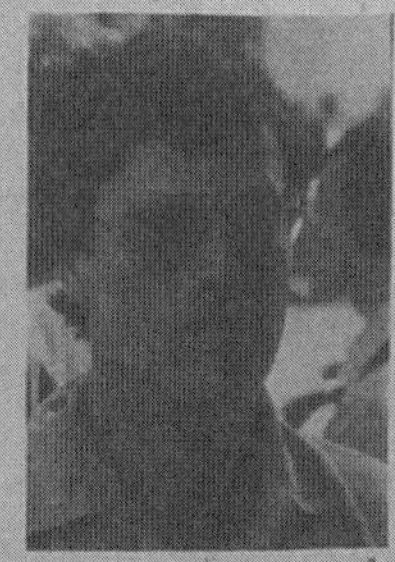

Wayne Hooper, free lance writer: Uniquity, each person's uniqueness. I need to get along and interact with others. I respond to someone who's really into what they're doing sponteneously and uninhibited, especially what Erica John caleld "the zipless fuck", where you meet someone and have fantastic sex without a word being spoken.

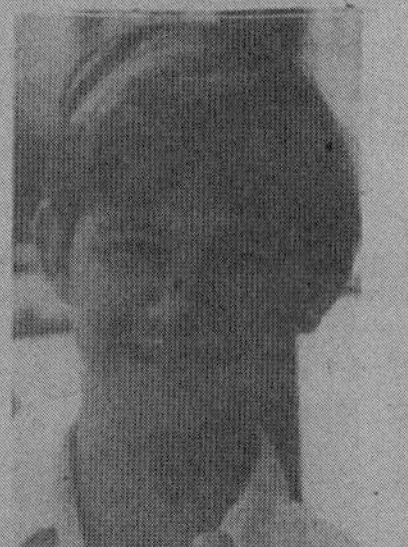

Kim Workman, floor refinisher: I think everybody on Castro St. turns me on. Men! Especially beards and mustaches . . . and leather. The last guy had a beautiful personality. I dig nice people.

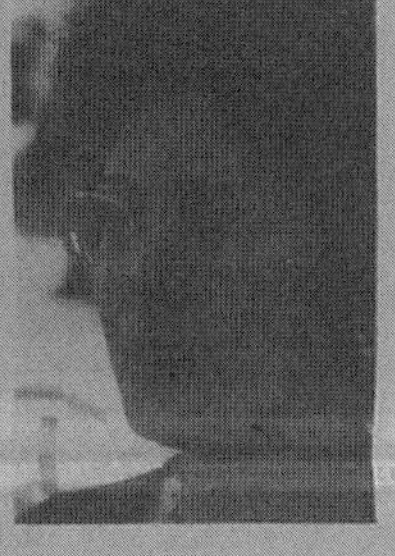

Seven Starrshaw, escrow officer: Of course the first thing is physical, then, a sense of humor, intelligence and money. I like blondes, blue eyes and someone who enjoys eating. People keep telling me I'm really into physical things.

Genealogy, geography, history

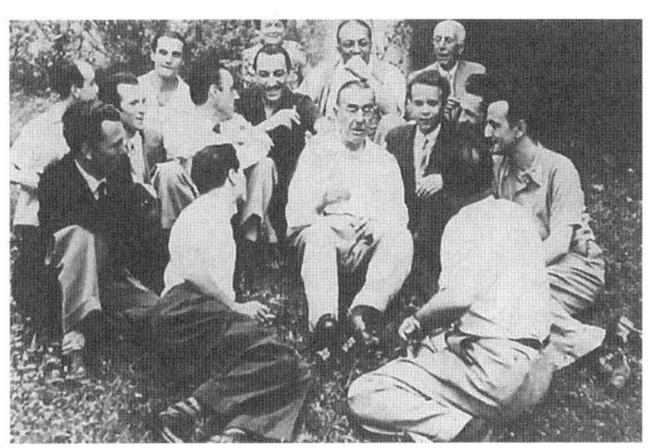

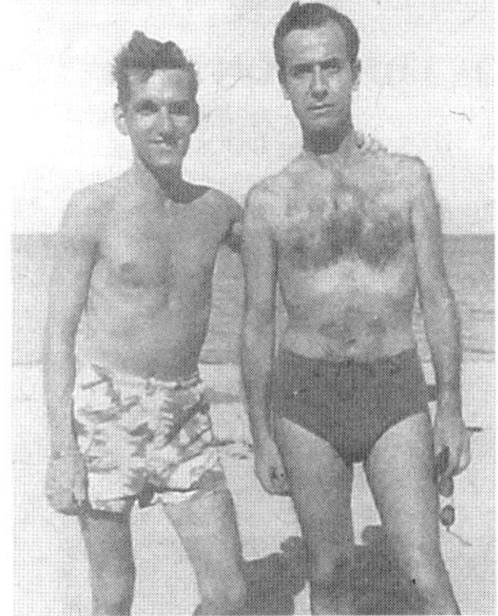

Gravity, Immunity and Soil

Dear Reader,

Below is a talk I presented at the Willem de Kooning Academy in Rotterdam on the 9th of June 2022. During this time I was half way through a research position in which I had promised to explore some myths of separability[1] that emerged out of (or were conceived under) modernity. Within this broad remit my research meandered and took tangents that included gardens, practices of death and dying, sleep, bacteria, healthcare, odour, environmental justice, viruses, toxic landscapes, plumbing and fossil fuel infrastructure but somehow always related to and through the body. Ultimately I focused specifically on the immune system and soil.

I initially thought of the collective study groups that I co-constituted as being a place to share, find and dialogue about content. In reality the method of collective study, in and of itself, taught me more than any individual thing we discussed.

One of these collective study moments was the Promiscuous Care Study Group. Initiated by Michelle Teran, the group drew together many of us from the academy working somehow around the theme of care. It opened a space for meeting under para- extra- intra- institutional forms of being and learning. We were invited to bring food, tea, concerns, our bodies, our fatigue and our pains, our needs, anger, joy, refusal and differences as well as our thoughts, research and references to our meetings. In this space we could acknowledge the whole of the person, not just the palatable parts we usually reveal at work. This acknowledgement became, in practice, a method for relating to one another: 'check ins', where each person in the group talked about pressing thoughts or feelings, while initially a way to introduce the sessions, gradually took over and became the ground from which our conversation grew. This was a lesson for me, that in trusting the intersectional and embodied knowledge(s) gathered within the room, rather than imposing thematics, what is most important can emerge.

1. Gesturing towards Decolonial Futures Collective (GTDF) define modernity as having built an ideological 'foundation of separability (separations between humans and the earth, and hierarchies of human value)' GTDF website: https://decolonial-futures.net/house-of-modernity-zine/.

2022... let's hope it offers more levity and grace.

This group was also a much needed and welcome relief from the usual tempo, pace, demands and formalities of the institution. It intersected with my own research in thinking about what care can look like and how it can be performed. Too often care is represented as only softness; as tea and cake and back rubs. The group importantly made space for radical softness, for rest as resistance and resilience, but also for care envisaged as protest, as solidarity, as rebellion.

I also initiated and facilitated the (toxic) soil study group: an informal group of teachers, BA and MA students and researchers who met during this period around the topic of the (toxic) soil of Rotterdam. Over the period of a year, we met in classrooms, gardens, a disused industrial greenhouse and 'studied' together; we read, watched films, took trips, dug and planted, told stories and made clay objects. Here too, experience, situated learning and doing were prioritised. It was a relief to move, to go outdoors, to read and learn with all of the senses. The group manifested a kind of learning that resembles soil. We slowly, laterally, composted together; some things were quickly metabolised, others slowly digested. I weaned myself from texts a bit and learned to trust process, relation and observation, to listen more closely to the ground.

Reflection: towards an ecology of soil

Revisiting the talk I presented in June 2022, six months later, I wanted to take the opportunity to preface it in a way that is mindful of these lessons.This involves thinking about what you and I might have in common, and the space between us, to address your body, and the knowledge it holds.

So, dear reader, how do you feel? How is your body? Are you breathing? Draw your attention to the pace of your breath. Is it deep or shallow? Notice where the air enters and where it goes. On the inhale feel how the cool, fresh air passes in through your nostrils and travels up and inside your body. Think about what else goes in along with the oxygen; there's nitrogen, also C02 in there and probably argon. Can you distinguish these gases as you inhale them? In one breath there is likely methane, helium, carbon monoxide, ammonia, water vapour, smoke, dust, pollen and fungal spores. As you inhale, open your ribcage to make space to host these molecules.

Every time you breathe out this composition shifts a little. Who inhales what you have exhaled?

What or who do you see? Probably you are focused here on these words but likely you have other impressions in your peripheral vision which you are mostly blocking out. What if you allow yourself to observe these peripheries? Are you inside or outside? What ground do you stand on? What is this ground made of? Is it solid? Who owns this ground? What history lies here?

What do you hear? Perhaps you can identify sounds with no clear origin. Is it quiet enough that you can hear something from your own body? Perhaps the sounds of the air passing through the back of your throat, your stomach digesting, or a soft squelch when you swallow? When did you last speak and to whom? How did the words feel as they left your mouth? How and where did your words land?

What can you smell? Are you close enough to smell another person? Can you smell yourself? Lots of things stink. Are you one of these things? Do these words have an odour? Sometimes it helps to close your eyes as you try to discern the subtleties. The olfactory bulb, like the immune system, remembers molecules without the help of the brain. What is the scent of memory? Can you describe the smell of someone you love? Are you sweating? Do you feel the edge of your body without looking at it? What is touching your skin now? Where is your body in contact with what holds your weight? How does this weight feel? When was the last time you were touched and how? Hold your ear lobe between your fingertips. Feel the place where soft skin meets cartilage and as you do think about where the sea meets the land, or where soil meets concrete.

What do you sense that you don't have a name for? Are you experiencing sensations that do not fit into a clear category? Are you comfortable with experiences that you cannot give a name to? When does perception become sensation?

As you read on, remember that you have a body and to keep observing it.

The Talk

I will start us off not with a part of the body but a complex network of parts; the immune system that governs and determines what is integrated into or rejected from the body. The immune system begins and ends with the largest organ—the skin, a watertight but permeable boundary crawling with microbial life, a soft edge of the self, highly respondent to environment, temperature, touch, bruising, humidity and pathogens.

The immune system is a kind of memory bank that requires encounters with antigens in order to identify threats correctly. In *Inflamed: Deep Medicine and the Anatomy of Injustice*, Rupa Marya and Raj Patel critique the dominant militaristic description of the immune system to 'fight off' infection and instead articulate it as a complex

Well just wondering how long this can go on, it's been two years now.

and nuanced, adaptive and acquired system which is highly dependent and attuned to its specific exposome (including social environments).[2]

Soil, a sort of skin for the earth, shares a surprising number of microorganisms that we have within our bodies.[3] Many antibiotics and fungicides used in industrial farming are the same that are used in medicine. The aspergillus fungus, for instance, has developed immunity to some fungicides through excessive exposure in farmed soil (where it is relatively harmless) so that when it gets into immunocompromised human lungs it can cause a deadly and untreatable disease (aspergillosis).[4] If given time, soil develops immunity to drought and other unfavourable conditions, learning from the previous season to make adaptations for the next.[5] Is it a stretch to call this a kind of memory?

Soil is a multifaceted material archive which does not fit within any single discipline: It contains bodies of plants, animals, humans, sedimentation and ancient rock and also remnants of human endeavour; ancient artefacts, lead, mercury, microplastics, arsenic, petrochemical run off, benzene. If probed just a little it can provide a murky mirror to our recent as well as our deep past.

The toxicity of Rotterdam's soil is often attributed to legacies of war-time bombing. Although perhaps a pleasingly simple explanation, this is not accurate. Most of the vast quantities of lead in Rotterdam soil doesn't come from war but industry: Through the 19th and early 20th centuries Rotterdam contained a high concentration of lead paint factories who dumped excess lead into the soil. As an industrial port city, Rotterdam is surrounded on three sides by oil refineries (Exxon, BP and VPR energy have one each, Shell has three). This has led to ground poisoned both with heavy metals and volatile chemicals, such as benzene. The contaminated soil is treated by the city as a problem to be solved rather than as a living, evolving material. Conducting interviews with toxicologists and professional remediators working in Rotterdam, they sternly warn me not to let my young daughter touch this soil with her bare skin.

2. Rupa Marya and Raj Patel, "Immune System: I Am Because You Are," in *Inflamed: Deep Medicine and the Anatomy of Injustice* (London: Penguin Books, 2021), 33-39.

3. Samiran Banerjee, and Marcel G. A. van der Heijden, "Soil Microbiomes and One Health," *Nat Rev Microbiol* 21 (2023): 6-20, https://doi.org/10.1038/s41579-022-00779-w.

4. Centers for Disease Control and Prevention, *Antimicrobial-Resistant Aspergillus*, accessed December 27 2022, https://www.cdc.gov/fungal/diseases/aspergillosis/antifungal-resistant.html.

5. Emma J. Sayer, John A. Crawford, James Edgerley, et al., "Adaptation to Chronic Drought Modifies Soil Microbial Community Responses to Phytohormones," *Commun Biol* 4, 516 (2021), https://doi.org/10.1038/s42003-021-02037-w. org/10.1038/s42003-021-02037-w.

Botanist and citizen of the Potawatomi Nation Robin Wall Kimmerer states that we are all immigrants. In so doing she calls upon her reader to begin a process of developing their indigeneity with where they are at now. For her this involves developing a different sense of time—having accountability to the future and developing reciprocity with that which you stand on; both in terms of soil and of history.[6] This resonates with the squatting ideology outlined by Jay Jordan and Isabelle Fremeaux in their description of inhabiting la zad autonomous zone in France. In *We Are 'Nature' Defending Itself: Entangling Art, Activism and Autonomous Zones*, they define squatting as a process of building structures and relations through planting roots to live in and care for, as if you will be there forever despite knowing you will not.[7] I am confronted with the question; how to responsibly establish roots and develop reciprocity here in Rotterdam with(in) such toxic material?

If both soil and the immune system are a sort of memory bank, they are not static; they are constantly in processes of reconfiguration, adaptation and becoming. Soil self-remediates and metabolises toxins—just not effectively within capitalist time frames.[8]

The word 'soil' itself may be an overly simplified misnomer. It tries to encompass something complex, non-linear, mutable and slippery. As María Puig de la Bellacasa puts it:

> *Are living organisms part of soil? We would include the phrase "with its living organisms" in the general definition of soil. Thus, from our viewpoint soil is alive and is composed of living and nonliving components having many interactions… When we view the soil system as an environment for organisms, we must remember that the biota have been involved in its creation, as well as adapting to life within it. In this conception soil is not just a habitat or medium for plants and organisms; nor is it just decomposed material, the organic and mineral end product of organism activity. Organisms are soil. A lively soil can only exist with and through a*

6. Robin Wall Kimmerer, "Skywoman Falling," in *Braiding Sweetgrass: Indigenous Wisdom, Scientific Knowledge and the Teachings of Plants* (London; Penguin Books, 2013), 8-9.

7. Isabelle Fremeaux and Jay Jordan, *We are 'Nature' Defending Itself: Entangling Art, Activism and Autonomous Zones* (London: Pluto Press/Journal of Aesthetics & Protest, 2021).

8. By this I mean, microbes in soil can self-remediate but not for example within the time frame of a housing development planned on toxic soil. María Puig de la Bellacasa makes this argument: See: María Puig de la Bellacasa, "Soil Times: The Pace of Ecological Care," *Solitude Journal* 1 (2017).

Multiple studies have recently been done on microbial remediation techniques such as this one from 2020: https://www.nature.com/articles/s43017-020-0061-y.

But I can't even visit her because of COVID.

multispecies community of biota that makes it, that contributes to its creation.

María Puig de la Bellacasa, *Soil Times: The Pace of Ecological Care*[9]

9. de la Bellacasa (n 8) 103.

If soil is both the habitat and organisms that inhabit that habitat, and at once those organisms are habitat for one another and are adapting to the habitat they co-constitute, then what single word can contain such a multiplicity? Soil can be seen more as a process than an object, an adjective rather than a noun. Soil soils; it is soiling. Learning this, I ask myself what about our societies' above ground and collective rememberings can we learn from soil's entangled intra-dependent operation?

10. The amazing *ACT UP Oral History Project* is available at: https://actuporalhistory.org/.

Looking down to the soil, rather than up to the heavens I think about grassroots movements and histories from below. Sarah Schulman's incredible *ACT UP Oral History Project*[10] gathers 188 interviews on the devastating history of the HIV/AIDS epidemic and ACT UP; the social movement that grew in defiance of the societal and governmental neglect faced by the communities most affected. In Sarah Schulman's 2021 book on the history of ACT UP[11] as well as in the online *ACT UP Oral History Project*, the form of remembering evokes collective action itself; complex and messy, negotiated, woven and decentralised.

11. Sarah Schulman, *Let the Record Show: A Political History of ACT UP New York, 1987–1993* (New York: Picador / Farrar, Straus and Giroux, 2021).

The HIV/AIDS epidemic is still ongoing, particularly for those without access to adequate care and antiretroviral drugs. Its impact has just been eclipsed by subsequent pandemics. At its height during the 80s and 90s it presented a moment when societies were faced with questions about the parameters of care and inclusion, whether to choose to ignore, stigmatise and sacrifice a part of the social body in the marginalised communities most devastatingly impacted by that pandemic; namely queer communities, sex workers and drug users. In Schulman's careful and collective representation, ACT UP generated an affirmative practice. It took in and asserted difference, made no apologies for what bodies are and do, it built solidarities and refused to cast blame onto individuals. Rather than policing its marginal constituents, it focused insistently on those in power, demanding systemic, cultural shifts, acknowledgement of rights to visibility, recognition, care and ultimately to life.

12. Gran Fury poster campaign, New York City (1989).

This is summed up succinctly in the slogan from artist collective Gran Fury *Kissing Doesn't Kill: Greed and Indifference Do.*[12]
The link between bodies and soil can also be between life and death. While alive, the immune system resists bacteria, fungus and viruses just enough to hold the body together. When we die and the immune system stops mediating, we rapidly are overrun and metabolised, we become

soil and (if given the opportunity) return to the earth. We are constituted by soil (it grows the food we eat) and we are the soil of the future. As Donna Haraway famously states "we are compost, not posthuman."[13] For ACT UP, death was an implicit presence not to shy away from, grief and loss were rendered explicit. In the famous *Ashes Action* of 1992, ashes of AIDS victims were marched by friends, lovers and family to the White House and thrown onto the lawn. Protesters chanted "Bringing our dead to your door / We won't take it anymore."

Soil, as a mix of composing and composting matter, can reveal muddy spillovers between life and death. Until recently the reason for the amount of viruses in soil was not evident. It was discovered[14] that these viruses have a parasitic function, to kill and feed on the bacteria in soil. During this process a sticky glue called 'necro-mass' is released from the dead bacteria which is the substance that holds carbon in the soil. Viruses, through killing bacteria, are vital to soil health, carbon sequestration and subsequently to every organism living on earth.

In her writing on immunity, Eula Biss makes a parallel point about the human body:

> *A virus can, on occasion, infect an organism in a way that ensures the viral DNA will be passed on to that organism's offspring as part of their genetic code. A rather surprising amount of the human genome is made up of debris from ancient viral infections. Some of that genetic material does nothing, so far as we know, some can trigger cancer under certain conditions, and some has become essential to our survival. The cells that form the outer layer of the placenta for a human foetus bind to each other using a gene that originated, long ago, from a virus.*[15]

Biss argues that we cannot, and should not, try to isolate or protect children or ourselves, against the world. Instead she posits that we understand ourselves as forming each other's ground, part of a commonly negotiated immune system and collectively responsible for our most vulnerable parts. Collective immunity shows, on a molecular level, that we, like soil, co-constitute our shared environment. We are each other's social and molecular ground. To quote Biss again:

> *If we do not yet know what the presence of a vast range of chemicals in umbilical cord blood and breast milk might mean for the future of our childrens' health we do at least know that we are no cleaner, even at birth, than our environment at large.*

13. Donna Haraway, *Staying with the Trouble: Making Kin in the Chthulucene* (Durham: Duke University Press, 2016), 55.

14. Partly by scientists at Leiden University. Research into viruses in soil began around 2015 and is ongoing. https://www.sciencedirect.com/science/article/abs/pii/S0038071718303432.

15. Eula Biss, *On Immunity: An Inoculation* (Minneapolis MN: Graywolf Press, 2015), 31.

I tested positive with COVID.

We are all already polluted. We have more micro-organisms in our guts than we have cells in our bodies—we are crawling with bacteria and we are full of chemicals. We are in other words continuous with everything here on earth. Including, and especially, each other.[16]

To be grounded is to be weighted, rooted, secure but also to be stuck and limited. The immune system evolved to be terrestrial, it seems to require literal grounding or gravity to work:[17] without it astronauts in space can experience the resurgence of childhood illnesses such as chicken pox. On earth these dormant viruses that are carried within us are held at bay.

So here we are, polluted bodies on damaged earth, held by gravity and holding one another. I end on this note with an excerpt from the tape journals of David Wojnarowicz:

> *'Survival is such a lovely thing, such a transient thing.' Survival is a moral good, possibly the only moral good. But my survival is not for myself but for others. I alone don't get to decide what matters. It's only when we meet that this becomes something. My body is precious and special because it's yours. If you want it.*

David Velasco, *The Weight of the Earth: The Tape Journals of David Wojnarowicz*[18]

16. Ibid 76.

17. This is attributed to immune cells becoming dysfunctional in zero gravity, specifically T-cell activation, https://www.sciencedirect.com/science/article/abs/pii S0038071718303432, https://www.nature.com/articles/s41526-021-00141-z. S0038071718303432, https://www.nature.com/articles/s41526-021-00141-z.

18. David Velasco, "No Motive," forward in *The Weight of the Earth: The Tape Journals of David Wojnarowicz*, eds. Lisa Darms and David O'Neill (South Pasadena CA: Semiotext(e), 2018). Velasco's passage opens with an embedded quote from David Wojnarowicz, from his book *Close to The Knives: A Memoir of Disintegration* (New York: Vintage, 1991), 168.

Let Us Meet in the Margins[1] [Barzakh]

١. البرزخ

Dear Barzakhiya,

حضرة البرزخية،

I'm very glad I have not been materializing for a while. I do not belong in this realm of matter, I need breaks here and there to go to the surface and breathe. So,

stop

breathe.

In.

----

pause

---------------------------- out.

Repeat however long you need. I'll still be here, waiting.

1. برزخ

2. برزخ

I will not leave. Unless you displace me, which is also okay. I'm used to it. Continual displacement is my preferred means of travel. It means I can be found somewhere else, by someone else, another Barzakhiya lost between the layers of life which she can only maybe squeeze into if she tries hard enough. Sometimes it feels like we still need to wear Victorian underwear, just metaphysically now. Sometimes it is good to be clothed naked in solitude. Unmaterialized. Unseen. I also don't mind if you don't know what I am talking about, I'm trying to retire from intellectualism. To submit to the desire of feeling. Understanding intuitively. To make the master in me submit to its servant, the raw unscreened input only filtered through the act of writing. Or typing. I think it's time for another break.[1]

Pause.
Take your time.

There's no need to rush back here.

Barzakhiyaat are here to stay. Between the lines,[2] the parameters, the categories. Making transparency opaque for the sake of conjuring up a story, a figure to embody. To narrate yourself into, if you wish. This story can be about you. If you wish. Feel free to take from the words which are not mine in the first place. If you cannot own a letter why would you be able to own a word or a sentence or a story. Feel free to participate. Write to me. Write to you. Become me and you at the same time. Lose your borders in reading, they were never yours to begin with. Forget the borders of the text, they were never intended to be there to begin with. Begin, not anew, but in a debt that cannot be paid back, only forward. It is still okay if you do not know what I am talking about. I hope you know that. I am also just practicing freedom in writing. I think that's what this text is about. Feel free to enter it when you feel like it. Feel free to write with me if you feel like it. I am here to host you and the metaphysical back fat that is squeezed out of your corset. By reading this you are hosting me too, so thank you.

Yours, Barzakhiya مودتي، البرزخية

Dear Barzakhiya, حضرة البرزخية،

There is so much I would like to write. There is so much I need to say. But right now, what is urgent, what I would like to highlight from my writing is that I am trying to propose our Islamic framework as an alternative value system to Western liberal values which have, more than ever right now, been proven to be so very selective. Which have been proven, again and again, to be themselves rooted in white supremacy. The "humanity" of the west which it so very much prides itself on is a mere hollow shell for their crimes. A hollow shell which borders and protects white lives. A military checkpoint we can maybe pass through after violent interrogation. Like the ones in occupied Palestine, which European Christians and Jews, practicing or not, can easily pass. While for Muslim and Christian Palestinians, these places exist not only to restrict their movement, but to intimidate, to humiliate, and harass. Western humanity selectively recognizes some lives as protectable, while actively keeping up the organized violence against others. This is the practice of bordering, or *borderizing* bodies as Mbembe would put it. Some bodies are *discounted*, are thought of as not containing life. "They are, strictly speaking, bodies at the limits of life,[3] trapped in uninhabitable worlds and inhospitable places. The kind of life they bear or contain is not insured or is uninsurable."[4] "They are trapped in fragmented spaces, stretched time and indefinite waiting.[5]"[6]

Again and again, we are reminded that we are not human enough. Not until we manage to belong to the other side of the border. Not until we go through checkpoint after checkpoint. Not until we prove our souls to be sellable to neoliberalism. We must pledge allegiance to Progress with a capital P. We must prove interest in the current order. Must prove our willingness to invest. Some bodies are allowed to move, while others are stopped at the border. Are made to wait at the limits of life.[7] What I propose is that we might as well get comfortable here, at the border, where some of us already are.

Some of us don't need theory to realize this. Don't

3. برزخ

4. Achille Mbembe, "Bodies as Borders," *From the European South*, no. 4 (2019): 10.

5. برزخ

6. Julie Peteet, "Closure's Temporality: The Cultural Politics of Time and Waiting," *The South Atlantic Quarterly* 117, no. 1 (2018): 43-64, quoted in Mbembe (n 4).

7. برزخ

8. برزخ

9. Arabic for "veil".

10. Subhanahu wa ta'ala" translates as "may he be praised and exalted".

11. Arabic for "the Real, the Truth, the Right", also one of the 99 names for God in Islam.

12. Naomi Klein, *The Shock Doctrine: The Rise of Disaster Capitalism* (London: Picador, 2008).

need academia to explain organized violence against our very own bodies. Others of us have to work harder to see the borders.[8] To not forget the violence that is there. So let's not reject the written word now. We need words now more than ever. And we do have words, divine words that are being illuminated again, that are acquiring different meanings now that we see clearer the hollowness of our comfort. An earthly حجاب [hijab][9] to Allah (SWT)[10] has been lifted. But we have work to do. We have studying to do. What other lenses are clouding our vision? We are, by force of seeing our brothers and sisters in Palestine being brutally murdered, redirecting ourselves towards الحق [Al Haqq].[11] Towards the Rightful, towards Justice. I hope and pray and write so that we stay directed towards justice. So that we don't fall into illusion again once the genocide unfolding in front our eyes goes back to a slower pace.

You see, the Muslims around me in the West have also often been living their lives chasing luxuries. Personally, my activism has barely ever been seen as something that is sprouting from my "Muslimness" or something that comes from my "Iraqiness" by other Iraqi Muslims. Reading Marx and critiquing capitalism is something that is feared for it may put you on the path of atheism. But not knowing the material reality that you are navigating will have you worshiping the wrong gods. The clergy that have historically made Muslims believe that to be an anticapitalist is to be a kafir have had a vested material interest that they were protecting. Just like the Emirati and Saudi imams that are now going as far as saying that a boycott of Israeli products is haram. They have a material interest that they are being led by. Not a spiritual one.

Our understanding of religion is imprisoned by modernity. We Muslims are not immune from the societal illnesses that are capitalism and colonialism. On the contrary, we are purposefully infected with them. Speaking of my own country, Iraq, it has been a victim of the most comprehensive implementation of "shock therapy" at the hands of the US.[12] Currently, we

برزخ. 13

برزخ. 14

see the same technique being deployed by the Israeli army in Gaza. A military strategy designed to leave you in shock by its use of an overwhelming amount of force. It is meant to paralyze. Apart from the material destruction it produces, it works on its opponents also on the level of imagination. It creates, of its opponents, victims to be merely spared. It displaces us into their paradigm of Progress. It puts us under the mercy of their colonial control.

Some bodies are allowed to move, while others are stopped at the border.[13] Some bodies even stop the Others at the border.[14] As a very real remnant of colonialism, modern society and its institutions shape us into violent individuals. They shape us according to a particular type of script—Man[15]—which enforces colonial power dynamics and leaves no space to identify with "the other." This is a direct functioning of Western *humanism* (which is not to be confused with humanity).

We must remain steadfast and re-root ourselves in our own paradigms. Let it be known that the ongoing terror of the Israeli army is being committed as a response to Palestinian resistance. Let it be known that the Palestinians, after 75 years of forced displacement, violent apartheid and a growing occupation of their land, still believe in liberation. Despite their own government selling its integrity, they dream of freedom. The people of Gaza dream of being released from their 365 square kilometer prison. The people of the West Bank dream of going to the beach. Let us not forget their dreams for a dignified life, let us remember the, by now over 30.000 Palestinians killed, as martyrs, as شهداء [shuhadaa],[16] bearing witness to the dream of liberation and justice. A dream we also bear witness to and must not wake up from. We, as Barzakhiyaat, stay in this dream world,[17] in عالم الخيال [Alam Al Khayal].[18] We have faith, we believe in the power of the divine, and the divine power of resistance. We believe in living outside of imperialist rule, in Iraq, in Palestine, in Armenia, in Congo, in Sudan, in our lands, on our terms, in liberation.

Yours, Barzakhiya مودتي، البرزخية

not being able to breathe at night and feeling really freaked out by that.

15. The specific genre of Man we are facing today has come to self identify with the idea of the human through a historical process.

In *Unsettling the Coloniality of Being/Power/Truth/Freedom*, Sylvia Wynter writes up the trajectory of the genre of Man from its first political conceptualization in the Renaissance period which constituted the emergence of Man1 or *homo politicus*; to its religious reinvention in the Enlightenment period as Man2 or *homo economicus* and finally to its naturalization under the colonial distortions of Darwinism.

See: Sylvia Wynter, "Unsettling the Coloniality of Being/Power/Truth/Freedom: Towards the Human, After Man, Its Overrepresentation—An Argument," *CR: The New Centennial Review* 3, no. 3 (2003): 257-337. http://www.jstor.org/stable/41949874.

Man thus constituted himself as the master of the world and as the regulator of primarily racial and sexual classifications set himself apart from other beings who—through sexism, humanism, Eurocentrism and modernity—are either excluded from the category of human altogether or come to be seen as lesser beings.

See: Walter Mignolo and Catherine E. Walsh, *On Decoloniality: Concepts, Analytics, Praxis* (Durham NC: Duke University Press, 2018), 168.

The overrepresented human genres of Man1 and Man2 are thus a humanist imaginary that has come to be synonymous with being human itself.

See: Mignolo and Walsh, 157.

Man1 and Man2 = Human: this universalization is a claim for totality which discursively overrides other genres of being human.

The starting point of Wynter's theorizing comes from Fanon's claim that "beside phylogeny and ontogeny stands sociogeny" which rejects the idea of the human as a purely biological being.

See: Frantz Fanon, *Black Skin, White Masks*, Translated by Charles Lam Markmann (London: Pluto Press, 1986), 4.

She exposes Man as an invention and traces its origins and evolution "through colonial capitalism, inextricably linked with transatlantic slavery, and back to the origins of the discipline of the humanities."

See: Sarah E. Truman, *Feminist Speculations and the Practice of Research-Creation* (Oxfordshire UK: Routledge, 2021), 2.

Wynter builds upon Fanon by extending Butler's insight that gender's existence depends on its performative enactment to include race, class and sexual orientation which she posits as also being "genre-specific, fictively constructed, and performatively enacted roles/identities." She thus reads Fanon as being the first to articulate how this performative enactment of the self in the mimetic terms of "white masks" causes self-alienation for black and colonized people. The white mask being an "artificially speciated genre (or Mask) of being human" which Fanon exposes by writing from the underside of Man-as-human.

See: Katherine McKittrick, *Sylvia Wynter: On Being Human as Praxis* (Durham NC: Duke University Press, 2015), 195.

16. The Arabic word شهداء [shuhadaa] means both martyrs as well as witnesses.

١٧. برزخ

18. Arabic for "the imaginal realm", another way of conceptualizing the Barzakh.

Dear Barzakhiya, حضرة البرزخية،

Onze liefde is terroristisch[19]
Çağlar Köseoğlu

> *I tell myself that we are terrorists, not terrorists in the political and ordinary sense of the word, but because we carry inside of our bodies—like explosives—all the deep troubles that befall our countries... and traveling doesn't change anything in any way. We are the scribes of a scattered self, living fragments, as if the parts of the self were writing down the bits and ends of a perception never complete.*

Etel Adnan, *Of Cities and Women*[20]

As an Iraqi woman born in The Netherlands, I was raised by fragments. I was born in the exilic condition, in an "unhealable rift between the self and its true home"[21] as Edward Said puts it. I have become an inhabitant of the collective state of estrangement. The immaterial برزخ [Barzakh][22] is what has filled the material loss. I started building my imaginary home on spiritual land after having lost the material land, and I invite you to join me there.

A lot of you, children of loss and longing, I have already met here. Let's stay here, remaining yearning for our lands, present with their reality in the realm of the imagination. We have not abandoned you, oh palm trees. We have not abandoned you, oh olive trees. We remain with you, carry you
on our backs, in our stomachs,
on our tongues,
in our minds, in our pockets.
Etched in our skin is your memory.

19. Title of the poem Onze Liefde is Terroristisch. English translation: Our Love is Terroristic. Çağlar Köseoğlu, "Onze Liefde is Terroristisch," DIG (De Internet Gids) (digital literary magazine), December 12, 2023, https://www.de-internet-gids.nl/artikelen/onze-liefde-is-terroristisch.

20. Etel Adnan, *Of Cities and Women* (Sausalito CA: The Post-Apollo Press, 1993), 96-97.

21. برزخ

22. *Barzakh*: the liminal or imaginal realm between the corporeal world and the spiritual world resides between existence and non-existence as a non-existent thing [al shay' al ma'dum]. See: Amira

El-Zein, *Islam, Arabs, and the Intelligent World of the Jinn* (Syracuse NY: Syracuse University Press, 2009), 6; Salman H. Bashier, *Ibn al-'Arabi's Barzakh* (Albany NY: State University of New York Press, 2004), 3.

Barzakh as both the separator and uniter of the corporeal and spiritual realms, is a transitory meeting place, the place for difference to reside and unite. It is the intermediate state between life (al-dunya) and the hereafter (al-akhira), where the souls dwell in their awaiting of the day of judgment.

23. Adnan (n 9).

24. The fall of Granada in 1492 resulted in the ethnic cleansing of Andalusia's Muslims and Jews and marked the destruction of its multi-religious culture; and as the year 1492 is also the year that the colonization of the Americas began, this moment in history marks the "emergence of a firm imperial Europe conceiving itself as the center of the whole world and as the telos of civilization."

See: Nelson Maldonado-Torres, *Against War: Views from the Underside of Modernity* (Durham NC: Duke University Press, 2008), 3.

The consequences of this, we still onto-epistemo-logically experience today.

> *Spain (or should one say the Inquisition?) has carefully erased the traces of its Arabs. And this cultural genocide was soon followed by the slaughter of the Indians... and Spain will tomorrow celebrate the quincentennial of its conquest!*
>
> *These last few days we have spoken of Ibn Arabi as if we were dealing with a ghost or a shadow. Where is his house? Where are the places he frequented, the libraries of his parents, the gardens in which he played?*
>
> *Hearing the Arabic words behind the Spanish ones, I tell myself that Andalusia is the first loss, the death of the Mother, and of the orchards of which Lorca was the last tree.*
>
> *Ibn Arabi pursued the Whole when all the details were falling one after the other around him. He had foreseen the fall.*[23]

In pursuing the Whole, Ibn Arabi offers an antidote to our fragmentation before it historically arrives. *He had foreseen the fall.*[24] In his writing Ibn Arabi gives us a taste (Dhawq) of wholeness, of a Unity. Like Adnan, or maybe like in my own reading of Adnan, I believe Ibn Arabi's understanding of being can help us de- and re-construct humanness. The Islamic epistemological grounds set by the Sufi writer Ibn Arabi can offer us a different origin narrative to base our humanity on. The foundation I am proposing to work from is located in the Iberian peninsula in the 13th century. This is the specific historical context of the Andalusian (Sufi) Muslim Mystic Ibn Arabi, a history which coincides with what can be seen as a key event in the development of modernity/coloniality.[25]

As an alternative to the "zero-point epistemology,"[26] Ibn Arabi's cosmology not only represents the "historical outside of those worlds of sensing and meaning, that has been under erasure," his very understanding of the process of acquiring knowledge encourages this unveiling (مكاشفة [Mukashafa][27]) of modernity's underside, its negated alterity, and the freeing of these multitude "worlds of sensing and meaning" that lie there[28].[29] I am probing Ibn Arabi's cosmology here as a fertile ground to grow ourselves in, as well as roots to water and get tangled up with. Ibn Arabi's cosmology necessarily shatters our disciplinary ways of knowing. Like coloniality's matrix of power, it reaches into all realms and is not limited to epistemology but structures amongst other things our understanding of ontology, pedagogy and ethics. For these reasons, I posit Ibn Arabi's framework as a beneficial companion to "thinking from and with the lived experience of coloniality."[30]

Thus, let us return to Ibn Arabi, return to the Andalusia before the fall, and return to pre-1492 Spain. I hope to return here to reverse modernity/coloniality's effects on our understanding of knowledge and being. Let us reclaim the uncredited heritage of knowledge upon which Europe has built itself upon, to rebuild our understanding of ourselves and our worlds on. Let us bathe in the richness that Ibn Arabi offers us
to piece together our fragments
piece ourselves together as fragments
and Realize (we were always already carrying)
the whole.

Yours, Barzakhiya   مودتي، البرزخية

And then the storm came with everything kind of crashing down.

25. The battle between Islam and Christianity in the Iberian Peninsula lasted from the eighth to the fifteenth century.

See: Walter D. Mignolo, *Local Histories/Global Designs—Coloniality, Subaltern Knowledges, and Border Thinking* (New Jersey: Princeton University Press, 2012), 74, quoted in Zuleika Bibi Sheik, "Liminagraphy: Lessons in Life-affirming Research Practices for Collective Liberation," PhD diss., (Erasmus University Rotterdam, 2021).

During this time, there were three main Christian victories over the Muslims. Alfonso el Sabio and the School of Toledo thus came to power three times: after the reconquering of Cordoba in 1236, Valencia in 1238 and Seville in 1248 (Ibid). During his reign, el Sabio had ordered the translation of the classical Greek teachings from Arabic and Hebrew into Spanish. The classical Greek teachings had been preserved by Muslim and Jewish scholars, and this preservation had served as the precondition for Europe's emergence out of the dark ages. Europe's modernity/"enlightenment" was directly indebted to the work of these Muslim and Jewish scholars in preserving these translations of the Greek philosophers as well as in translating them from Arabic and Hebrew into Spanish.

This indebtedness could however not be acknowledged by the West, as this would mean to acknowledge the technological and philosophical achievements of the colonized "This unacknowledged debt, erased by the "Purity of Blood" principle is the lynch pin to the coloniality that persists today," Sheik writes.

She explains that this Purity of Blood principle, which is called *Limpieza de Sangre* in Spanish "saw the ethnic cleansing of Muslims and Jews, who were residing in Andalusia (controlled by the Catholic Monarchy), as a means to destroy the sultanate of Granada, the last Muslim political authority in the Iberian Peninsula (Maldonado-Torres quoting Dussel)."

Bibi Sheik, 57.

26. In the "zero-point epistemology", as Santiago Castro-Gómez calls it, the researcher's position remains hidden in the universal. Santiago Castro-Gómez, *Zero-Point Hubris* (Lanham MD: Rowman & Littlefield Publishers, 2021), 18.

27. Arabic for "unveiling" or "uncovering". In Sufism it's the inner knowledge that mystics acquire through uncovering the heart's veils to God.

28. برزخ

29. Rolando Vázquez, *Vistas of Modernity: Decolonial Aesthesis and the End of the Contemporary* (Amsterdam: Mondriaan Fund, 2020), 171, quoted in Bibi Sheik (n 25).

30. Catherine E. Walsh, "Decolonial Pedagogies Walking and Asking. Notes to Paulo Freire from AbyaYala," *International Journal of Lifelong Education* 34, no.1 (2015): 9-21, DOI: 10.1080/02601370.2014.991522.

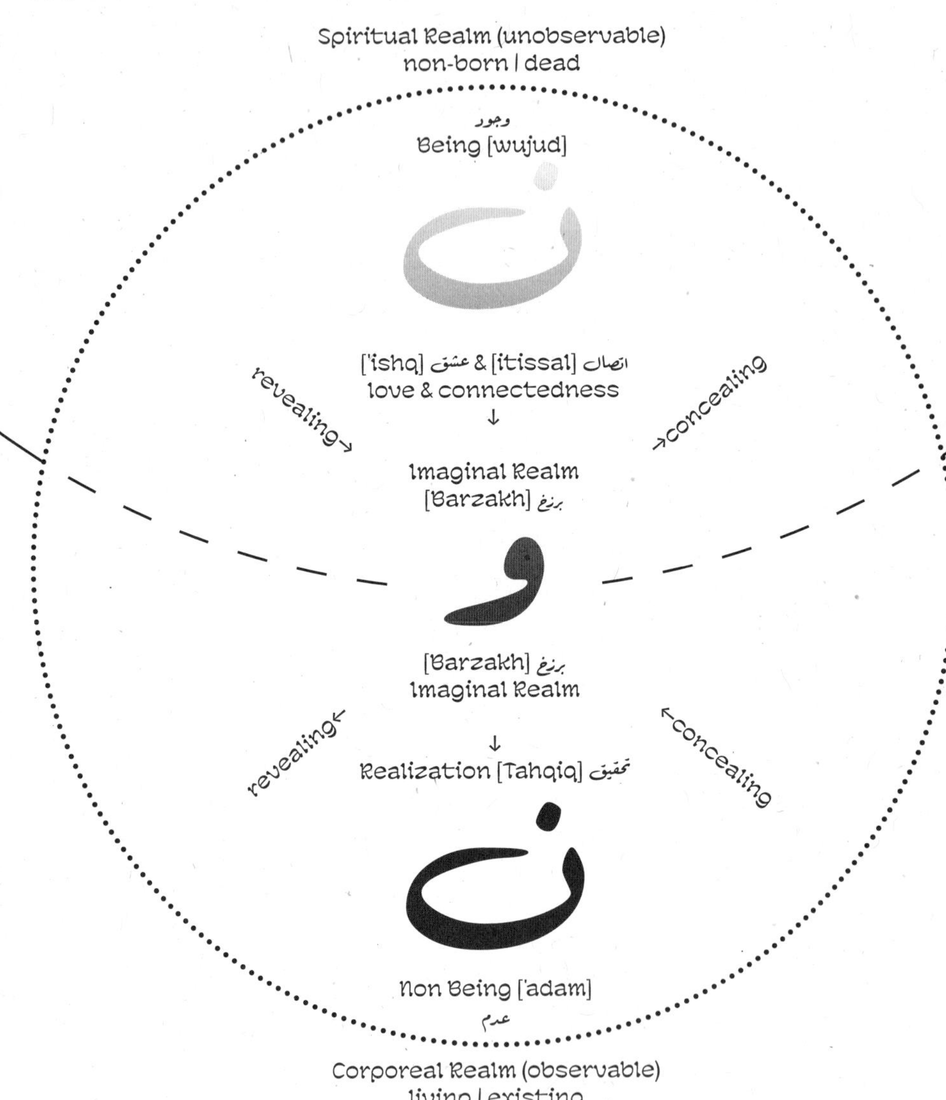

"Sufis believe that the world was created out of Divine love and that the entire cosmos is the result of God's primordial imagination. From this perspective, imagination is not in us; rather, we are in imagination. When we are engaged in actively imagining, from the Sufi perspective, we are emulating God and engaging in a co-creative process on a microcosmic level".

D. Steven Nouriani, *Islamic Cultures and Jungian Analysis*[31]

31. D. Steven Nouriani, "Islamic Cultures and Jungian Analysis," *Jung Journal: Culture & Psyche* 11, no. 3 (2017): 9-25.

32. Maldonado-Torres (n 24) 116.

33. McKittrick (n 5).

Dear Barzakhiya, حضرة البرزخية،

Do we dare to work somewhere else? To work at enacting something else? To see language as something to inhabit rather than merely exercise? I want to perform the words I read and hear with my whole being. Words are there to be exchanged. We build with them not castles of thought but bridges upon bridges. Roads and routes. To الحق [Al Haqq] I hope. I pray for us to face that way.

In order to unveil الحق [Al Haqq], we must first be facing it. So please see this as my attempt at redirection to الحق [Al Haqq], the Just, the Divine, God, Allah (SWT) and all the 99 names. In *Against War*, Maldonado-Torres writes that "Imperial Man wants to become necessary Man, a man whose existence is ontologically justified. The divine, the social, and the realm of things cannot but testify to the necessity of his being. Empire is this order of things whereby Man is elevated to the status of God."[32] The white masks have us facing the wrong way, looking towards the White Man as الحق [Al Haqq] to be realized through our being. We become not vessels of the true حق [Haqq], not vessels for the true God as "Necessary Being" which encompasses all essence as the ultimate presence or وجود [Wujud] which encompasses all creation through compassion; but vessels for Man and his specific "normalized origin narrative of survival-through-ever-increasing-processes-of-consumption-and-accumulation."[33]

What is necessary is a refusal of mastery in service of emergence. I have been struggling with Man where I would have much rather been struggling with the Divine. A rejection of Man is still a relation to Man. A refusal of Man would mean to engage in a liberatory project rather than an emancipatory one. A project built on different grounds. Can the [34]برزخ be such grounds? Can we see the border[35] as a space of struggle rather than suffering? The space at the limits of life[36] is also a space closer to God. A space that brings us closer to the Truth. Can we see the margins, as bell hooks suggests, as a space of possibility[37]?[38] Can we choose the margins, as our site of resistance?[39] As a place we are not only confined to but a place we actively choose to inhabit. A place we choose to make more habitable, together. To see [40]برزخ when we think *border*[41].[42]

From an Islamic perspective that centers the divine, the place at the limit of life is a privileged space. The margins[43] are closer to the true center: Allah (SWT), which Empire has tried to replace. Reintroducing an Islamic approach which centers the Divine is able to take us "beyond the confines of modernity and the imprisonment of what Jacqui Alexander in *Pedagogies of Crossing* refers to as its 'secularized episteme.'"[44] Instead of being human as a teleological suspension of Man, Ibn Arabi conceives of the goal of life as an unending process of the تحقيق [Tahqiq] of knowledge. تحقيق [Tahqiq],[45] as the realization of الحق [Al Haqq] in خلق [Khalq][46] offers another onto-epistemological basis for being.

This basis is ultimately rooted in the [47]برزخ as the realm of imagination, which one can access through imaginatively seeing "with two eyes" both the immanence and transcendence of الحق [Al Haqq]. Through imagination we can grasp the logics of reality [حق] as being neither/nor and both/and. Through imagination we can see the

34. *barzakh*

35. برزخ

36. برزخ

37. برزخ

38. bell hooks, "CHOOSING THE MARGIN AS A SPACE OF RADICAL OPENNESS," *Framework: The Journal of Cinema and Media*, no. 36 (1989): 15–23. http://www.jstor.org/stable/44111660.

39. Ibid.

40. *barzakh*

41. برزخ

42. Etymologically the word *barzakh* is said to come from the Persian word pardah, which means "barrier".

See: Salman H. Bashier, *Ibn al-'Arabi's Barzakh* (Albany NY: State University of New York Press, 2004). However, the reality of our paradoxes. Through imagination we can see the برزخ[48] not only as the border to death, but also as the place for us to meet.

تحقيق [Tahqiq], as the process of embodying meaning, thus leads us to a poetic onto-epistemological existence in which the material of one's life becomes metaphor. It opens up our perception to the divine in all parts of life. It makes way for a different type of sensing, one which transcends the limits of reason. It allows us to materialize the imaginative and grasp the radical openness of being. To reach تحقيق [Tahqiq] we must partake in مكاشفة [Mukashafa], which we can now see as a poetic working at the margins.[49] It is the space beyond the semiolinguistic confines, at its very borders,[50] where it allows us to be neither/nor and both/and. Aimé Césaire, in poetry and knowledge, calls this state in which the antinomy between the Self and The World is resolved "the poetic state."[51] From this poetic state, "pregnant with the world, the poet speaks."[52] He posits the poetically conjured up image as a manner to transcend the limitations of scientific knowledge. He writes that "It is by means of the image, the revolutionary image, the distant image, the image that overthrows all the laws of thought that mankind finally breaks down the barrier."[53]

To situate oneself at the برزخ[54] is to source from its unactualized reality. I want to direct us towards a giving of words to possibilities, possible futures that reside in the برزخ[55] through being potentialities. This is a different way of being with words and working with words for feminist practice than a mere "having names for problems."[56] While giving words to structural

barrier that is the Barzakh works by uniting that which is at the same time separating. Ibn Arabi ascribes imagination the power to synthesize extreme opposites and transcend the confines of an either/or logic. Instead, through imagination we can grasp the logics of reality as being neither/nor and both/and.

See: William C. Chittick, *Imaginal Worlds: Ibn al-'Arabi and the Problem of Religious Diversity* (Albany NY: State University of New York Press), 141.

43. برزخ

44. Jacqui Alexander, *Pedagogies of Crossing* (Durham NC: Duke University Press, 2006), quoted in Catherine E. Walsh (n 16).

45. Arabic for *Realization*, a way of knowledge seeking that takes the form of immediately perceiving knowledge.

46. Arabic for *Creation*, all which exists.

47. *barzakh*

48. *barzakh*

49. برزخ

50. برزخ

51. Aimé Césaire, *Lyric and Dramatic Poetry, 1946-82*, Translated by Clayton Eshleman and Annette Smith (Charlottesville: University Press of Virginia, 1990).

52. Ibid.

problems is extremely important as a way to rewrite past personal experiences into a collective history of struggle against racism/sexism and other violent isms; having words to structure the potentialities of our worlds is a struggle on a different terrain, the terrain of the possible,[57] the terrain of the future[58] and the terrain of hope.[59] It is a way to affirm our autonomy as not just subjects which are being subjugated to these isms and the scripts they carry. It is a way to affirm our autonomy as possible (co-)writers of our own scripts. I see this as a liberatory logic, a reclaiming of the power in our own modes of perception.

Positioning oneself in this profound margin[60] and working through there is an act of resistance, as "most of our oppressors" do not even have access to seeing through this margin.[61] What becomes clear from the position of those within the margins of society, within that [62]برزخ, who navigate between it and the world of the living on the daily, is that this [63]برزخ is not a meta-physical [64]برزخ placed upon us through God, it is one which has been placed by its imitators, in positioning themselves as the universal all-seeing being. And thus, as this [65]برزخ is not one installed by God, it is not holy, it is not uncrossable, and by seeing its possibility, we become able to transcend to it. Hooks' *Choosing the Margin as a Space of Radical Openness* reminds us of the importance of not only seeing the [66]برزخ as imposed reality, but working through the [67]برزخ as active choice, as "a central location for the production of a counter hegemonic discourse that is not just found in words but in habits of being and in the way one lives."[68] My writing is an extension of her invitation to meet there[69].[70]

Yours, Barzakhiya

مودتي، البرزخية

53. Ibid.

54. *barzakh*

55. *barzakh*

56. Sara Ahmed, *Living a Feminist Life* (Durham NC: Duke University Press, 2017), 22.

57. برزخ

58. برزخ

59. برزخ

60. برزخ

61. hooks (n 35) 20.

62. *barzakh*

63. *barzakh*

64. *barzakh*

65. *barzakh*

66. *barzakh*

67. *barzakh*

68. hooks (n 35).

69. برزخ

70. “This is an intervention. A message from that space in the margin that is a site of creativity and power, that inclusive space where we recover ourselves, where we move in solidarity to erase the category colonized/colonizer. Marginality as site of resistance. Enter that space. Let us meet there. Enter that space. We greet you as liberators.”
See: hooks (n 35) 23.

71. *barzakh*

72. برزخ

73. برزخ

74. *barzakh*

75. *barzakh*

76. *barzakh*

Dear Barzakhiya, حضرة البرزخية،

I’ve been trying to test the [71]برزخ as a space for us to come together, our margins[72] as a place to meet. It was my home before I knew what it was called, before I knew there were words for this place. Reading was the first and primary way I discovered that there are more people there. That there have been other people trying to build grounding with/in and between words[73] in the absence of its material presence. I know now that there have always been people there. That you might be here too. Estranged mystics or poets or teenage girls who feel out of place in this world and don’t know why. Like them, maybe like you, I see words as the primary material to build homes with.

I may not understand you completely, but I want to hold space for you. and I want to find a way, a place, a ground for us to stand on. I want us to stop floating in a wound that is mine, yours and at the same time entirely not ours. There, on that ground, I want us to lie down. I am tired of standing up for and against everything. I want us to learn how to lie down in the [74]برزخ. To lean into it, and reach out for each other there. The [75]برزخ, where my being becomes yours and we do not recognize where I stop and you begin. Where we mistake form for meaning and learn to appreciate meaning as form. [76]برزخ as being simultaneously meaning and form is a place for us who understand that our form means a lot. Our form determines the way we are dictated. It determines which script is dictated to us, which scripts we are made to carry and in turn become. Who am I? The endless quest which starts at teenagehood stays relevant.

Yours, Barzakhiya مودتي، البرزخية

Dear Barzakhiya,

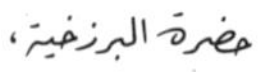

I am not the first to propose a liminal poetics. Not the first to try to engage in it. Just like I am not the first liminal being. Those who "were never meant to survive," who have been sitting in the برزخ[77] of modernity, have been partaking in poetry and poetics for their very survival.[78] As Audre Lorde writes in "Poetry is Not a Luxury": "Poetry is not only a dream and a vision, it is the skeleton architecture of our lives. It lays the foundation for future change."[79] The way that both Césaire and Lorde write about poetry is not as a mere wordplay, it is not "the sterile word play that, too often, the white fathers distorted the word poetry to mean," but rather "the revelation or distillation of experience."[80] It is a relation to the برزخ[81], an imaginative exercise in conjuring up الحق [Haqq]. It is a way of sensing and being in the world which is essential for liberation.

Let us situate ourselves there, in the poetic realm, in the realm of imagination, the realm of forms, in برزخ[82]. What do we need to get there? What do we need to reach, to in our disposition keep on reaching towards this space of radical openness? I want us to move from human to Barzakhiya, from a being being to a reaching being, to become our knowledge and act it at the same time, to exist as a performance of liberation. Let this be our ontology. Let our being be a trajectory towards the برزخ[83]. I will start at Man and end in poetics. Poetics not as wordplay, but as the material of the برزخ[84] itself.

I would like to free poetics from the discipline of poetry. To claim poetics without claiming poet. I have never felt comfortable or confident with the label poet. I think there are poetic ways of seeing which transcend the functions of our eyes, that require us whole, present, in the world in order to conjure up an arrangement of words in the same way that you

77. *barzakh*

78. Audre Lorde, *Your Silence Will Not Protect You* (London: Silver Press, UK, 2017), 200.

79. Ibid 10.

80. Ibid 9.

81. *barzakh*

82. *barzakh*

83. *barzakh*

84. *barzakh*

I'm not one of those people who is very good at asking for things.

would pick and create a flower arrangement. I say you here, but I realize not everyone picks their flowers with the same care. You need to be a flower lover for that. And so you need to be a lover to be poetic too. You need to stir and be able to be stirred. Something needs to move in you in order for you to move. Liberating sense in one way and reconfining it in another. Doing that again and again to uncover more and more meaning and beauty and tiny layers (maybe in the form of flakes?) of the world. Creating endless new confinements creates endless configurations in which liberation accumulates. There is so much to be liberated from. There are so many barriers, earthly احجبة [ahjiba][85] which separate us from connecting. Truly connecting is what دين [deen][86] is about. Working towards that is political. The love for liberation is poetic. Poetics is the love for liberation.

So let us enter that space.[87] Let us enter into the space of poetics where the human is a verb rather than a noun, a praxis rather than a being. Where the Islamic principle of تحقيق [Tahqīq] is the basis of our purpose as خلق [Khalq]. We enter now the space where Ibn Arabi meets Sylvia Wynter meets Aimé Césaire meets Audre Lorde, who all suggest letting imagination lead the way in order to liberate us from modern/colonial confines. So here I propose the Barzakhiya as a figure for us to embody. As an alternative to the posthuman, one which is not caught up in the Eurowestern logic of the human and thus does not replicate its mechanisms.[88] A speculative fiction that goes beyond our understanding of fiction. A mythical creature arising from different cosmological grounds. A fictional noun proposing a rejection of ontological being. A new story proposed as one of many. My own origin story that I invite others to inhabit. Come join me in the [89]برزخ. Let us dwell among the jinns. Come, join me in imagining. This[90] is not a place to fear.

Yours, Barzakhiya مودتي، البرزخية

85. Plural of حجاب [hijab], Arabic for "veils".

86. Arabic for "faith".

87. برزخ

88. As Mignolo already explains, the posthuman can be seen from Wynter's framework as merely a "feminist" man3, a remolding from within the Eurowestern paradigm. Walter Mignolo and Catherine E. Walsh, *On Decoloniality: Concepts, Analytics, Praxis* (Durham NC: Duke University Press, 2018), 171.

The Barzakhiya on the other hand is not one being. It is a name I propose for the borderbeing.

89. *barzakh*

90. برزخ

Slow, Situated & Reparative Reading: THE GARDEN EDITION

(This is not a manifesto; it's a manifestation.)

Together in the garden, we share books, poems and essays as ways of tuning in and turning towards. To do this, we go against the pace of the emergency, resisting its terms and conditions, which numb us from so much. Instead, we engage in a counter practice of slow, situated and reparative reading, pouring over the works of Amitav Ghosh, Jamaica Kincaid, Robert Macfarlane, Anna Lowenhaupt Tsing, Robin Wall Kimmerer, Donna J. Haraway, Rachel Carson, and so many other canaries in a coal mine who continue singing across time, sometimes in a whisper and at other times, in a chorus.

it's quite nice to have my kitchen in the background, usually it is a bookshelf.

–*The garden* referenced in this text can be any garden, yours, mine or a friend's, or it could be the commons collectively cared for, or a balcony filled with beloved plants. That isn't to suggest these leafy encounters are generic or interchangeable. Each has its own qualities that tune the reader and the reading. That's certainly the case with my garden and how it has and continues to work upon me.

For over fourteen years, I've had an allotment at the SNV complex in Rotterdam. During this time, it has been a place of growth and gathering for plants, family, friends, and acquaintances. It is also integral to how I've come to understand what it means to teach and learn. In my garden, I have met with students to discuss their work. During COVID and lockdown, when I witnessed students, especially those without family nearby, overwhelmed by isolation and the impenetrability of the screen, I would suggest meeting at my allotment. Walking along the complex's intersecting pathways, we would keep our prescribed distance while still in a shared physical reality. Step by step, we would unpack our thoughts together.

As I continue to meet students at my allotment, I see there is something about the distraction of the green or feeling a breeze, which short-circuits the strictures associated with academic settings. Maybe it is the simultaneity of existence that relativises and gives air for breathing outside of the ever-spinning mental narrative that falsely casts the self as the protagonist. Instead, the mind falls in line with the body, and subsequently, the senses connect to the surroundings. Or, as the artist, gardener and initiator of this publication, Michelle Teran, and I have discussed on numerous occasions, *gardens are learning grounds that, in turn, ground learning and the learner.*

These thoughts about my garden have been *germinating* for a while. In the past, together with literary scholar Frans-Willem Korsten, I taught a course called *Critically Committed Pedagogies*. During the seminar, we held sessions in our respective allotments. Although in two different cities, our gardens faced similar threats from the municipality. We discussed possible strategies for resistance and coalition forming. We talked about how a site and situation shape hierarchical, non-hierarchical and emergent ways of learning and practised the pedagogical differences between explanation and demonstration. Together in our gardens, we discussed how traditional classrooms arranged like factories with desks lined in rows reinforce centralized authority or how more contemporary settings mimicking the open offices of tech industries promote surveillance. In contrast, gardens bring insights more akin to forest schools where the site of learning is not a disciplining tool or simply a backdrop but dialogic and with a curriculum that is irreducible to words.

More recently, I have been teaching *Issues in Contemporary Art Education: Learning with Others* with designer, curator, and fellow gardener Irina Shapiro. The course considers how we might learn with and from others in multi-species environments and how education all too often foregrounds human experience and know-how at the exclusion of all other intelligence and ways of existing. Such oversights have devastating consequences on a large scale that is hardly fathomable for the mind. However, our gardens, with their limited square meters, offer humble starting points where we can share listening practices, tuning methods and intimate forms of observation aimed at undermining our sense of human sovereignty.

Threaded throughout these experiences is a fundamental lesson I don't want to learn. It is a pedagogy of perishing where, sadly, extinction is the final exit qualification. Like many green spaces, my garden stands at an all too familiar precipice. Having faced countless threats from the municipality in the past, the complex, now only a third of its original size, continues to be under pressure from urban expansion, housing development and climate crises. When I listen to the dawn chorus of birds and witness the seasonal shifts, I can't help but consider what will be lost if it disappears. It is a library, an archive, a storyteller, a testimony to the many—living, non-living, human, and more than human. Under its influence, I'm the one being gardened. It is a caretaker that simultaneously needs care. My garden is indexical to everything at stake around us, near and far. As I was writing this manifestation, I wondered if I was writing a love letter or a eulogy. I suppose these modes of address may be indistinguishable in the end, or rather, our end.

This "we" is not the kind of "we" that levels difference or proclaims to speak for others. Maggie Nelson writes in her book *On Freedom*, "...our entire existence, including our freedoms and unfreedoms, is built upon a 'we' instead of an 'I,' that we are dependent upon each other, as well as upon nonhuman forces that exceed our understanding or control."
Maggie Nelson, *On Freedom: Four Songs of Care and Constraint* (Minneapolis MN: Graywolf Press, 2022), 10-11.

Whether enacted collectively or alone, silently or aloud, slow reading allows time to pause, rewind, doubt and pursue what at first sight may be tangents. Analogous to gardening, it is a means of *tending to* and *being in attendance with* what is read. As the Belgian philosopher Isabelle Stengers points out: "speed demands and creates an insensitivity to everything that might slow things down: the frictions, the rubbing, the hesitations that make us feel we are not alone in the world." Urgency abounds, but we must not become desensitized under the pressure of its pace. Stengers argues for deceleration, noting: "Slowing down means becoming capable of learning again, becoming acquainted with things again, reweaving the bounds of interdependency." Although counter-intuitive amid multiple crises, slow reading hits the pause button and summons, as if by séance, an incongruous temporality.

Within that parallel time zone, slow reading acclimates itself to subtle movements and listens closely to declarations of doubt. *Wait, I'm confused. There's just something I'm not getting.* Without hesitation, we recalibrate, adjusting to linger with the lost or even admit that we ourselves are lost too. There is solidarity as we have all been there. R-E-A-D-I-N-G, in this way, is a practice that consciously aligns itself with the seemingly negative associations of slowness—of not being clever, lacking efficiency, not getting things done and simply not knowing. Rather than a hindrance, these qualities are generative. They create an opening for exploring questions, giving attention to shimmering lights in the margins and accounting for things escaping words altogether. As the British nature writer Robert Macfarlane observes:

> *There are experiences of landscape that will always resist articulation, and of which words offer only a remote echo—or to which silence is by far the best response. Nature does not name itself. Granite does not self-identify as igneous. Light has no grammar. Language is always late for its subject.*

In reading, ever so slowly at a snail's pace, we listen to distant echoes. Continuously thumbing through pages and fumbling for words, we preserve placeholders for the unsaid and silences. We nurture places for *what may have been* and the *yet-to-be*. Rather than championing the avant-garde, slow reading fosters falling behind, failing to comprehend, stopping and taking time to follow up. *Sorry to interrupt you, but can we go back and read that last part of the sentence again?* Yes, slow reading allows space for falling behind, failing to comprehend, stopping and taking time to follow up. Slow reading rejects hierarchy, cold, critical analysis, disavows any illusions of mastery and does not surrender to the linear. Without seeking definitive interpretations, it relishes in the

It is also akin to the Aboriginal Rights group in Queensland and indigenous artist and activist Lilla Watson's declaration: "If you have come here to help me, you are wasting your time, but if you have come because your liberation is bound up with mine, then let us work together." In these paradigms, "we" are tightly and inextricably knotted.
For more on Lilla Watson, see: https://en.wikipedia.org/wiki/Lilla_Watson.

Slow reading is a methodology collectively developed by the *Slow Readers* during COVID and lockdown. Initiated as a part of my research fellowship at V2 Lab for the Unstable Media, the project took place online over the course of six months. Through reading relevant texts, we looked at AI and gender inequality. Aside from informing my approach, reading *Autopoiesis and Cognition: The Realization of the Living* by Humberto Maturana and Francisco Varela was especially relevant to understanding our interdependency. I still remember that day sitting in my garden cottage, reading it aloud together while being apart in isolation. Confined to tiny squares on the screen, as we talked about the intricacies of living systems, messages from other gardeners suddenly poured in on my phone. An eagle owl had escaped from the neighbouring zoo and was sitting in the Dawn Redwood on my plot. I ran outside and tilted my laptop upwards for the Slow Readers to see it. While I wasn't sure if it was visible on the screen, that moment nonetheless felt stranger than fiction, a reminder in a surreal and mostly online time that the physical world was still out there and shared with other creatures. I am eternally thankful for that owl disrupting and simultaneously grounding our reading. And my heartfelt gratitude goes out to all the *Slow Readers* whose sharpness and generosity anchored me during the untethered life of lockdown.
The *Slow Readers* are: https://v2.hotglue.me/the_slow_reading_group.
Humberto Maturana and Francisco Varela, *Autopoiesis and Cognition: The Realization of the Living* (Dordrecht NL: D. Reidel Publishing, 1980).

Isabelle Stengers, *Another Science Is Possible: A Manifesto for Slow Science* (Cambridge: Polity, 2018), 70.

Ibid.

Robert Macfarlane, *Landmarks* (London: Penguin Books, 2016), 10.

Within my teaching practice, the presence of silence has always interested me. What does it do, how is it palpable, and how might its impact, if not lessons, be understood? I am fascinated by more abstract notions of silence as articulated and evoked by John Cage and Pauline Oliveros. But also, there are political understandings of silence. In the *Mother of All Questions: Further Feminisms*, Rebecca Solnit writes about layers of silence, saying: "In the landscape of silence, the three realms might be: silence imposed from within; silence imposed from without; and silence that exists around what has not yet been named, recognized, described, or admitted. But they are not distinct; they feed each other; and what is unsayable becomes unknowable and vice versa, until something breaks." In another life, with more time and, yes, silence, I would like to explore and unpack these ideas further.
Rebecca Solnit, *Mother of All Questions: Further Feminisms* (London: Granta, 2017), 28.

Eve Kosofsky Sedgwick, *Touching Feeling: Affect, Pedagogy, Performativity* (Durham NC: Duke University Press, 2004), 146.

complexity of entwined and contradictory knowledge(s).

However, slow reading does not happen in a vacuum or in the imagined ethereal solitude of the mind. It is a situated and embodied practice operating from the perspective that all texts are permeable and influenced by material conditions, place, time, mood, memories, histories and the present. Borrowing from Donna Haraway, it is the opposite of "a view from above, from nowhere." Instead of objectivity, it holds dear the modesty of a partial view and the premise that context matters and matter forms and informs.

In the garden, situated reading roots firmly with feet planted into the ground. It is immersed in the muck and imbued with a mixture of scents, and sensations; the itchy sting of mosquitos in summer, and the frosty bite of cold in winter. As an unfolding process amongst us humans and more-than-humans, reading is subject to diurnal, crepuscular and nocturnal stretches and flows. Here, porosity is a virtue, connecting us to ourselves and various others, with their own rhythms of being. *I'm a blip on that rock's timeline, and that annual has gone to seed.* Here, lessons abound, or as the anthropologist Tim Ingold notes:

> *The world itself becomes a place of study, a university that includes not just professional teachers and registered students, dragooned into their academic departments, but people everywhere, along with all the other creatures with which (or whom) we share our lives and the lands in which we—and they—live.*

Here, there are no heads down with noses buried in books to escape reality. On the contrary, poetry and prose are fleshy, connective tissues weaving us into the world, binding the animate, inanimate, singular, plural, the ground elder, the stone, the bumblebee and the tiniest shrew. Here, at last, we are not alone and potentially greater than our sum. To repeat, we are *tuning in and turning towards* when we read in the garden. It is not because it's Edenic, it's not because it's stress-free, it's not that we are liberated from distraction. Again, to the contrary, it's because the garden is, as Jamaica Kincaid observed in her essay *The Disturbances of the Garden*, a contentious site of past trauma and ongoing crisis. Any urban or rural garden bears witness to the violent legacies wrought by colonisation. Think of Carl Linnaeus and his binomial nomenclature of plants, or hydrangeas, introduced to Europe by the Dutch East India Company. History seeks reckoning even in our garden. Or consider the scorching summers bereft of rain and how such parched conditions speak to forests burning across the globe. Here, the grand narratives and minor stories crisscross so tightly they cannot be unpicked.

Pandemic and the loss of tactility and the loss of the relation to touch.

Donna Haraway, "Situated Knowledges: The Science Question in Feminism and the Privilege of Partial Perspective," *Feminist Studies* 14, no. 3 (Autumn 1988): 575-599.

One of my cherished reading experiences was with Kate Price, an artist whose work engages in garden practices and Irina Shapiro, who I mentioned earlier. In the middle of winter, we sat under the dying tomato vines in the waning warmth of the allotment's glasshouse. Snacking on the few remaining yellow tomatoes, we discussed whether the vines should be cleaned away or allowed to collapse from the trellises and self-seed. We read two chapters, *The Garden in Winter* and *The Glass House*, from Jamaica Kincaid's *My Garden (Book)*. Kincaid's words reminded me that the glasshouse is a colonial legacy where the bounty of *there* is violently extracted to accrue wealth for *here*. It was the first time we ever read together, and for some reason, that session stuck with me the most. I am grateful to Kate and Irina for that day in the greenhouse. Both have been pivotal in expanding my thoughts and garden bibliography. While we struggle to synchronise our schedules, our scarce and gem-like reading time has been invaluable to me. Jamaica Kincaid, *My Garden (Book)* (London: Vintage, 1999).

Tim Ingold, *Making: Anthropology, Archaeology, Art and Architecture* (London: Routledge, 2013), 2.

Jamaica Kincaid, "The Disturbances of the Garden," *The New Yorker*, (August 30, 2020).

You see, when we gather in this humble bit of cultivated green, we engage in what Eve Kosofsky Sedgwick, poet, teacher and queer scholar, would call a reparative reading. In her beautiful meditation on queerness, literature, and the AIDS crisis, *Touching Feeling: Affect, Pedagogy, Performativity*, she writes:

> *Hope, often a fracturing, even a traumatic thing to experience, is among the energies by which the reparatively positioned reader tries to organise the fragments and part-objects she encounters or creates. Because the reader has room to realise that the future may be different from the present, it is also possible for her to entertain such profoundly painful, profoundly relieving, ethically crucial possibilities as that the past, in turn, could have happened differently from the way it actually did.*

With each word, pause, hesitation, or stammer, we pick up pieces, mourn, imagine a whole that resists being stitched too tight, and dream, if not plot otherwise. While wide-eyed and sober about what is, we seek reparation in the gaps. This is a labour of tenderness, and care. To read is to hold words, touch them and be touched by them. And although this can be a centering act, we read not to centre ourselves but instead to feel our interdependency. María Puig de la Bellacasa writes in *Matters of Care: Speculative Ethics in More than Human Worlds*, “Affirming the absurdity of disentangling human and nonhuman relations of care and the ethicalities involved requires decentering human agencies, as well as remaining close to the predicaments and inheritances of situated human doings.” Here in the garden, we vibrate amongst other reverberations. As we engage in slow, situated and reparative reading, we are quilting ourselves back into an imperfect but illustrious patchwork. This is not a manifesto; it’s a manifestation. By tending to and being in attendance with all that surrounds us in the garden, we are in a state of becoming in our differences together.

You should not have to apologise. Please cry!

I want to acknowledge the many animated conversations I had with the artist and writer Amy Pickles while she was studying at the Piet Zwart Institute. At that time, she was thinking through scripts and what it means to read aloud and hold the words of another in your mouth as an act of care. Together, we talked about the work of Sedgwick and the potential of reparative reading. I was graced and grateful to have such thoughtful exchanges with Amy, where I truly learned so much. In her educational work, she has a way of transforming the most theoretical concepts into something lived and grasped through all of the senses.

Kosofsky Sedgwick, 146.

While the educator and curriculum designer Lisanne Janssen worked on her thesis at the Piet Zwart Institute, we had numerous discussions about the relationship between gardening and education. *Tending to, being in attendance with*, and *tenderness* were words that continually punctuated our talks. We also spoke of the history of women's labour, often invisible and repetitive and of darning socks, mending clothes, and giving attention to something or someone through small gestures as a form of care and love. Through Lisanne's sensitive and nuanced reflections, she helped refine my thinking about the value of these subtle acts.

María Puig de la Bellacasa, *Matters of Care: Speculative Ethics in More Than Human Worlds* (Minneapolis MN: University of Minnesota Press, 2017), 2.

In the Autumn of 2022, an early version of this text was read aloud together with the *Reading Rhythms Club* in my garden house. I want to thank all of you for embodying these written words, liberating them from the page and making them manifest through speech. Your polyphonic voices remain in my ears.

The Reading Rhythms Club at my garden house, Rotterdam, SNV allotment, Winter, 2023 (Photograph: Michelle Teran).

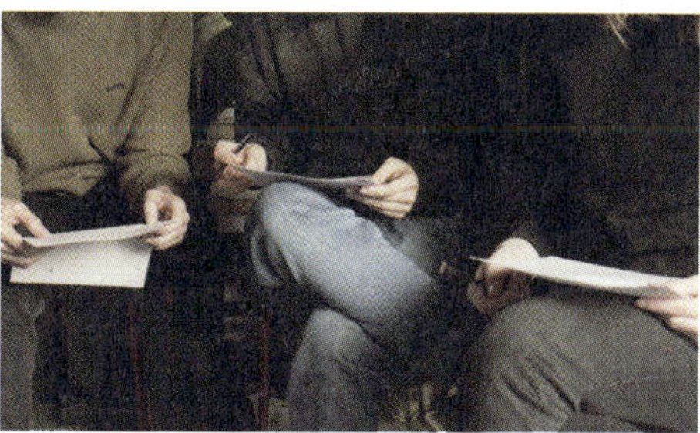

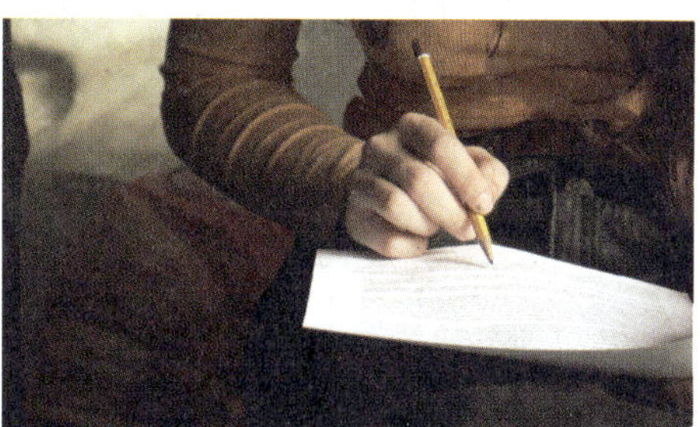

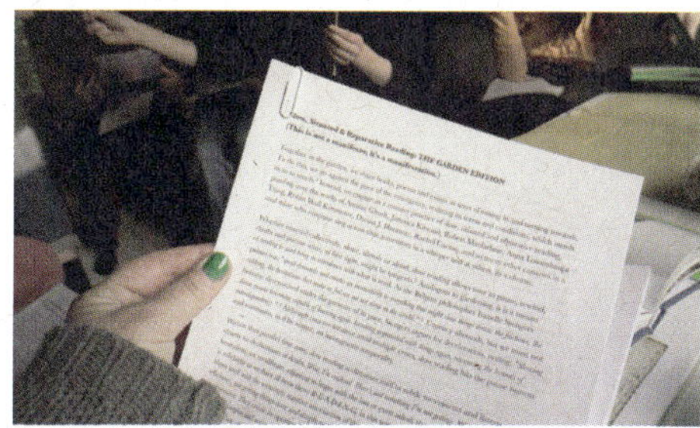

Seed / Earth: An Exchange of Relational Knowledge

A photo-narrative presentation

****************************** SLIDE 1 ******************************

Are you inside? Are you by a window? If so, what do you see out of it? I hope you're comfortable, content, even happy wherever you are at this moment. Where you lived during the COVID19 pandemic, were you required to stay inside and isolated for long periods of time? What did you think about during those days and nights that stretched senses of time? I don't want to bring up difficult memories and then gloss over what it meant for you. I apologize if this happens while you read this. Instead, I hope this narrative of a period in my life, one that was layered with many other realities that were being lived simultaneously, brings you a sense of solidarity; a connection with the words, the images, and between you and me.

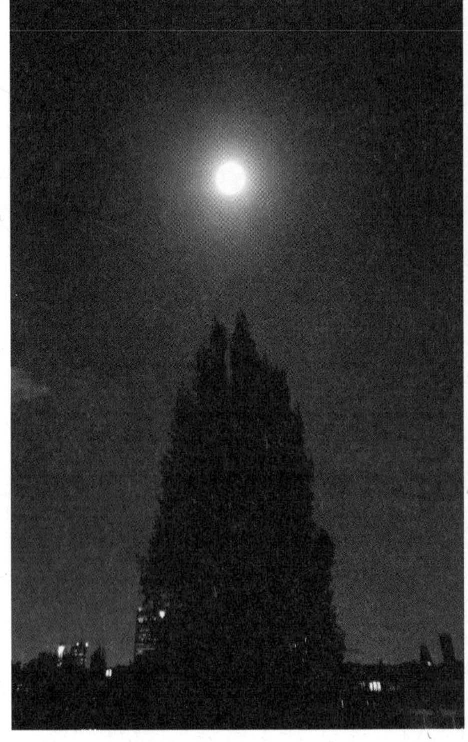

All photos were taken by Skye Maule-O'Brien between 2019 and 2023, unless noted otherwise.

This story[1] is about me and a poplar tree in the north end of Rotterdam.

It is customary for me to begin a presentation by speaking to my relationship to the land that I'm currently on. When in what is now called Canada, this is about acknowledging and paying respect to the Indigenous peoples and lands, and the unceded territories where I was raised and lived most of my life as a settler. As a child this was on the Omàmiwininiwag and Anishinabewaki territory, and then as an adult on the island of Tiohtià:ke / Mooniyaang—commonly known today as Montreal—where the Kanien'kehá ka Nation are recognized custodians.[2] Now I live in Rotterdam. It is a city built on deltas and floodplains, with most of it lying below sea level. My apartment is sinking into the sand, and I'm not always sure that the waters which course, with great calculated control, through the city and the whole of the Netherlands, always appreciate the adversarial ways they've been treated over the centuries of settlement and development. I consider myself a guest on this land; learning about the sandy soils[3] and the lives of those who have built roots in it.

1. is a love story.

2. Sourced from Native Land Digital, https://native-land.ca/.

3. I regularly see seashells in the sand on the sidewalks of the city, reminding me I live below sea level.

As you read, I'd like to ask you to think about your own relationship with the land you live on, its trees and plants.

The title I chose, *Seed / Earth: An Exchange of Relational Knowledge*, is a reference to Octavia Butler's book *Parable of the Sower*. The book is about collectively surviving an apocalyptic future. The protagonist envisions and creates a new religion and community she calls Earthseed. Its core principle being:

All that you touch
You Change.

All that you Change
Changes you.

The only lasting truth
Is Change.

God
Is Change.[4]

4. Octavia E. Butler, *Parable of the Sower* (New York: Grand Central Publishing, 1993), 3.

I begin here because my practice and research are rooted in change—specifically a critical and transformative pedagogical strategy that prioritizes relational knowledge building. Not just any knowledge, but embodied knowings that if activated may help create social, political, and environmental shifts. I call this *intimate pedagogy*.

Those who have experiences as educators or learners of critical pedagogy may agree that transformative learning can be difficult work that requires vulnerability and discomfort. I have found this to be especially true when addressing subjects of gender, sexuality, race, anti/decoloniality, and/or grief work. I created intimate pedagogy as a tool to address the limits I was coming up against, and to support the difficult, but required, shifts that happen within our bodies when engaging in transformative or social justice forms of education. I wanted to name this embodied learning I was witnessing as something integral to the type of education I'm committed to in my teaching and learning practice, but also in my own life.

At its core, intimate pedagogy is a theory and method of recognizing and strengthening connections in daily life that I understand as always, already present. It is a practice of learning through intimacy making with the self, with other forms of life, and their knowledge.

Maybe in my stress, I produce more stress.

****************************** SLIDE 2 ******************************

5. adrienne maree brown, *Emergent Strategy* (Chico CA: AK Press, 2017).

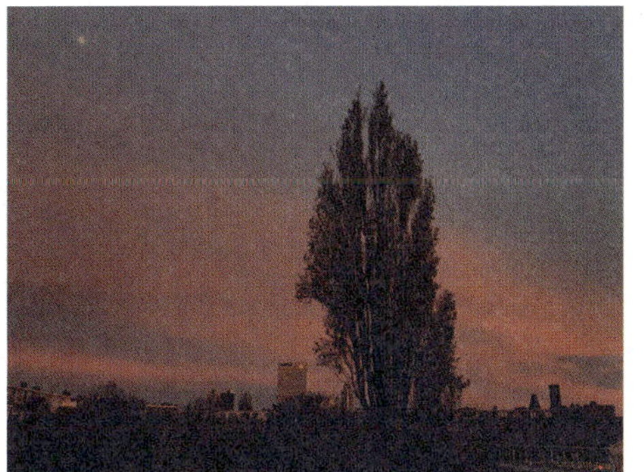

I tell this story of the tree to consider how theory, the visual, and sensorial impact how we learn together. Using a photo narrative I ask, can an intimate pedagogy help us transgress divisionary boundaries to produce transformative outcomes of accountability to ourselves, each other, and the planet? Intimate pedagogy prioritizes attending to a connected and relational life. This story puts attention on participatory learning with plant life. The writing and accompanying images invite an understanding of how mundane moments can be recognized as relational exchanges that work to deepen our knowledge of a place and our connection to it. It shows how being attentive to a non-human life can root us in ways that feel both comforting and unsettling. And articulates how as an emergent practice,[5] intimate pedagogy encourages the awareness of botanical life as affective and effective in shaping how knowledge is formed.

****************************** SLIDE 3 ******************************
(video still)

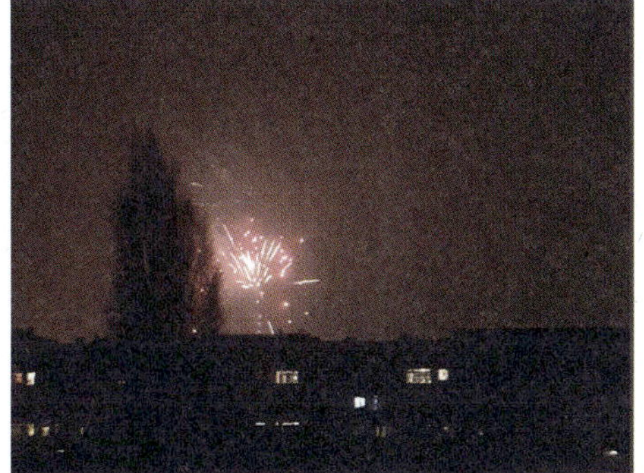

I saw the cottonwood tree for the first time in possibly late October and certainly November 2019. It is a Populus nigra or black poplar. This type of tree is known for its invasive pollination and expansive roots systems that enable it to grow tall and fast.

This is the first visual record I have in my photo gallery of the tree. It's a video taken on December 31, 2019 (before the firework ban in Rotterdam) that shows a cloud covered night sky, apartments and the top portion of a leafless tree with fireworks going off behind it.

****************************** SLIDE 4 ******************************

I moved to Rotterdam with my partner in the Fall of 2019. We briefly lived with friends until we found a temporary (illegal) apartment. Within the second month of living there the news began to reach us of a novel virus, and subsequently this apartment is where we were for the first lockdown of 2020. Like most people, I experienced a wide range of emotions during this time. I was grateful for having safe housing but simultaneously felt a deep unease / rage at being stuck in a small, precarious living arrangement; jobless, isolated from family and friends in a new city, on a new continent.

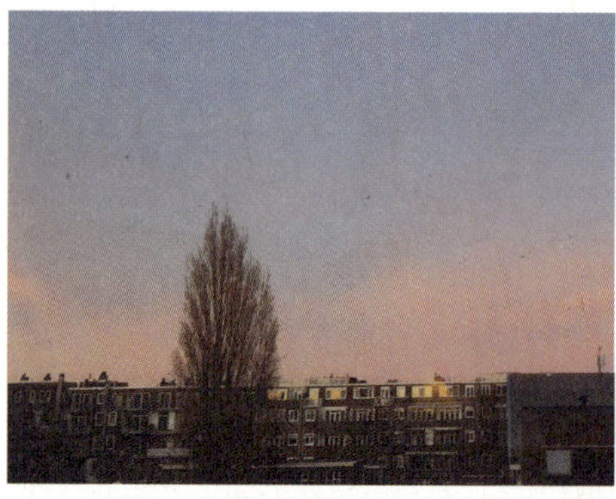

Also, probably like many people during this period, I spent a lot of time looking out the window. For me this meant staring at a tall leafless tree on the grounds of the public swimming pool across the street. The tree towered above everything else in the skyline. And honestly, I felt resentful at being forced to look at this skeletal tree daily as it swayed eerily in the wind that felt more aggressive than any wind I had ever experienced before.

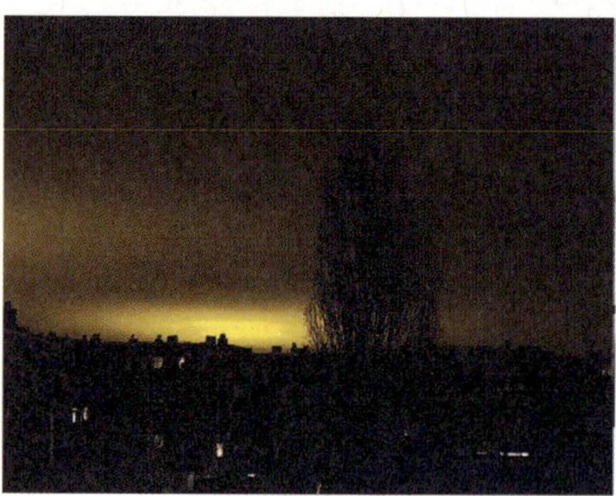

****************************** SLIDE 5 ******************************

But as the temperatures rose, the rain was replaced with relentless sun (it was the sunniest spring on record in the Netherlands), daylight increased, and life began to bloom. Birds sang louder, and COVID19 numbers dropped. My resentment and anxiety slowly eased, making room for hope. I watched the tree fill with leaves and become the most popular poplar—a hot spot for birds. I started to grow an appreciation at having so much life to watch from

Sometimes I think we just need to be kinder to ourselves.

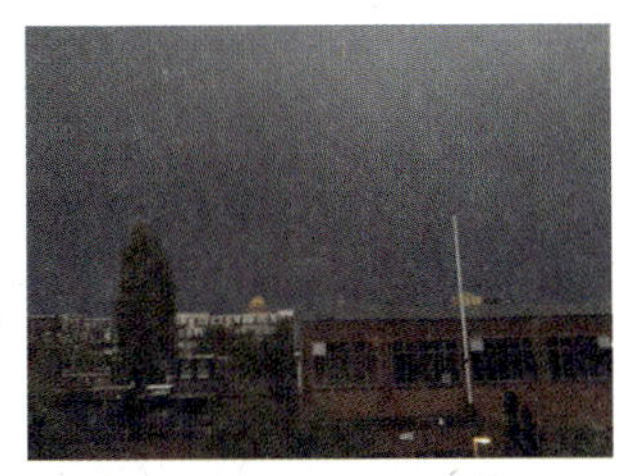

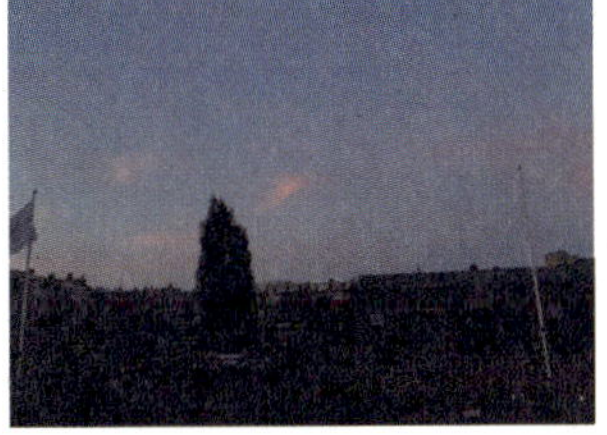

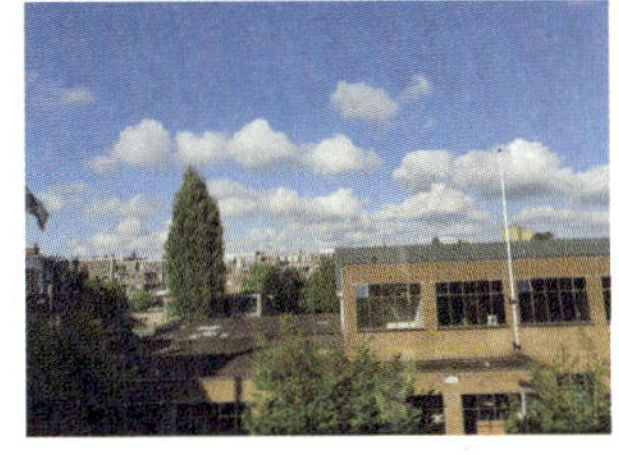

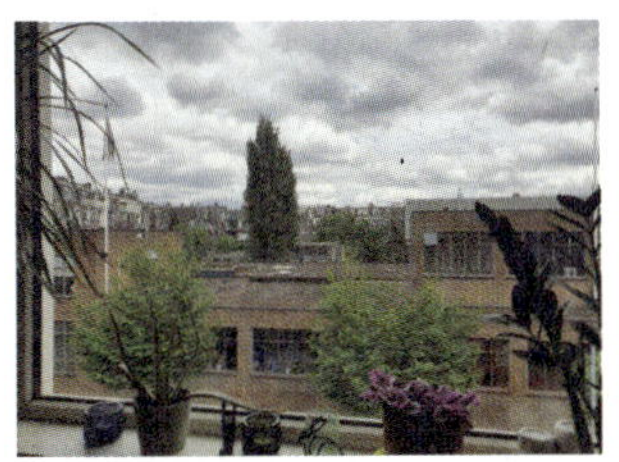

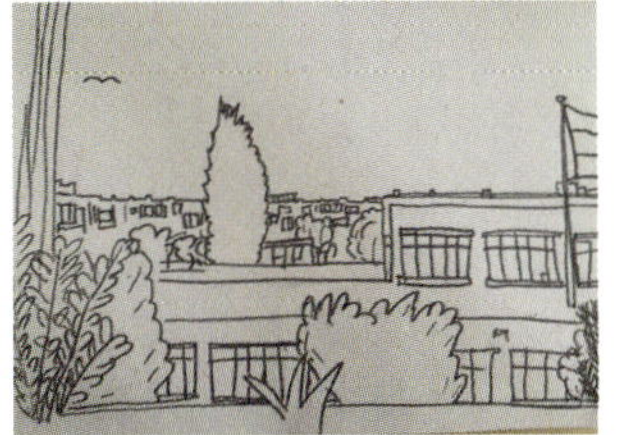

my apartment window; even drawing a picture of the view on a birthday card for my partner that April.

That spring I had made it my full-time job (instead of finishing my PhD) to find my partner and I permanent housing. My partner was working and with some creative navigation (lying) about my income, this enabled us to search for a legitimate rental whose address we could legally register with the gemeente (municipality).[6]

However, the housing search was not easy in the competitive rental market. It was months of messaging, calling, and visiting places all over the city, with nothing coming through. I tried not to get discouraged / panicked, but the frustration certainty kept me up at night.[7]

Then on June 16th I opened Funda (the local house-search website), like I had every morning for months to scour any new posts. I saw a fresh orange dot in my area instantly, and as I read the details of the posting a tidal wave of excitement filled my body. Then came the moment when I realized that the apartment was one block away, and that it was right beside THE TREE. I was flooded with emotion and my body kicked into extreme polite, but fierce, Canadian girl mode. There was no way someone else was getting that apartment.

We got the keys within a week.

6. In the Netherlands, residents are legally required to register with their municipal government. There is a limit to how many individuals may be registered at each address depending on the size of the home.

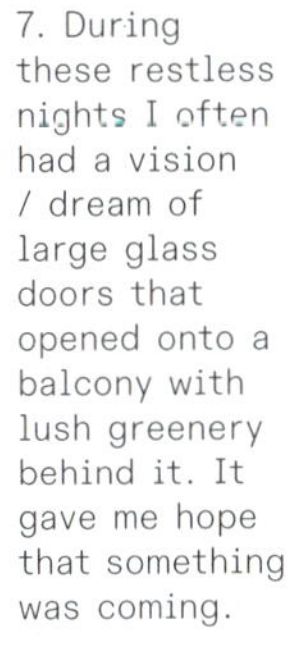

7. During these restless nights I often had a vision / dream of large glass doors that opened onto a balcony with lush greenery behind it. It gave me hope that something was coming.

****************************** SLIDE 6 ******************************

New view! This was the first photo I took of the tree from the new perspective. It was so close that I could hear its leaves rustling in the wind. I can't even express how lucky and thankful I felt at that moment.

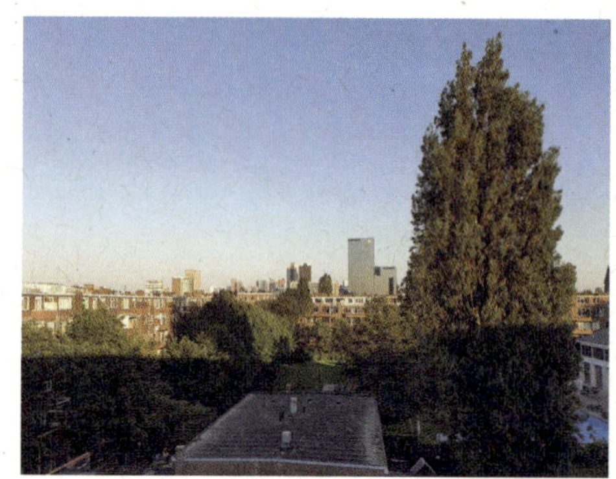

But, as life goes, it's always a messy mixture of joy, pain, gratitude, and unresolved trauma that we experience and carry in our bodies.

****************************** SLIDE 7 ******************************

Video of a black bird singing his evening song in the top branches of the tree. It's spring and the buds are just starting to bloom into small leaves making it difficult to see the bird.

10 days after getting the keys, I experienced my first instance of extreme metrorrhagia (abnormal uterine bleeding that occurs outside of the period of menstruation). In my case it was due to five large uterine fibroids, that meant I needed to undergo an urgent total abdominal hysterectomy the following month, during a global pandemic with travel bans in place and the Atlantic Ocean between myself and my family in Canada.

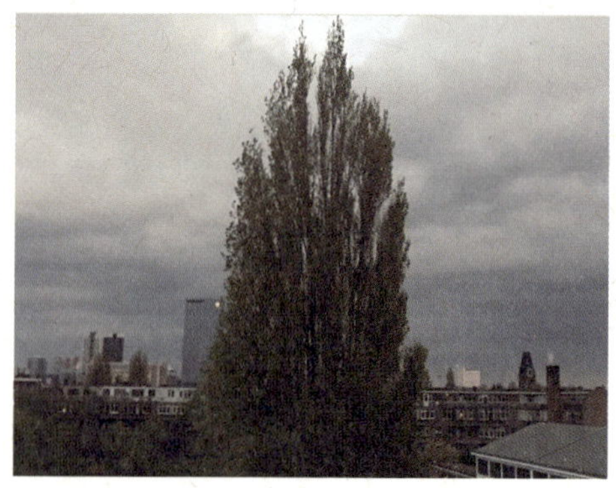

SLIDE 8

As I healed, and the pandemic waves continued with various lockdown measures, I spent more time looking out the window, but interspersed with working at a new job, meeting more people, and learning about Rotterdam. Even though much of my time was spent at home, I was building intimacy with a view of a city while also forming a new community. The tree dominates my view, and I don't take their[8] presence lightly. This poplar has become as much a part of my Rotterdam community as anyone I have met since moving here.

Sometimes their leaves blow on to my balcony and I save them.

8. I use the pronouns they/them/their when referring to the tree.

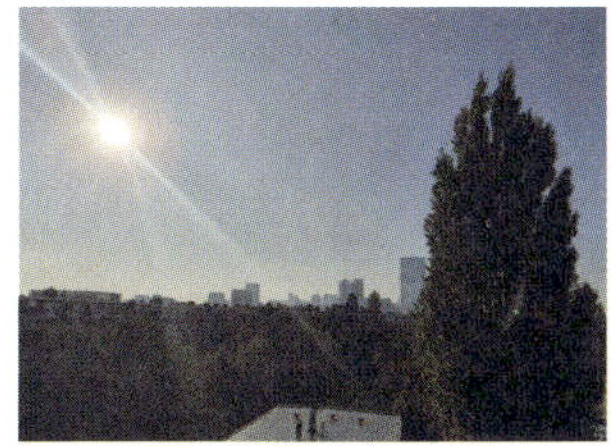

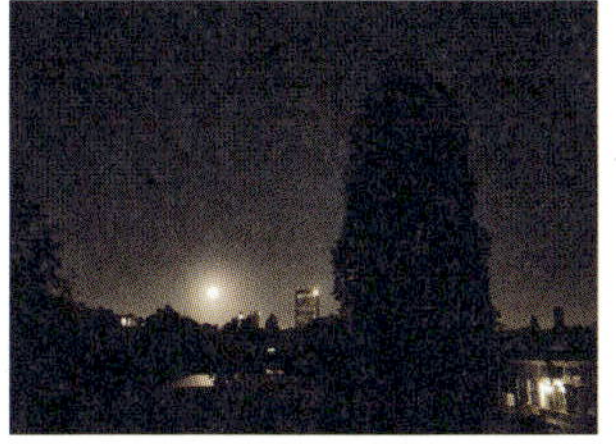

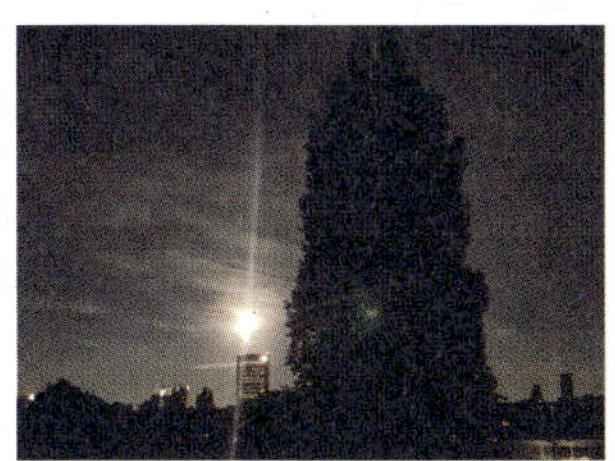

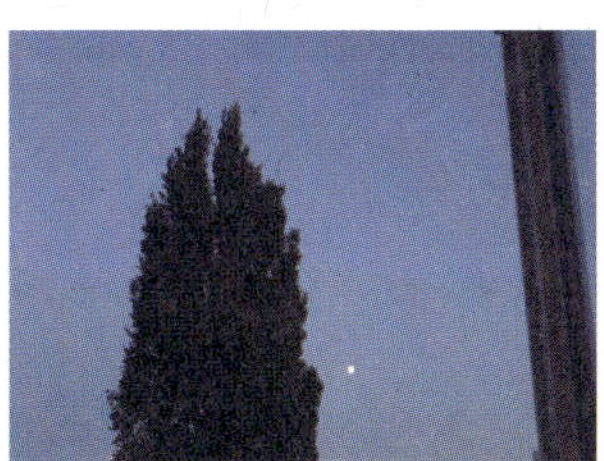

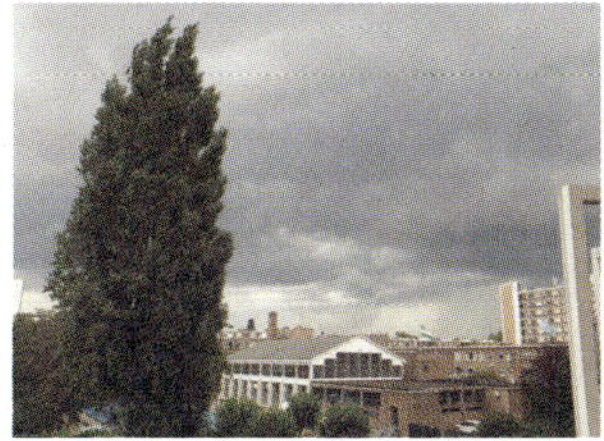

****************************** SLIDE 9 ******************************

Collage of photos with a video of a tiding of magpies chattering to each other and jumping between the leafless branches of the tree.

The love and respect I have developed for the tree is clearly big. I've never liked a tree this much, but maybe I've just never taken the time to listen and learn from one. It has been a durational practice of attention: watching, listening, and living life beside each other. The memories that make up this narrative hold a mixture of joy and gratitude with the initial anxiety, resentment, and fear I experienced during the early pandemic days. Some of my most life altering events—not all bad, but some extremely hard—have occurred during my short time in Rotterdam and in the presence of this tree.

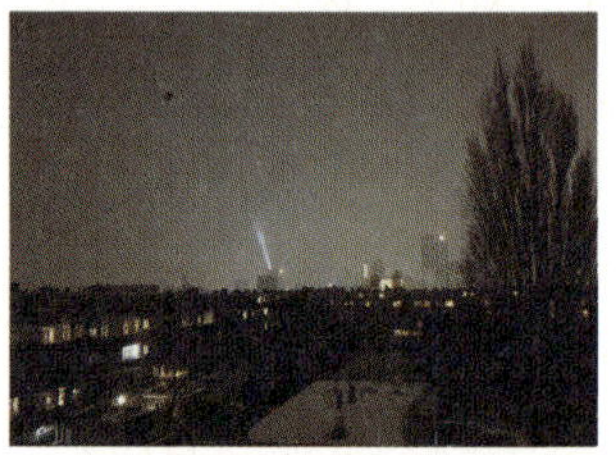

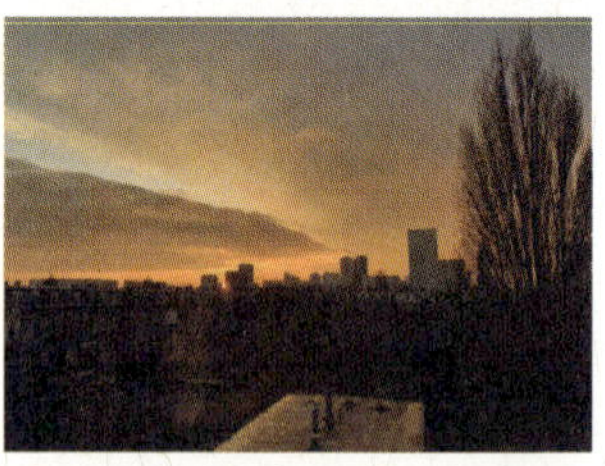

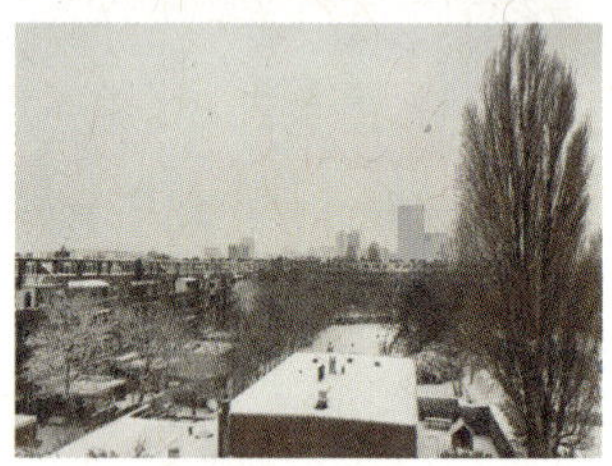

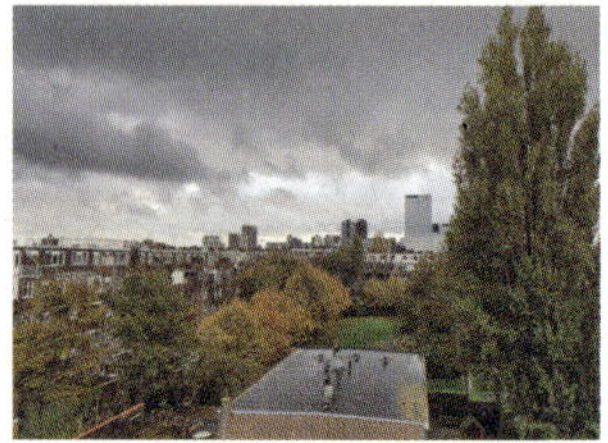

I was thinking how nice it would be if I can hug you now, give you another hug.

***************************** SLIDE 10 *****************************
(1 photo, 1 video still)

Video still of a tree trimmer cutting the lower branches off the tree with a chainsaw and photo of the results / aftermath.

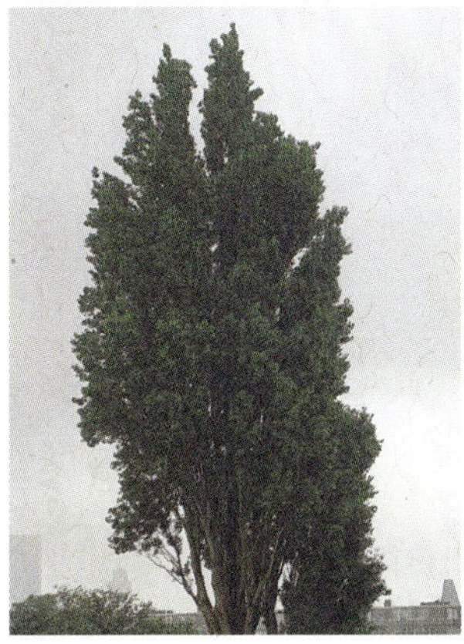

I've also been witness to some of its difficult moments.
Like when it got a dramatic haircut!

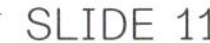

***************************** SLIDE 11 *****************************

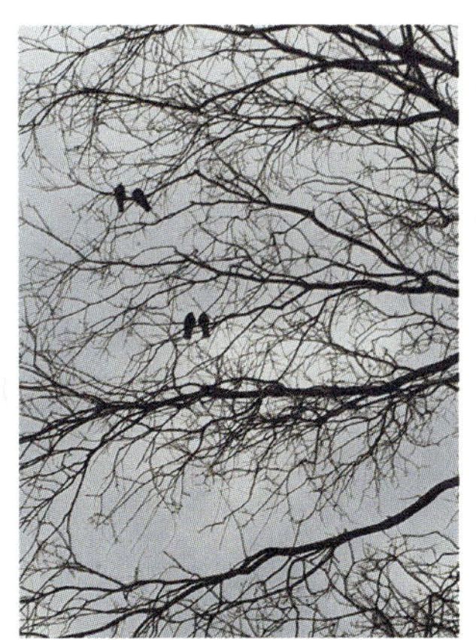

In the winter of 2022, we thought we might have to move. Our landlord (who we loved by the way) wanted us to buy the apartment from her, but figuring out if that was even possible or something we wanted, and then navigating the multiple processes, rules, and paperwork in Dutch was stressful, to say the least.

My anxiety already high, my chest felt like it would burst when three back-to-back storms that February shook and bent the tree in ways I had never seen. As I watched, I knew that if the tree fell, we were definitely moving.

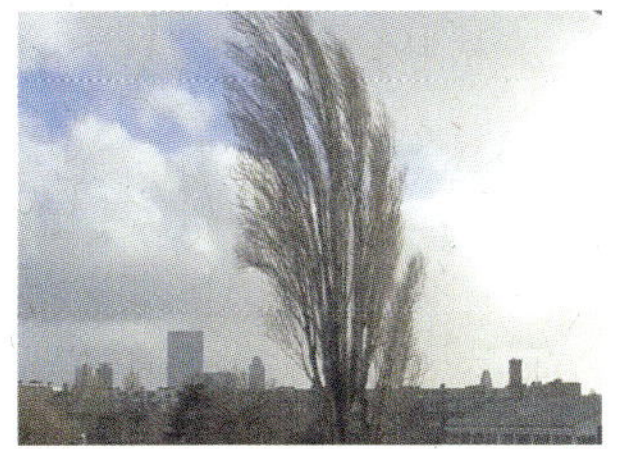

A tree pal beside them didn't make it, and the poplar lost many branches, but they survived!

We were able to buy the apartment.[9]

9. There have been multiple moments where I have been forced to face the contradictions of living, and thriving, in a neo-liberal state in ways that I did not expect when first arriving in the Netherlands. For example, the status of housing and its legislation meant that for my partner and I, we could apply and be approved for a mortgage of 100% of the value of the home, and it was cheaper to do so than finding another rental apartment of similar size.

**************************** SLIDE 12****************************

I feel rooted to Rotterdam in ways that don't always feel easy or in my control. Creating home and community often result in feelings of un/belonging that are rarely simple or linear for anyone in a new place. My experiences of building roots have unfolded in ways that have been surprising and at times have caused resistance inside me. As someone who is invested in listening to the earth as a method of learning and action, I ask myself, how can entering a profound dialogue with the landscape be done so respectfully and with accountability to life I share space and place with? I think this tree, and many trees, hold knowledge that can be learned from if we are open to listening and hearing about how these roots implicate us.

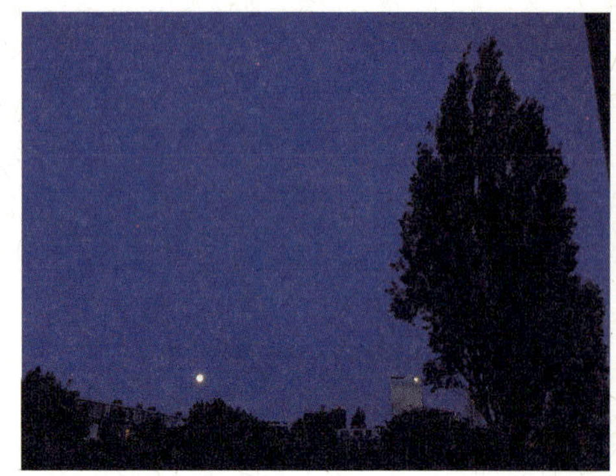

**************************** SLIDE 13****************************

let's pause

and

breathe

and

drink water

**************************** SLIDE 14****************************

Trees and plants have always lived in both political and spiritual dimensions, being used in reparation, resistance, and counter-knowledge production.[10] The stories people tell about plants hold social memories and important historical dimensions of citizenship that are woven through the public and private spheres of life.[11] For me, this tree holds

10. Skye Maule-O'Brien, "Intimate Pedagogy: Visual Explorations of Race and the Erotic," PhD diss., (York University, 2021).

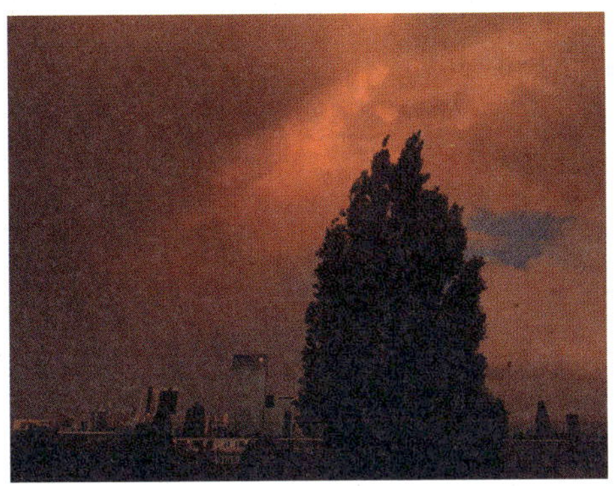

an intimidating power that I admit sometimes scares me. It seems to know of things I cannot yet know. Holding information from elsewhere that expands across time, to a past and future simultaneously; between the worldly and otherworldly. Trees are not merely passive beings. They are teachers that hold knowledge to be learned from, which stretches beyond the visual, towards sensory and layered bodily knowing.

Mimi Sheller's chapter "Arboreal Landscapes of Power and Resistance" develops a spatial methodology for tracking citizenship on the land through the communicating root structures of trees and plants that reach underneath gardens, plots, plantations, and history.[12] She argues that botanical life is fundamental to understanding relations between bodies and landscapes. Stating that attention needs to be paid to life burrowed beneath human interactions as a way to make visible and rethink the gaps or silences in our histories.[13] Her work suggests that claims to power and land, as well as our politics of freedom and control, must include nature as sites of conflict. Meaning the darker histories held within the soils, and the reading of the landscape's underside as a site of multiple and contested histories, is needed to unsettle fixed colonial discourses of a region.[14] Landscapes are always textured with living histories that speak back with particular agency.[15] In agreement, Elizabeth DeLoughrey and George B. Handley write that "the environment stands as a nonhuman witness to the violent process of colonialism" and it makes this engagement with alterity "a constitutive aspect of post (or de) coloniality."[16]

11. See, for example, Ibid. and also the following: Mimi Sheller, *Citizenship from Below: Erotic Agency and Caribbean Freedom* (Durham NC: Duke University Press, 2012); Amar Wahab, *Colonial Inventions: Landscape, Power and Representation in Nineteenth-Century Trinidad* (Newcastle Upon Tyne UK: Cambridge Scholars Publishing, 2010); Elizabeth M. DeLoughrey and George B. Handley, *Postcolonial Ecologies: Literatures of the Environment* (New York: Oxford University Press USA, 2011); Édouard Glissant, *Poetics of Relation* (Ann Arbor MI: University of Michigan Press, 1997).

12. Maule-O'Brien (n 10).

13. Sheller (n 11).

14. Wahab (n 11).

15. Maule-O'Brien (n 10).

16. DeLoughrey and Handley (n 11) 8.

****************************** SLIDE 15******************************

I want to return to what this means for this story and intimate pedagogy. Practicing an intimate pedagogy to me means to grapple with being human and living in relation to all expansive forms of life (known and unknown), and creating intimate knowledge with decolonial[17] purpose. Within our ecosystems the interconnectivity of life is awaiting our recognition. This story does not ask whether we are intimately connected to all life on earth; the connection is understood as always already present.[18] I have argued previously, "we belong to each other across biological categorization, territory lines of geography, and social organization."[19] For example, the tree and I share the same biological material and we live in the same neighbourhood. The purpose of an intimate pedagogy is to make these connections—our bodies next to other bodies (including plant life)—tangible in our learning and teaching strategies, and to recognize that teachers take multiple assemblages. An aesthetic of the earth acknowledges that nature's multitude of life contains a density of experience and knowing,[20] and it is to privilege a non-linear embodied knowing as part of our practices.

What does it mean to be openly drawn in by another life; to share or witness experiences, and feel connected outside of the normative limits of what is recognized as human perception? What would including this form of relational (at times intangible) knowing mean to our practices of learning, teaching, and research? Intimate pedagogy as a theory offers a way of listening, being, and learning with and in the world. As a transformative learning practice, it asks us to stay with the discomfort that deeper knowledge requires of us. As a theory and practice together (praxis), intimate pedagogy challenges us to transform.

****************************** SLIDE 16 ******************************

My understanding of home and perspective/perception of life in the city have been shaped by this relationship. And it would be irresponsible to think that my human presence has not impacted the tree in some way, even if I cannot trace how. This poplar and I know each other in inarticulable ways; our past, present, and futures are intertwined through our shared environment. They remind me that life has longevity and is transitory, temporal, immaterial, and ephemeral all at once. The tree acts as a force of stability; a rooted image that flourishes with life, bends with flexibility and grace. It holds a staying power and has welcomed me to remain / linger with the trouble that an intimate knowing requires. A relationship that began from resentment and anger around feelings of being trapped, transformed into grounded and intense appreciation and care that are reiterated in community life here. This story of relationship / knowledge building with the tree and the grounds of Rotterdam is not over. It is ongoing, as is my reflective praxis of intimate connectivity and care.

17. Decoloniality to me means practicing alternative and relational forms of living and learning that challenge the normative exploitative, extractive, destructive, and divisionary ways colonial projects have interacted with life.

18. Maule-O'Brien (n 10).

19. Ibid.

20. See, Ibid. and also DeLoughrey and Handley (n 11).

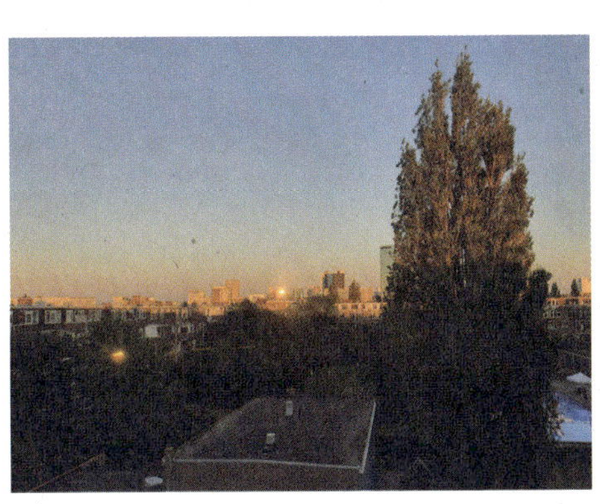

****************************** SLIDE 17******************************

In closing, I will share a second, much shorter, narrative.

The purpose of this presentation was to introduce you to a learning theory and practice.
A small seed of change.
I hope you let this seed of intimate learning grow.
I hope that you let it resonate within you and spread beyond.
I hope you feel more connected.

In the summer of 2021, as a way for myself to feel more connected in Rotterdam, I joined a sunflower growing competition, fully knowing I wouldn't win with my pots on my balcony. But I didn't care. I just wanted to grow some flowers with people around the city for the bees. I was given three seeds, and all three turned into beautiful and fairly tall sunflowers that the bees definitely appreciated. These flowers then provided me with countless more seeds that I want to share with you.[21]

21. As a relational gesture, after the June presentation everyone was invited to plant a sunflower seed that they could take home and grow. The final photo of the slideshow was sent to me by marjolijn kok (friend and participant) a few months later.

Thank you.

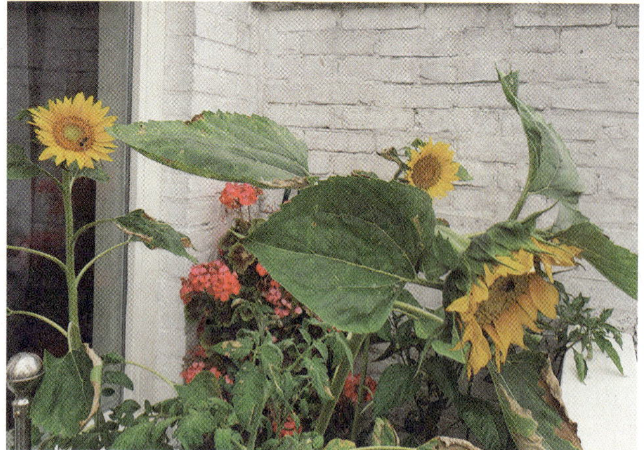

I'll totally hug you.

****************************** SLIDE 18******************************

Afterword

The writing and editing of this text was all done either at my desk beside a window that looked out on the tree, or sitting on my balcony listening to their leaves rustle.

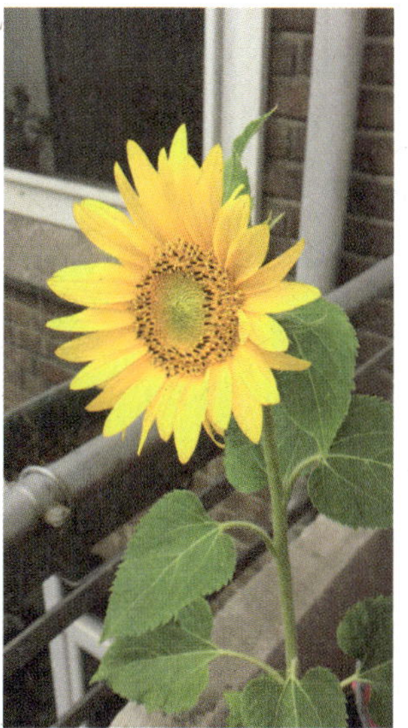

This text began as a talk I presented twice to two different audiences in SNV Volkstuin, a community garden in Rotterdam. Both times I was invited by educators working in the Master Education in Arts at the Piet Zwart Institute. The first time, in early June, the talk was presented as part of Piet Zwart Institute: *Learning with the Garden; Learning from the Land*, a day-long educational event of talks, actions, and workshops. Then in late September, I was a guest lecturer in the *Learning with Others* seminar. Both events were an opportunity to expand and deepen my community within Rotterdam, and invited reflection on a practice of intimate knowledge building. The editing process that followed allowed me time to further articulate some of the intricacies that came up in conversations with those who engaged with the text. The process meant unsticking some of the difficult memories that lingered and stirring up some hibernating ghosts. The text published here is a combination of the presentations that included lighter moments to welcome sharing and ease tension in the public setting, with an expansion and deepening in certain areas that seemed to ask for more attention. A further unpacking, have you will, to contend with the difficult or at times contradictory work (even promiscuous nature) of care within a social and ecological justice framework. The narrative had to be told in stages. Like the durational practice of building a relationship, the meanings and implications of the story and the theory holding it have taken time and are still taking time to emerge.

Carrier, A Deficit, A Surplus

Seecum Cheung and Renée Turner talk about care, the limits of what one can carry and how a sense of belonging can be incrementally fostered over time. Looking at Cheung's simple gesture of carrying books from Hong Kong to the Netherlands, they discuss how such a simple act of care is the work of many.

> RT: When thinking about your gift of books to the Willem de Kooning (WdKA) library, one of the things that strikes me is that care often manifests itself in the smallest of acts and in your case, it is a series of linking connections between people, geographies, identities and initiatives made through this gifting these books. Can you talk about how you acquired them and what the selection of books means to you?

Seecum: Two events came together around this gift. In October 2022, Hong Kong re-opened its borders after its COVID

→

Transported books from the Asia Art Archive

HKG↗

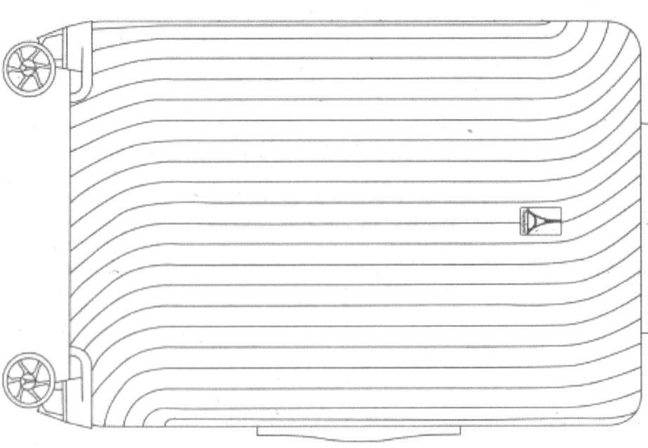

1. Ai Weiwei and Juliet Bingham, *Sunflower Seeds* (London: Tate Publishing, 2010).

2. Ai Weiwei and Hans Ulrich Obrist, *Ai Weiwei Speaks: With Hans Ulrich Obrist* (London: Penguin House, 2011).

3. Joris Escher and Martijn Kielstra, *The Selected Scriptures of Hong Hao* (Amsterdam: Canvas Foundation, 1999).

lockdown, and during that summer in which I realised I was burning out, I decided and was able to drastically reduce my workload at the Willem de Kooning Academy which gave me my first semester off from teaching in around three to four years. At this moment, I chose to leave the Netherlands and travel to Asia to reconnect with my heritage and my family.

Hearing that I would be in Hong Kong for a few months, colleagues, peers, and friends offered to connect me to their contacts to help me settle in a little more. Meeting one person and the next, I quickly connected with various arts organisations in Hong Kong, including the Asia Art Archive, which became a new research home for me. The Archive is a study, library and event space with sites in Hong Kong, New York, and New Delhi, and it is the first and largest repository of printed matter focusing on East and South East Asian contemporary art in the world.

In March of 2023, Wan Chi and Carol Choi from the Asia Art Archive circulated an invitation to collect books from the organisation's depot in the Fo Tan Industrial Centre, which was set to close due to a funding reduction. Around a thousand duplicate copies of artist monographs, exhibition catalogues, magazines, art reference books, and periodicals were consequently offered to the teaching networks around them. As I was affiliated with the WdKA, they extended this invitation to me

→

1.

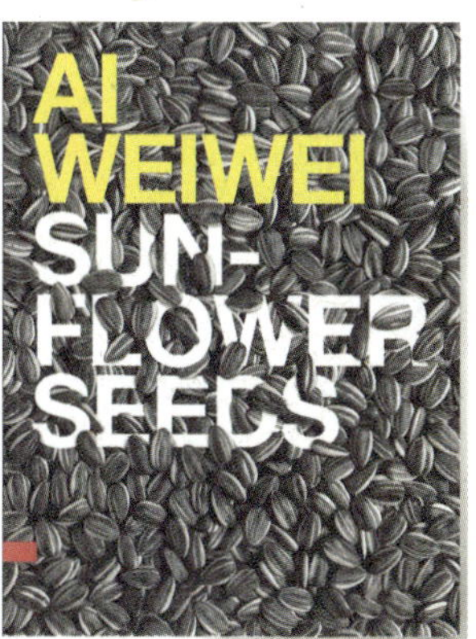

2.

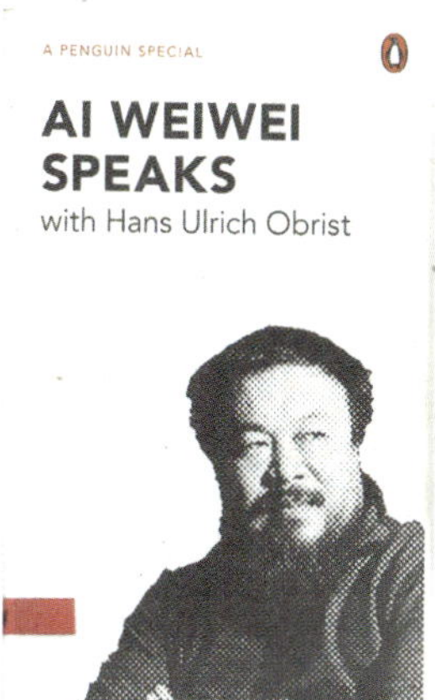

3.

and so on a Tuesday, I went with my suitcase to collect books for our students.

As a student, I struggled to find books which featured modern and contemporary Asian artists, though I knew powerful art movements were happening on this side of the world. This information was not available on English or Dutch library shelves and not having such resources made it difficult to reference and discuss these happenings with my tutors and peers. So, when selecting the books at the Asia Art Archive depot, I thought about the Asian collective diaspora within the WdKA student body; Korean, Indonesian, Japanese, South Asian, Chinese and elsewhere. I looked for materials that would be culturally relevant to them and selected monographs, exhibition catalogues, and theory books. Most were already translated into English. The only book I selected that was not in English is a Chinese edition of Yoko Ono's *Grapefruit*. Originally published in 1964, the book contains different event scores or scripts, which, in the Chinese version, are written in the centre of each page. The students can easily overcome the language barrier by using the camera function on Google Translate, and see a different language aesthetic.

Interestingly, however, my favourite book from the collection is; *FESTAC '77: The 2nd World Black and African Festival of Arts and Culture* in 1977, which was a coming together of the

4. *Artomity*, no. 12 (Spring 2019).

5. *Artomity*, no. 13 (Summer 2018).

6. *Artomity*, no. 14 (Autumn 2019).

4.

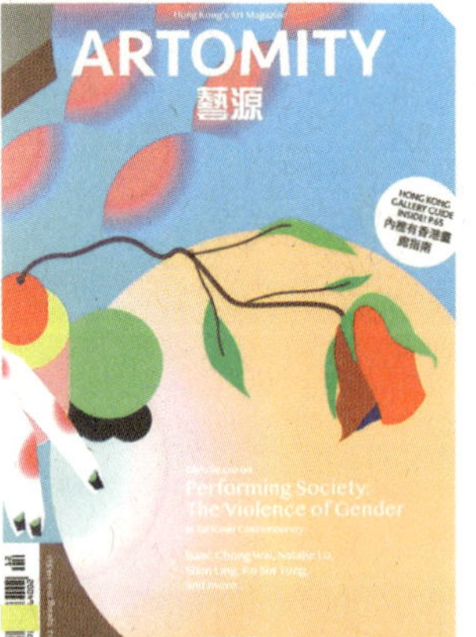

5.

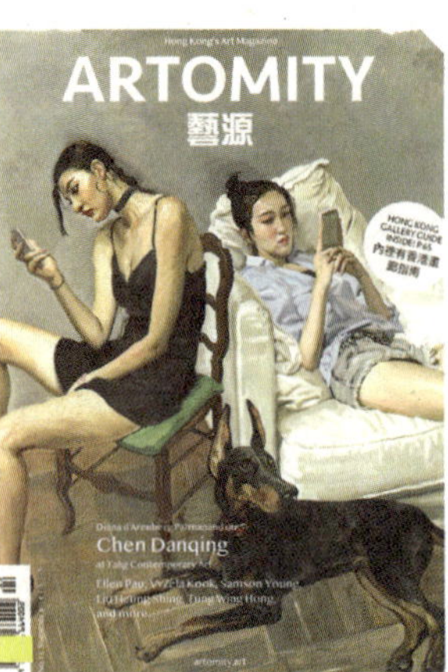

6.

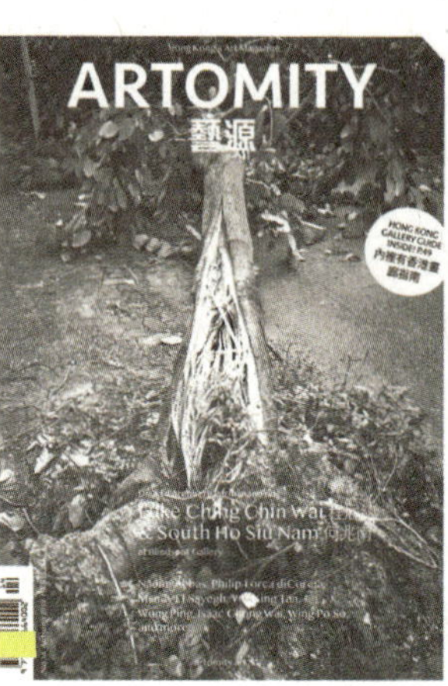

7. *Artomity*, no. 10 (Autumn 2018).

8. Fei Dawei, *Cai Guo-Qiang* (Paris: Publication Fondation Cartier pour l'art contemporain, 2000).

9. *Bentu: Chinese Artists in a Time of Turbulence and Transformation*, eds. Laurence Bossé, Suzanne Pagé, Claire Staebler, and Philip Tinari (Paris: Editions Hazan/ Foundation Louis Vuitton, 2016), exhibition catalogue.

cultural diaspora including Audre Lorde, Sun Ra, and many other famous names. Although this event didn't hail from Asia, one of the catalogue contributors was a researcher for Asia Art Archive which is why there were a few copies inside the library. FESTAC was an activist event in Nigeria, which celebrated the coming together of a "half-century of transatlantic and pan-Africanist cultural-political gatherings." This book documents a very rare cultural and political moment in our recent history, and I think, is a great contribution to our WdKA library and a gift of knowledge for all of our political and cultural diasporas.

To address your observation about small acts of care, it's important to acknowledge the attention given by others, too. Getting these books to WdKA is, as you say, an involved accumulation of gestures, time and physical energy. It was first borne from the Asia Art Archive's initiative and generous offer, ensuring that a wider student body could benefit from their surplus resources. Wan Chi often worked overtime until eleven in the evening, so the teachers and school caretakers could come to select books for their collection. Rather than one week as initially planned, this exchange and transfer process lasted over a month, which was exhausting work for Wan Chi and the team. Their dedication marks, for me, the necessary invisible labour carried through the transference of these books.

7.

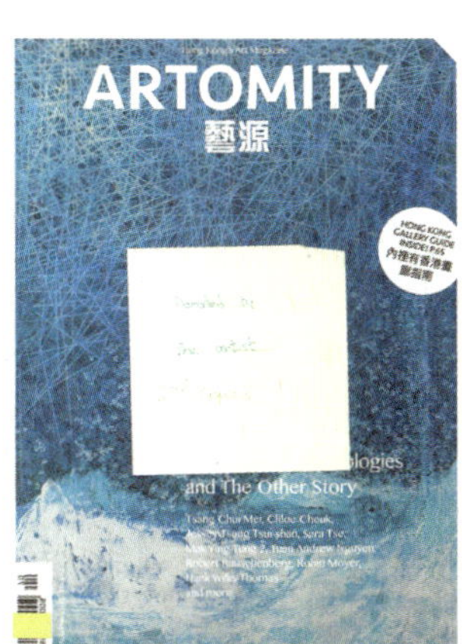

8.

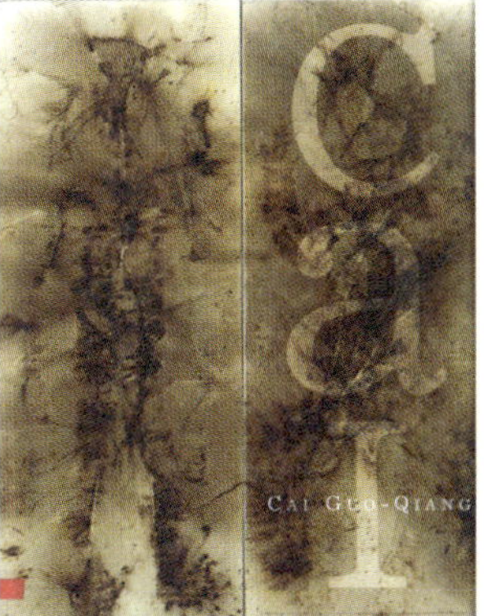

9.

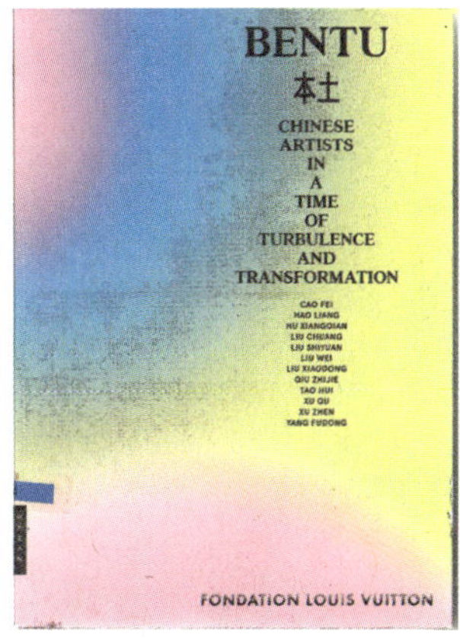

Asia Art Archive came into existence out of certain realisations by Claire Hsu. While studying at the SOAS in London, she observed there was very little access to materials reflecting, recording or documenting contemporary East and South East Asian art. So, along with Johnson Chang, founder of Hanzart TZ Gallery, they set up the Asia Art Archive in 2000 and have been procuring, processing and cataloguing ESEA art practices and artistic knowledge ever since.

Although the Asia Art Archive was initially established to fill a lack; at this moment, it found itself with a surplus. And now, I have carried that surplus to fill a lack at the WdKA. I hope this act, however modest, can, as you say, connect or reconnect people to other geographies and identities and open a small space to build wider collective knowledge, together.

> RT: You were restricted by the number of books you could carry due to the size of your luggage and its weight. Concerning care, there is something almost poetic about the notion of "*no more than I can carry*" or "*as much as I can carry.*" It is an embodied intervention framed by practical limits and it makes do with what is possible. It demonstrates what it means to find agency on the fly. Can you talk about the journey of bringing the books from there to here and what that process evoked?

SC: Every gift begins with conjuring a form of energy of some

10. Laura Murray Cree, *Ai Weiwei—Under Construction* (Sydney: University of New South Wales Press, 2009).

11. Ntone Edjabe, *FESTAC '77: 2nd World Black and African Festival of Arts and Culture* (London: Afterall Books and Chimurenga, 2019).

12. Cai Guo-Qiang, *Hanging Out in the Museum* (Taipei: Taipei Fine Arts Museum, 2010).

→

10.

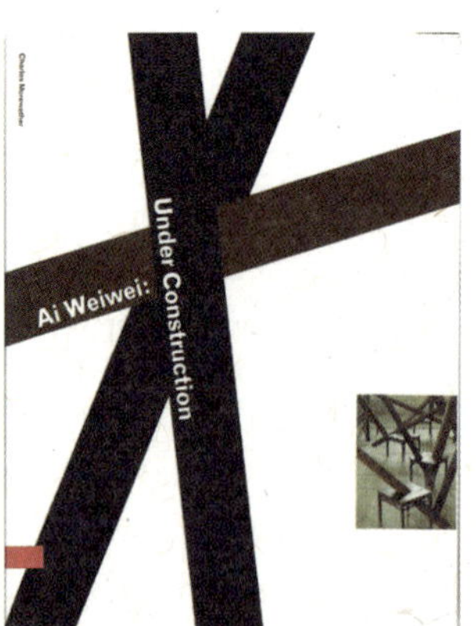

11.

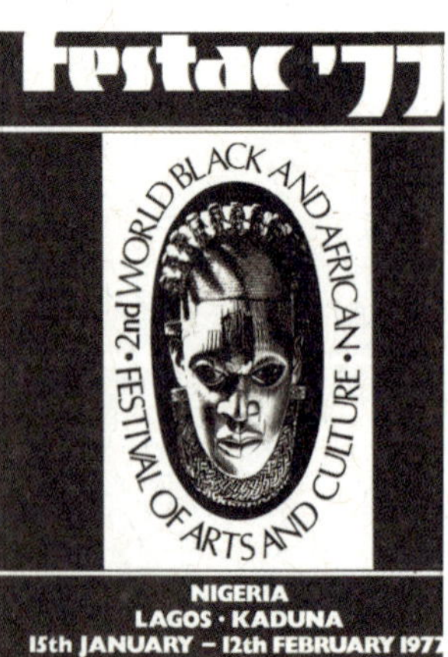

12.

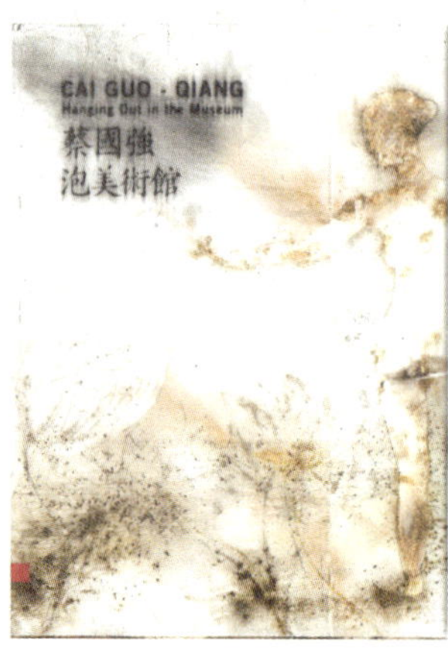

13. Heman Chong and Melissa Lim, *The Sole Proprietor and Other Stories* (Guangzhou: Vitamin Creative Space, 2007).

14. *2003 Hermes Foundation Missulsang*, (Seoul: Artsonje Center September 27-May 15, 2003), exhibition catalogue.

15. *2008 Hermes Foundation Missulsang*, (Seoul: Artsonje Center 2008), exhibition catalogue.

sort. For example, it requires physical exertion, material resources and hours of coordinated time. Unfortunately, for various reasons, I had felt utterly depleted on all of these fronts. As a practitioner and documentary filmmaker who likes to work with groups of people facing tough social issues, I have been giving more than I could give and carrying more than I could carry for several years. As a result, I felt the need to move away, take distance, and decompress by using my time in a different, yet culturally familiar home, in order to reflect and replenish.

I have been in Hong Kong since October 2022, with one month of this time spent in the Netherlands and the UK in June 2023. The main reason for this European trip was for my younger sister's wedding, though I included a stopover to Rotterdam so that I could see my friends and colleagues at the WdKA, and to drop off a portion of these books. Knowing that I had to carry books as well as a range of traditional wedding materials for my sister, I was concerned by my luggage restrictions of 23kg. I had already paid €100 fee for these kilos, and as there was no budget from WdKA to cover the book transfer costs, I knew I had to make it work with the luggage that I already had.

My suitcase was filled with such cultural items as traditional wedding silk pyjamas, lai see, decorations, celebration ribbons, hair pieces, guest books, outfits and shoes. There were gifts for my friends and loved ones including Chinese runes, traditional

→

13.

The Sole Proprietor and other Stories
私营者
及其他轶事

Hu Fang
Binna Choi
Astrid Mania
Joselina Cruz
Russell Storer
Cosmin Costinas
Rodney Latourelle
Leif Magne Tangen

编辑
Edited by
Melissa Lim
Heman Chong

出版
Published by
Vitamin
Creative Space

14.

15.

bracelets, fragrant Buddhist incense, and unique toys found only in Asia for my friend's children and my family and their children. My personal belongings were folded into my small hand luggage, as it could no longer fit within the larger case. And next to this, I was already carrying a traditional wedding umbrella and two large wedding pillows that also couldn't fit into the suitcase... so once again I realised I was carrying too much for others. As usual, I wrote it off as a one-time effort and bundled my items together onto the aeroplane, the Eurostar, and the many buses... home.

This makes me think that the idea of "*as much as I can carry*" is a weight determined by people's own capacities. I'm used to carrying more than what is possible for my size, so when handing over these ten or so books to the WdKA Research Station, it felt so small and somehow I wished that I could have brought more.

There are around thirty books still to make the journey, which will gradually be transported to the Netherlands in my future luggage. The books will be catalogued and placed onto the WdKA bookshelves by the WdKA Research Station team. Through long journeys, small bundles, limited luggage, bodily constraints and an accumulation of small acts and transfers, these books will arrive and hopefully become a resource that a few more people can find meaning in connecting with.

16. *Imprint of the Heart: Artistic Journey of Huang Xinbo*, (Hong Kong: Leisure and Cultural Services Department, 2011), exhibition catalogue.

17. Alexandra Munroe and David Joselit, *Cai Guo-Qiang: I Want to Believe* (New York: Guggenheim Museum Publications, 2009).

18. *Orientation*, (Yogyakarta: Cemeti Art Foundation, 1996), exhibition catalogue.

→

16.

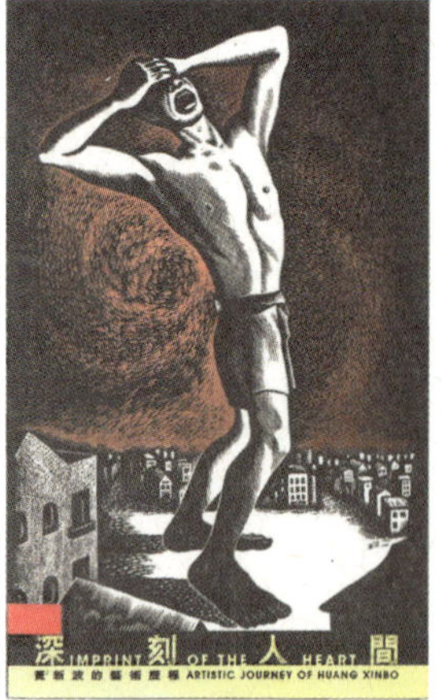

17.

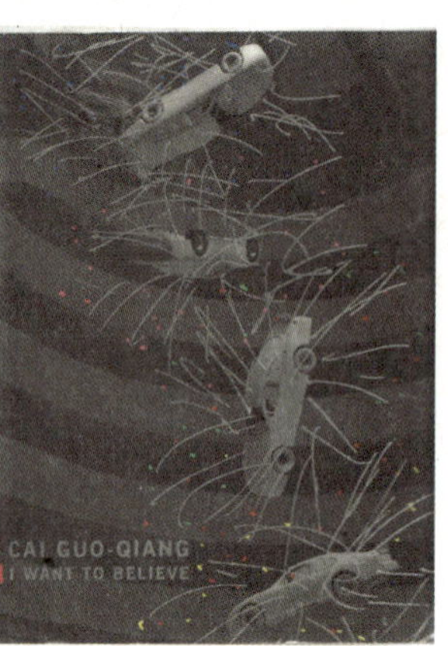

18.

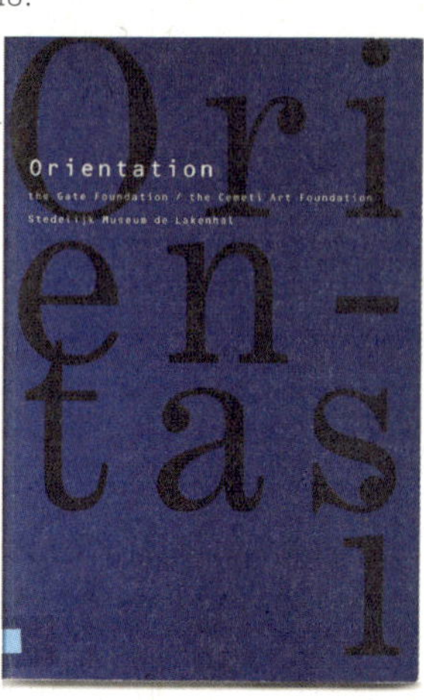

19. Chankyong Park, *Ghosts, Spies, and Grandmothers: Modernities Against Modernity* (Seoul: Hyunsil Books/ Seoul Museum of Art, 2014).

20. 編集東京都現代美術館 and 東京都現代美術館 (henshū Tōkyō-to and Gendai Bijutsukan), *Selected Works from Museum of Contemporary Art, Tokyo* (Tokyo: 東京都現代美術館, 1995).

"You came back here looking for missing pieces, for missing wordless pockets of air left floating, or written and kept by others, to link your collected texts of ether to, in hopes of perhaps forming a library, an archive of air to read communally.

What you found here was more than you could have known. What happened to you has itself become another porous zone of formless words made of air, legible by those who know, those whose air stories float nearby. They come together and form an airborne archipelago: an archive. An atmospheric singularity - it may be invisible and soundless, but it provides navigation referents for other seafarers of that airy archive.

Sometimes, when theses singularities come together, the air gets denser.

A

storm

forms."

Nine Yamamoto-Masson, *Air Tides (Zine, Asia Art Archive)*

19.

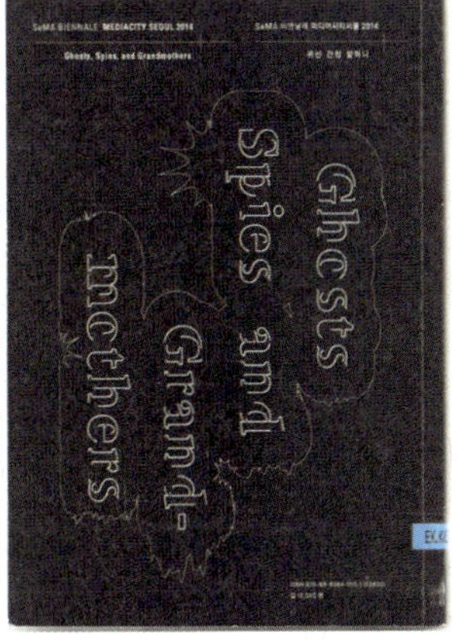

20.

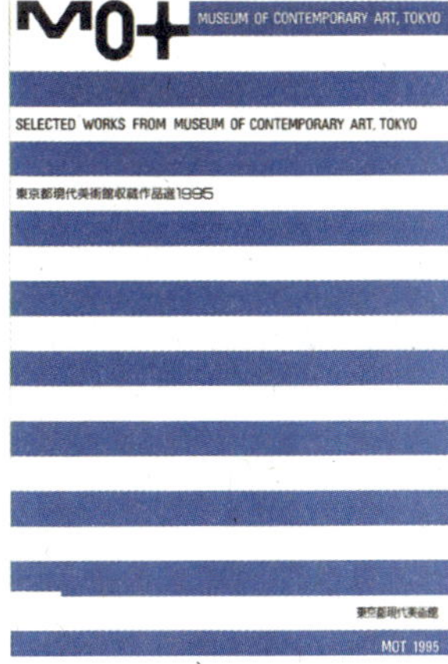

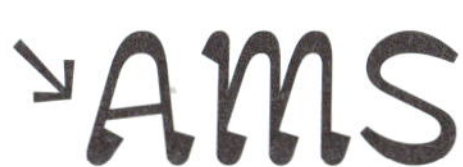

Learning and Dreaming Together through Social Uncertainty

Intro

We feel the uncertainty of these times. We wonder about ways of learning that are centered upon uncertainty, that do not hide from challenges we face. Institutions of higher learning have promised never-ending progress based on reason and science, but today we are unsure if this is real, or desirable. Rather than modeling education around a heroic narrative of individuals overcoming challenges, towards unquestioning progress, we think about how learning can be oriented towards learning together in difference. By facing it, we wonder how uncertainty can be embraced, or, at worst, how we can avoid panic around uncertainty. For this reason, we created an experiment, "Learning and Dreaming Together through Uncertainty." The experiment of "Learning and Dreaming…" was to host a collective overnight dream-in that asked its participants to focus on the emotional fragility of uncertainty and how experimental social and education practices could deal differently with this uncertainty.

When we get into the matter of uncertainty, we think about several aspects of it. On the one hand, there is the individual feeling and thinking self that may feel constitutionally fraught by self doubts and a sense of personal uncertainties. Then we have external impulses that normally help us orient ourselves within the world regardless of our own constitution, that because of the state of our world may or may not be stable. It is this second kind of uncertainty that we think about when we ask about living and dreaming through uncertain times. Among these uncertain things are social relations between people that are mundane and overarching, which constitute social and cultural

Sorry, I am making a cup of tea.

assumptions around how we should individually and collectively be—despite the actual state of ecological, economic, psychological affairs.

Turning toward education, we see how learning is evermore oriented toward a unipolar notion of "progress" or "development," determined by individual mastery, market competition and profit. This is not what the world needs right now. The educational model that holds sway within most schools replicates a business as usual *attitude, perpetuating the individual and systemic that brought us to this point of severe uncertainty. We ask instead if higher education could make space for collective practices of critical generosity, reciprocity, respect, and togetherness? Can it hold space for social learning around how to hold each other through uncertainty?*

In preparing for this pedagogical experiment, some of the question that we considered were:

How might we collaboratively deal with uncertainties, as a prerequisite for any kind of learning process?

What is social practice for, if it does not actually help us socially work through and care for our collective dreams?

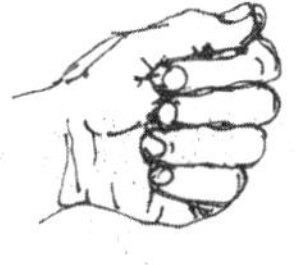

How would we like it to feel in the learning and caring space we share?

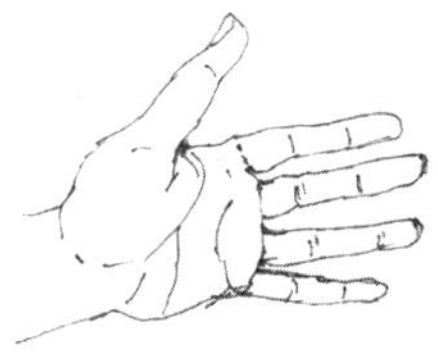

How do we develop capacities for sitting with discomfort, of feeling overwhelmed, anxious or rudderless—when facing uncertain times?

What are our commitments to ourselves and others through uncertainty? That is, what are our ideals for our being human despite the difficulties that we may face?

Illustrations: Marc Herbst

Below is a skit that we wrote between the Voice of Higher Education *and its alternative. The skit was an introductory text to the dream-in, and was used to focus the attendees on the institutional question of how we might learn together through uncertainty.*

Skit

Voice of Higher Education: The Ministry of Education, Culture and Science has sent along a brief that requires higher education institutions to review current educational practices. They are asking different stakeholders to participate in conversations around education. For this reason, we invited you to this meeting. We are hoping to have an open and frank dialog. What are your specific concerns around the state of education today?

Voice of an Other Education: Ok, if that's what you want. The first question that comes to my mind is, why is institutionalized education failing us?

Voice of Higher Education: What do you mean?

Voice of an Other Education: Our current system of Higher Education is unable to meet the actual social challenges we are experiencing.

Voice of Higher Education: Oh?!?

Voice of an Other Education: It's about the way that you insist we teach, how we are asked to address climate change, extreme weather conditions, right-wing populist government… the glacier ice spilling into the ocean, rising water levels... pandemic. You know, global crises.

Voice of Higher Education: Yes, these are things we study. I don't follow you.

Voice of an Other Education: We are speaking about the suffering and the anxiety we feel right now about all these things—pain that is ignored by your idea that this is a distant reality. It is all happening here and now, and is the result of the damage done by choices made by the best educated among us. This is where you are failing.

Voice of Higher Education: Ok, so you want to focus

I thought a lot about you over the holidays.

on the apocalypse—on unprecedented challenges in unprecedented times. And on how to meet those challenges in order to move forward?

Voice of an Other Education: Uhr, no, I'd really rather not. I'm not interested in this modernist fantasy of forward. And this 'we can fix it' mentality. Rather, I'd like to tend to the frayed but life-sustaining social relations that will hold us through the uncertainty of these unprecedented times.

Voice of Higher Education: I still don't understand. We are doing this innovative work. Take, for example, the art academy where we are currently speaking together. In this art school, these are our fields. And in these artistic and social practice skills, these are our practices.

Voice of an Other Education: What are you talking about?

Voice of Higher Education: Your concerns are what we've identified as the "urgent issues" for study and practice in 21st century arts and design. And that these are not just themes to be addressed and reflected upon, but they redefine the "very way artists, designers and educators work" through the emerging field of social practice.[1]

Voice of an Other Education: Highly evocative words, like a battle cry. But how do you think of it as a practice? What is your understanding of social practice?

Voice of Higher Education: Social practice is a discipline where "art and design projects become direct interventions in society and politics," focusing on addressing "wicked societal or environmental issues."[2]

Voice of an Other Education: So by your measure, social practice focuses on urgent matters in urgent times?

Voice of Higher Education: Yes, we ask "What can social art and design do to meet these unprecedented global challenges?" How can social practitioners be innovators and change-makers, by engaging directly with complex societal issues? Issues that are so

1. Nana Adusei-Poku, Iris Schutten, Roger Teeuwen, and Peter Troxler, "Social Design as a Political Act: Position Paper Social Practices WdKA," Beyond Social (website), 2017, https://beyond-social.org/wiki/index.php/Social_Design_as_a_Political_Act.

2. Ibid.

complex that they require co-creation with non-artistic fields and audiences.[3]

3. Ibid.

Voice of an Other Education: You can do this while also graduating business students who will become managers at Shell Oil, designers who will greenwash Airbus, and HR managers at ABN AMRO. What if what you offer is nothing more than a transdisciplinary Swiss-army knife for facilitating and managing financial growth? In this model, a social practice is just one tool in a toolset to meet "global challenges" and "societal needs" as defined by the Higher Ed Complex and its capitalist imperatives.

Voice of Higher Education: That's a funny way of phrasing it, but yes. We can do this, with the right data, the right plan, the right policy, the right expert, and the right methodology for societal development. We need more skill sets, strategies, and tools.

Voice of an Other Education: This is the thinking that got us into the mess in the first place! This problem-oriented approach to something that is, at its root, problematic. By trying to offer solutions while at the same time offering present and future generations a promise of moving forward you are bypassing the systemic causes inherent in business as usual. I hear you say: "Don't worry, we got this." We have a way out of this mess. We created the problem, but we will solve it. It is also as though you are saying that in order to build a better world, we must essentially destroy it.

Voice of Higher Education: I don't get it.

Voice of an Other Education: It's as though you are saying that in order to build a better world, we must first completely destroy the Amazon Rainforest because we can then devise innovative reforestation programs... The way I see it, there is an emergency in our systems of learning, and not in what we are learning about.

Your approach loves symptoms and hates root causes. You keep on making the same mistakes. We keep on putting bandaids over festering wounds. Time and

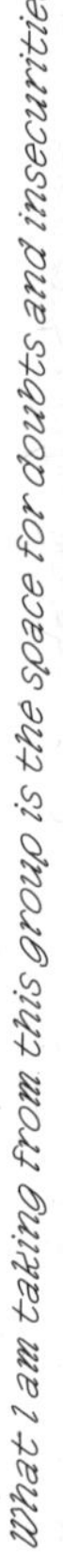

again. Because you are afraid to look deeply into those wounds. Because that wound is us, we are wounded. And this band-aiding numbs us to the actual realities of what we are supposed to be addressing.

Voice of Higher Education: So what would you have me do? Nothing? Give up hope? Binge-watch Netflix in my underwear eating Cheetos?

Voice of an Other Education: How about we deal with uncertainty as a prerequisite for a learning process? Can we hold onto that rather than just paper over challenges so that "other sectors" can get on with their business?

Voice of Higher Education: And what does this mean in concrete terms, for arts education?

Voice of an Other Education: It means that we are not interested in petro-capitalism's "green economy" that allows for more of the same consumption, as well as violence and inequality, but with less guilt. We are interested in how to learn and live within uncertainty. We are interested in deepening relations and developing a vocabulary for relationality. We want to sit with difference and not feel that we must either run from it or destroy it... by having the strength to ask together: How are you feeling? How are you doing? We also acknowledge the limitations of our own agency. Like, what can we actually affect? What might I really be able to solve?

Let's deal with this.

What is a social practice if not actually caring and working through the social capacity suggested in our dreams?

Voice of Higher Education: Are you talking sitting together and holding hands, and discussing our feelings? Some kind of peace-love-and-understanding kumbaya scenario?

Voice of an Other Education: No. We do not want the same kind of toxic positivity you've always offered.

Voice of Higher Education: I mean in actual practice,

what would you have us do? How should we teach? What do we need to learn?

Voice of an Other Education: How about holding a space for long processes of relation-building based on trust, respect, reciprocity and accountability, and through difficulties? For building the capacity for resiliency for holding difficulty while also building the capacity to dream collectively. Put that on your recruitment brochure.

Voice of Higher Education: But it is unethical to tell students that we cannot offer any clear economic pathways and financial outcomes. Or even a foreseeable future.

Voice of an Other Education: And it's unethical to offer students false promises or empty platitudes. Education should be about supporting people to face the world in its full spectrum. The "good, the bad, the ugly, the broken, and the messed up."[4] And to acknowledge our own complicity in systemic, historical, and ongoing harm and unsustainability so as to stop it from repeating itself. This is the benefit you can offer them. You can also tell them about the limits of this education, that we can only do so much to correct the generations of harm we have caused for the world. Not to absolve ourselves of it, but rather, to be honest.

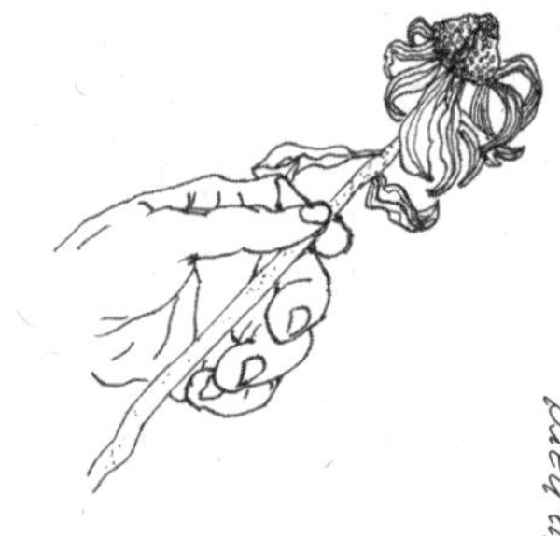

Voice of Higher Education: But this goes against our ideals, and the financial reality that we've constructed education as a highway of prosperity-as-progress? Our promises, our strategic planning, our doing, our making for a better future?

Voice of an Other Education: Look, we are at a crossroads where we have to start to learn from the ruins of modernity. We should understand what needs to be activated through relational change rather than technical or solution-oriented change for distraction's sake.

I'm curious, where is this conversation sitting right now in your body?

Voice of Higher Education: [thinks for a bit though feeling annoyed decides to play along] Well, there's anger and my sense of righteousness. I'm thinking to myself,

4. Vanessa Machado de Oliveira, *Hospicing Modernity: Facing Humanity's Wrongs and the Implications for Social Activism* (Berkeley: North Atlantic Books, 2021), 121-122.

was really sick. And it was awful. It was really hard.

"this is not right!" I feel frustration, and then denial—that everything is and will be alright. And then I get defensive. Now I feel nothing but fear in the pit of my stomach. It's still there.

Voice of an Other Education: And what if we were to start to work with this feeling in the pit of your stomach. It's difficult, discomforting, it's complex but can I ask you to stay with this feeling? As somehow a shared, communal or common experience with individual expression. And with this as what we learn from, this is where we act from. Within uncertainty, within the burgeoning cracks of the business as usual.

Voice of Higher Education: I am still getting visions of everybody standing in a circle hugging each other. Isn't that a little too naive? Too kumbaya?

Voice of an Other Education: Oh come on! I'm fucking terrified and you just said you are as well. I'd rather not have to do this.

Social practice begins with teaching and learning together. By design, our learning space is not naive. We need schools that do not assume neutrality, as yours does. Your dream that you can manage the world—its climate and people—has screwed us. For us all to learn together, you—and this also means we—need to acknowledge your and our deep entanglement and complicity with the worst of the world. In your "Higher Education," social practice is an elite science or just stuff that women and brown people do. You have to circle this square before we talk. Social practice is what we all do to relate to one another, but your "educational highway-as-progress" screws this all up.[5]

[END]

5. In writing this script, we have been inspired by the speculative dystopian fiction scenario Education 2048 by the collective Gesturing Towards Decolonial Futures (GDTF), the book *Hospicing Modernity* by Vanessa Machado de Oliveira, Resmaa Menakem's work on somatic abolitionism, and Stefano Harney and Fred Moten's work on the undercommons, among many others. See: Gesturing Towards Decolonial Futures Collective, "Education 2048 version 2," Gesturing Towards Decolonial Futures (website) https://decolonialfutures.net/portfolio/education-2048-v2/; Resmaa Menakem, *My Grandmother's Hands: Racialized Trauma and the Pathway to Mending Our Hearts and Bodies* (London: Penguin UK, 2021); Stefano Harney and Fred Moten, *The Undercommons: Fugitive Planning & Black Study* (London: Minor Compositions, 2013).

Additionally, some of the statements made by the Voice of Higher Education were directly, and somewhat irreverently, lifted from "Position Paper WdKA Social Practices: Design as a Political Act," a mission statement written in 2017 for the Social Practices department at the Willem de Kooning Academy in Rotterdam. This text was revised in a collective writing process undertaken by the teaching community in the Social Practices study programme at the WdKA. Renamed *In Search of Otherwise: (A) positional Paper Social Practices*, the co-writers ask: "What are the possibilities of living and learning differently?"

See: Sumia Jaama and Michelle Teran, et al., *In Search of Otherwise: (A) positional Paper Social Practices*, Research Center WdKA (website), 2022, https://research.wdka.nl/index.php/news-activities/in-search-of-otherwise-apositional-paper-social-practices/.

Learning Grounds[1]

Re: next meeting - visit to Pablo's exhibition in Amsterdam

Turner, D.R.(Renée) <████████>
Thu 24/03/2022 16:23

To: Julia Wilhelm <████████>; Lerma Gonzalez, P. (Pablo) <████████>; Martinez-Quintanilla Rubio, C.J. (Carmen) <████████>; Teran, C.M. (Michelle) <████████>; Robertson, K.L.R. (Kari) <████████>; Rehberg, V. (Vivian) <████████>; Judith Leijdekkers <████████>

CC: Maule-O'brien, S.N. (Skye) <████████>; Cheung, S.C.K. (Seecum); Yusser Salih <████████>; Carla Arcos <████████>; Freeke van der Sterren <████████>

Hello all,

My apologies, but I cannot attend the embroidery workshop or the garden session because I still have Covid :(

I really wish I could be at both sessions.... I love the power of the subversive stitch (yes, yes, embroidery, weaving and beadwork!), and forms of lateral agency and solidarity that emerge through being busy sewing, cooking, and gardening.

As I don't want to spread the bug, the only thing I can remotely contribute is a few quotes below.

Enjoy the day together, and I hope to see you in the next session,

Renée

nobody had touched him for five days.

On the necessity of tactility:

> *We touch things to assure ourselves of reality. We touch the objects of our love. We touch the things we form. Our tactile experiences are elemental. If we reduce their range, as we do when we reduce the necessity to form things ourselves, we grow lopsided.*

(Anni Albers, *On Weaving* (pp. 44-45). Princeton University Press.)

The garden as a space of disturbance and colonial legacies:

> *The appearance of the garden in our everyday life is so accepted that we embrace its presence as therapeutic. Some people say that weeding is a form of comfort and of settling into misery or happiness. The garden makes managing an excess of feelings—good feelings, bad feelings—rewarding in some way that I can never quite understand. The garden is a heap of disturbance, and it may be that my particular history, the history I share with millions of people, begins with our ancestors' violent removal from an Eden. The regions of Africa from which they came would have been Eden-like, and the horror that met them in that "New World" could certainly be seen as the Fall.*

Jamaica Kincaid, (2020, August 26). *The disturbances of the garden*. The New Yorker. https://www.newyorker.com/magazine/2020/09/07/thedisturbances-of-the-garden

On March 25th, the day you are in Michelle's garden, Derek Jarman wrote this journal entry about his Dungeness garden in 1989:

> *The sun rose and remained for the rest of the day, warm with a light breeze. At ten, I walked down to the sea to pick up flints. The sand flats were quite deserted, except for a small boy sobbing as he dug for bait. I heard him clearly on the wind, he was far out near the breakers. My own sadness, which set in last night with the television screening of War Requiem, swept away. There are so many strangers crying in England these days.*
>
> *All along the Ness they are putting up fences—more people are travelling out to the lighthouse. The local, the Britannia, has changed its name to the Smugglers' to cash in. Even this remote spot changes. My neighbours brought me a purple sage—the first gift the garden has received. It grows apace.~ Salvia salvatrix, sage the saviour. 'He that would live for aye must eat sage in May.' A man's business thrives or falls like the herb in his garden. Pepys writes in his diary that he saw a churchyard in*

1. Through our ongoing generative and nourishing conversations, Renée Turner—artist, educator, researcher, Rotterdammer, and gardener—and I have often exchanged experiences on the ways we are collectively learning, dreaming, imagining, and cultivating practices through and with our gardens. Renée contributes the essay "Slow, Situated & Reparative Reading: THE·GARDEN EDITION (This is not a manifesto; it's a manifestation.)" in this publication.

which sage was grown on every grave. Gerard says: Sage is singularly good for the head and brain, it quickeneth the senses and memory, strengtheneth the sinews, restoreth health to those that have the palsy and taketh away shakey trembling of the members. Sage attracts toads. Boccaccio's toad that lived under the sage bush was one of a long line. Thomas Hill writes: Serpents greatly hate the fire, not for the same cause, that this dulleth their sight, but because the nature of fire is to resist poison, they also hate the strong savour far flying the gar/ike and red onions procure. They love the savin tree, the ivy and fennell as toads do sage, and snakes the herb rocket, but they are mightily displeased and sorest hate the ash tree, in so much as the serpents neither to the morning nor the longest evening shadows of it will draw near, but rather shun the same and fly far off. In the evening I walked to the Long Pits, the violets under the ash tree glimmering in the dusk. No serpents about, just the hum of the power plant. In the foundations of the ruined school house, periwinkle had run riot, covering an area of several hundred square feet.

Brought back a small piece to plant in the garden.

Derek Jarman, *Modern Nature* (The Journals of Derek Jarman) (p. 41). Random House

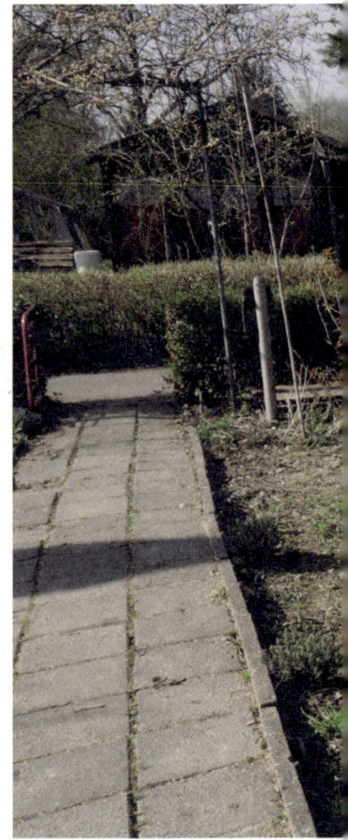

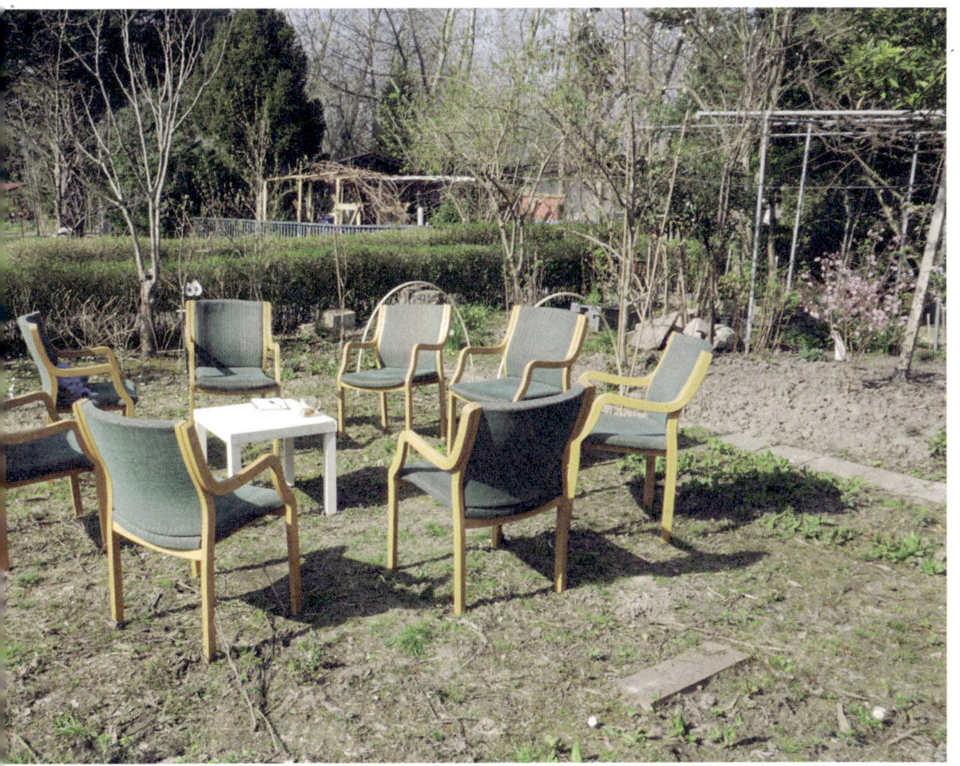

The Promiscuous Care Study Group arranges chairs in a circle for a meeting in Michelle Teran's recently acquired garden, March 25, 2022.

This is a text about personal loss. It is about losing my mother. It is also about collective grief and how practices of collective grief are, for the most part, absent in dominant Western cultures, in institutional spaces of higher education, community organizations, even family circles. Although this text will touch on these three areas, I will mostly be speaking from an educational context, with a focus on potential pathways to collective learning that can build capacities for holding painful experiences and conversations. In this text, I will also partly speak from my allotment garden in the South of Rotterdam where I ask how can we learn through and with collective grief?

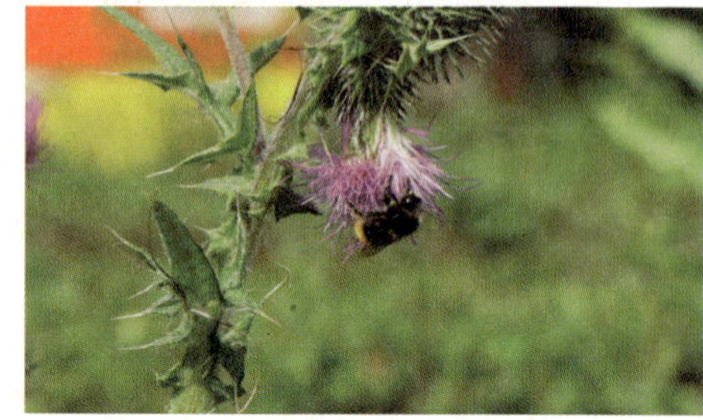

[Falling]

Last February, you fell. For one or two days, I am still unsure. You lay on the floor of your apartment, in the living room. I don't know what time of day it was, whether the lights were on, the television blaring, whether you tried to sit up if you were, at any point, conscious. I don't know your thoughts, whether you were afraid or felt yourself exposed and vulnerable. What little I know is that you fell, and you were alone.

[Breaking]

For many days, as you were lying on a hospital bed somewhere in Calgary, I was in Rotterdam between office and home. For days, for a week, then longer than a week, I kept up with you through daily check ins with my sister, who, because of proximity, could be with you. And I waited for a moment when my presence would be more supportive and less of a hindrance. COVID-19 restrictions limited the hospital visitors to two people; I was not one of them. To be honest, I was not ready to face the heartbreak that awaited me. Meanwhile life continued.

And so I continued working at the art academy where I work as a researcher and educator. My work calendar shows that during that period I prepared for and then: taught a seminar, attended a webinar for a new accounting system, had a meeting with my dean, read a book, printed out posters for a workshop, facilitated a workshop, continued with two research projects and prepared an abstract for yet another, perused a budget, submitted paperwork, sent and received emails,

But we decided not to isolate them or isolate ourselves.

moderated two panel discussions at an online conference, attended and facilitated multiple meetings whose atmospheres varied from the creative and inspirational to the mundane.

Also present on the calendar was my appointment for a COVID-19 antigen test but not that I waited for the results, which were positive. Apart from a brief entry stating "Go to Arif with tree work," there is no evidence of the red storm warning issued by the Dutch government for Storm Eunice, one of the worst storms in decades wreaked chaos across the country, as closed train lines, roads, and airports curtailed all travel. Schools, offices, stores and businesses shut down. For 24 hours I witnessed on television, social media and through my living room window the flying debris, ravaged rooftops, airbound cars, capsized boats, and felled trees. After the storm had passed, I, still infectious with COVID-19, decided to walk along the canal, through the park, to my garden, recently acquired a little over three weeks ago, to inspect for any damage. I discovered two large trees that had succumbed to the winds now blocking access to the garden. I climbed over the thick trunks, slick with mud. The following week, I planted two rows of potatoes in the back of the garden.

Not making any appearance on the calendar was a full-scale invasion by Russian ground forces of Ukraine, and their ballistic and cruise missiles striking multiple Ukrainian cities and airfields. That COVID-19 claimed 75,000 more lives and created 16 million new cases. A UN report warned of a climate disaster-fueled global wildfire crisis, while wildfires burned nearly 2 million acres of drought gripped Argentine wetlands. A Portland man opened fire on racial justice protesters, killing 1 and injuring 4 others. A jury found Ahmaud Arbery's murderers guilty of US federal hate crimes. Mining companies drove destruction of the Amazon and violated indigenous rights. Haitian police killed a journalist amid ongoing protests by exploited garment workers.

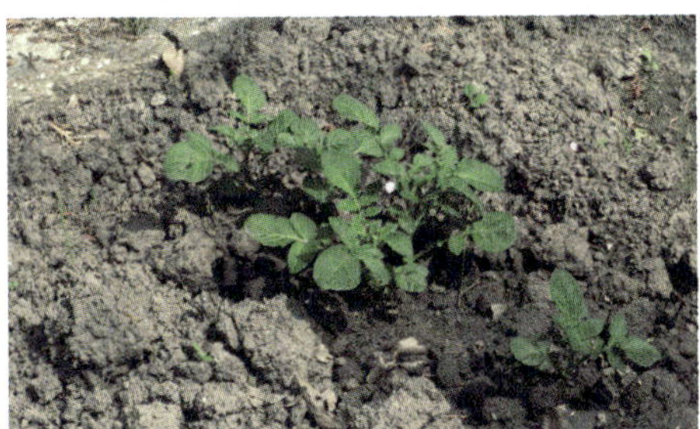

And then, as the world continued, frenzied, I was suddenly on a flight to Calgary, to your hospital bed where you lay quietly dying.

[Stopping]

Reading through what I have just written, I experience both a sensation of nausea and intense vertigo to the normative yet dizzying pace of the world, including my personal world.

I am sitting with the vulnerability of my sorrow and the disquieting stillness of your passing.

I am experiencing feelings of sorrow and heartbreak in ways that are more than just feeling 'sad'.

[Metabolizing]

Dear Cash, dear Malkia;

Thank you for your words. Thank you for your offerings. You both have often written about grief, pain, and suffering and how, through our socialization in dominant (modern, Western) ways of knowing, we are taught that they are unwelcome visitors that we must push away and eliminate.

Cash, as an esteemed scholar and Canada Research Chair in Indigenous People's Wellbeing, whose research focuses mainly on pain and our relationship to pain; you have often spoken about how "dominant ways of knowing and being (often called Western or modern)"[2] consider pain an individual problem linked to personal suffering. Translated into modern health and mental health practices, pain becomes a condition of individual problems and the elimination of it is the pathway to individual wellbeing and quality of life. You understand this as dominant ways of dealing with embodied problems where pain becomes an unwelcome presence in everyday life that must be regulated, managed, numbed, and eliminated.

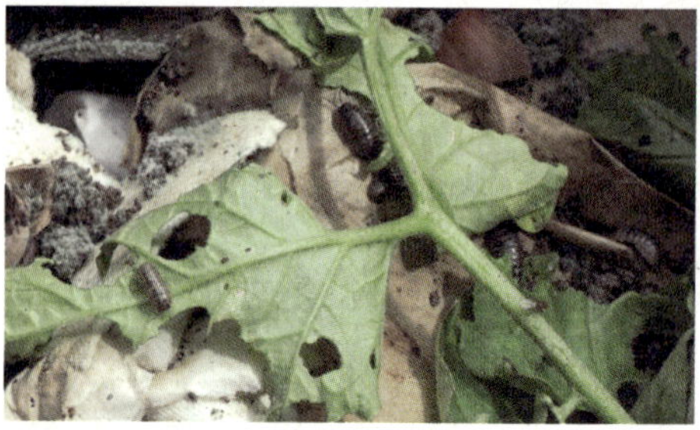

Malkia, activist, writer, and speaker on collective grief; you once referred to this numbing, overwriting and erasure of pain as a form of gaslighting. Grief—within the dominant narrative of business as usual, and predicated on productivity and the linear movement of progress at whatever costs—is this wild unruly, unwelcome presence. If grief were personified, it might be the one that stumbles in late to an important meeting, hair unkempt and unwashed, crumpled shirt showing last night's liquid dinner, mismatched socks, and torn pants. One who, before gobbling down the entire plate of pastries around the coffee table, struggles to find a seat amidst the discomfort and agitated others sitting around the table. “Security! Nobody wants this presence in the room. It's killing the vibe.”

2. Cash Ahenakew, *Towards Scarring: Our Collective Soul Wound*, (Guelph: Musagetes, 2019), 19.

3. Malkia Devich-Cyril, "To Give Your Hands To Freedom, First Give Them To Grief," in *Holding Change: The Way of Emergent Strategy Facilitation and Mediation*, ed. adrienne maree brown (Chico: AK Press, 2021), 75.

For example, when you write:

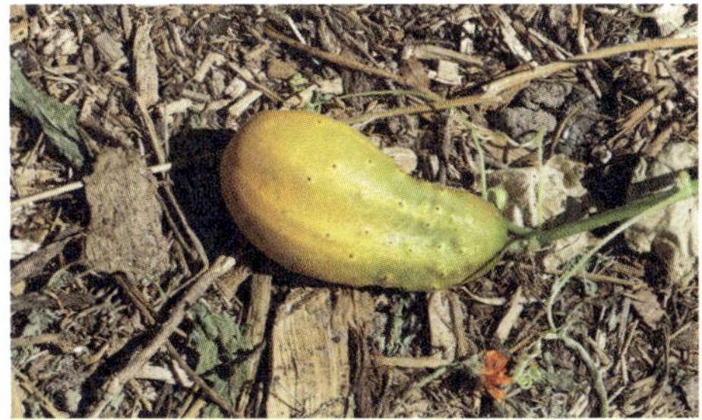

Dominant narratives about grief have turned gaslighting into an art form, convincing us that it is safer to deny grief than to feel it. At every turn, we are persuaded that grief is a wild, unacceptable emotion that must be handled, managed, overwritten, and hidden. We are pressured by political and even physical force to prioritize productivity over personal wellbeing, to seek eternity over embodied presence, even as we live through the most traumatic losses.[3]

4. This scenario is a creative adaptation of the methodology for critical inquiry entitled “The Bus” developed by the Gesturing Towards Decolonial Futures Collective. See: https://decolonial-futures.net/portfolio/the-bus/.

Yesterday, as I sat in my garden, writing, I imagined a scenario where you, Cash and Malkia, were invited to a meeting. At this meeting—let's say in an academic workplace—teachers, students, management, and support staff are invited to a conversation to speak openly about their grief and immense sorrows. You are not asked to speak but to observe the room. What are you observing? Hypothetically, you might witness visible embarrassment and nervous glances. There are some dull, vacant looks. One person becomes short-tempered and starts picking fights with the others, growing louder and shouting above the rest. Somebody, feeling overwhelmed, bursts into tears. One small group claims their pain is the only pain that matters. Another somebody, becoming increasingly withdrawn and shrinking into their seat, tries to ignore the conversation. Others check the time on their phones and numbly doom scroll through the newsfeeds. Someone else is trying to rationalize their pain by paraphrasing a text they read in a book. There is a to-do list made by yet another on what to do about the pain. Yet another still, increasingly impatient, asks in an agitated manner if there is any point to this meeting and when it will end.[4]

Cash, I wonder if you would think that what you are witnessing in the room is dominant culture's (read: Western or modern) way of saying, "This is embarrassing. Try to pull yourself together." In the room, multiple responses try to evade the conversation's painful discomfort by managing, assessing, evaluating, analyzing, critiquing, diminishing, or becoming otherwise overwhelmed in a way that reinforces separability and polarization. You might lament that it rules out the possibility to see pain as a teacher and to experience suffering's profundity as a way of listening beyond the limitations of the personal and the individual.[5]

Malkia, I also wonder if you might think this is what unprocessed grief looks, sounds, feels, and smells like. By getting to know your writing, I understand that unprocessed grief happens when grief that is not given the care and space to digest and reflect upon, nonetheless remains present.

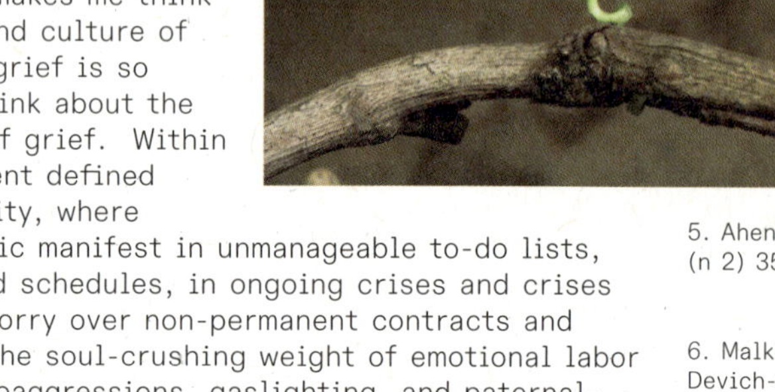

You once casually remarked, "How many people have lost their jobs because of grief? Getting into fights with people, being short-tempered because they were grieving."[6] It makes me think about how within the grind culture of my academic workplace, grief is so often left untended. I think about the presence and silencing of grief. Within an educational environment defined by precarity and insecurity, where pervasive stress and panic manifest in unmanageable to-do lists, deadlines and overbooked schedules, in ongoing crises and crises management, incessant worry over non-permanent contracts and future employment, and the soul-crushing weight of emotional labor in the face of daily microaggressions, gaslighting, and paternalism;[7] let's just say that grief is rarely acknowledged. It is not even part of a conversation. This state of affairs was exacerbated by the recent COVID-19 pandemic when many of us were asked to continue working and to keep classes running amidst an adrenaline-saturated double workload coupled with the individual and communal strife and loss occurring outside of the workplace. How is this grief being addressed?

In writing about grief and productivity, Malkia, you begin by revisiting your experiences of personal, profound loss and how it affected your work and life. I appreciate your willingness to bring in the intimate and personal into conversations on grief. I want to tell you about my experience of trying to return to work after suffering my own profound loss. I want to recount how personal loss and grief derailed my sense of time, obligation, and even my capacity to speak. I felt my grief a cursory hiccup, a floundering about, an embarrassment even, within the normal flow of the workplace. For weeks, I stumbled through the offices, classrooms, and corridors as a somnambulist, ill-equipped for the measured, machinic pace of institutional time. Cacophonic sounds of chatting and laughter, scraping chairs, loud pop music from the cantina reverberating off the smooth concrete walls and glass vitrines of the building. I experienced them as needle-like daggers piercing my raw unsteady and tender body. My returning self felt entirely out of sync with the rhythm and pace of the building that was ill-equipped to harbor grief, even of an individual nature.

5. Ahenakew (n 2) 35-36.

6. Malkia Devich-Cyril, "Radical Grievance with Malkia Devich Cyril," The Emergent Strategy Podcast (podcast), June 2022, https://open.spotify.com/episode/1AjW8v05FwDVuqC0Z6c5XJ.

From what I have learned about your social activism and organizing work, I recognize that when you write about grief, you also consider how it acts within the realm of dominant systems of modernity, capitalism, white supremacy, and patriarchy; systems that beget death to the land and also untimely and lonely death to bodies. You make palpable the ubiquitous undercurrents of grief though century upon century of harm; genocide and oppression, poverty and inequality, raging fires and rising sea levels. You see it every time somebody gets murdered because they have the wrong skin color, at the destruction of ecosystems and planetary collapse, the dispossession of land from Indigenous communities, and otherwise as the planet is treated as if it were nothing but a giant shopping mall for consumption without consequence.[8]

7. Alfrida Martis and Ali Şahin, *We Have to Change: Advisory Report by the Office for Inclusivity on the State of Equity, Diversity and Inclusivity at WdKA* (Rotterdam: Willem de Kooning Academy, 2022), 37-40.

8. Devich-Cyril (n 6) 74-77.

Reading, and nodding in agreement, I play an imaginary dialogue with you where I respond by saying that I also grieve whenever someone asks, "why can't we just stay positive?" but are not willing to do the work of critical inquiry; when they lack humility, or if they demonstrate boundless arrogance and an unrepentant ego that perpetuates business as usual, of which I am also complicit. I grieve for gratuitous waste and dispensability, of bodies, lives, and land. I grieve for a system prioritizing busyness and productivity, and also for simply aging, and for my own dying and for death.

The world continues spinning, with crises upon crises and days stretched to their limit with busy schedules. How is it possible to hold that much sorrow, that much grief without feeling completely overwhelmed?

And what happens if you don't?

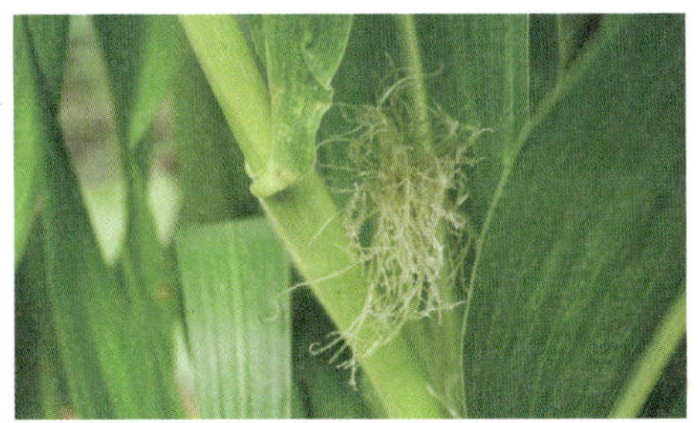

What happens when grief is left unattended, unprocessed, and left to its own devices? Just because you choose to ignore grief doesn't mean it goes away. Malkia, you mention that no matter how much one tries to silence, ignore, or overwrite grief, it will come back at you, in unhealthy patterns and self-destructive behavior for vengeance. Grief needs the space and care to be experienced fully. This space of care[9] works for grieving the people we have lost, those close to us, and all the societal ills and global loss. You note that unprocessed grief—insufficiently tended grief—resurfaces as burnout, as dissociation and detachment, numbness, apathy, unfettered rage. It resurfaces in addiction.[10] I understand what you are saying. Truly. At the same time, from my own uncomfortable place of loss, I understand that grief is such an overwhelming place of suffering, and of becoming untethered. I lose touch with the once familiar ground because the ground has shifted. Grief is such an uncomfortable place of loss.

I lost myself. I wonder how reconnection is possible after such complete loss of self and connection to the surrounding world?

Malkia, you write that "we should sit and take action from a place of grounded grief,"[11] because it could lead to feelings of joy. I freeze mid-page of your essay to stop and contemplate what you're trying to say. Because I was trying to imagine my or any other grief as joyful in any way. Upon further contemplation, I grasped it as your way of telling me that by taking note of grief by listening to what it needs, one can develop the capacity and stamina to open up to my and others' sorrows, big and small. And that by opening to others, in an embodied entanglement of grieving collectively, it could carve the path for other ways of becoming and taking action in societal transformation. Gargi Bhattacharyya refers to this as the revolutionary potential of collective heartbreak because it is only by making space for our collective sorrow that we can imagine remaking the world.[12] Grief, and by this I mean collective grief as you both have eloquently stated, can therefore be an intensely liberating and a communally joyful experience... That is, if you give grief the time it needs.

What would it take to *sit and take action from a place of grounded grief*? To do it in the profundity of sorrow and immensity of heartbreak that one person should not hold alone, to build stamina and capacity to hold grief collectively? Not as a pathway to healing, mending, to make everything whole again, but with the intention of fostering the capacity for discomforting conversations around the cracks of a crumbling, dying system that no longer serves.

What I am really trying to ask you, all of you, is how we can learn from grief? How can we learn to grieve collectively?

9. michelle cassandra johnson, "Episode 119: Michelle Cassandra Johnson—Finding Refuge Healing Collective Grief," Banyen Books Branches of Wisdom (podcast), November 2022, https://open.spotify.com/episode/5dAfZgHyJACfQ1IX-s5us5T.

10. Devich-Cyril (n 6) 75. See also: Steffi Bednarek, "Climate Change, Fragmentation and Collective Trauma. Bridging the Divided Stories We Live By," Future Foundation (website), https://futuref.org/climate_change_fragmentation_and_collective_trauma_en. Bednarek is a psychotherapist who works around climate psychology, studying the affects of collective trauma through the climate change crisis. Bednarek argues that "the efforts to meet the challenges of climate change need to go beyond a mere reduction in CO2 emissions. They require a maturing of the collective culture into a much larger capacity to process painful experiences whilst holding the interconnected, non-linear complexity in life. This includes the ability to acknowledge fragility, to bear the unbearable with dignity and to bring integration into the frozen and fragmented states of collective trauma."

11. Devich-Cyril (n 6) 75.

12. Gargi Bhattacharyya, *We, The Heartbroken* (London: Hajar Press, 2023).

[Noting]

What else needs to be said about grief?

I often feel a hankering to scream, "We are dying! We are dying, and we are killing one another. We are sick and we aren't interested in being well. We are entitled and our entitlement is causing oppression and suffering. We must stop. If we do not, we will not survive."[13]

Each day we lose valuable parts of our biosphere as species become extinct and ecosystems destroyed—yet where is their funeral service? If our world is dying piece by piece without our publicity and collectively expressing our grief, we might easily assume that these losses aren't important.[14]

When I speak of our heartbrokenness, I am trying to capture this sorrow that moves between individual grief and the consciousness of all that is so broken in our world [...] I don't believe we can build a different, better world without being heartbroken.[15]

I am inspired by grief, mourning, and lament. I feel like these places are vulnerable and generative spaces for healing.[16]

Denying grief denies humanity.[17]

Edges bleed into traces of becoming, melding, dying and living, beginning and ending, into an always pregnant middle. A thick middle.[18]

13. michelle cassandra johnson, *Finding Refuge: Heart Work for Healing Collective Grief* (Boulder: Shambhala Publications, Inc., 2021), 62.

14. Joanna Macy and Chris Johnstone, *Active Hope: How to Face the Mess We're in with Unexpected Resilience and Creative Power* (Novato CA: New World Library, 2022), 68-69.

15. Bhattacharyya (n 12) 4.

16. Tricia Hersey, *Rest Is Resistance* (London: Little, Brown Spark, 2022), 33.

17. Devich-Cyril (n 6) 70.

18. Bayo Akomolafe, *These Wilds Beyond Our Fences: Letters to My Daughter On Humanity's Search For Home* (Berkeley: North Atlantic Books, 2017), 19.

[Pausing]

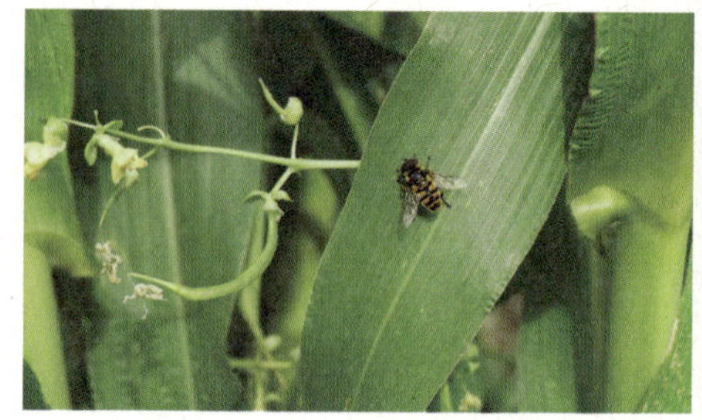

I am feeling quite full. Are you still breathing?

Can we please have one minute of silence?

How does that moment of reconnection happen?

19. On questioning: Bayo Akomolafe writes about the potential of generative and humbling questions. Rather than using questions as a logical means to solving the world's problems, Akomolafe offers questioning as means of opening up to how we are already mattering and showing up in the world. See: Akomolafe (n 18) 243.

[Tending]

My allotment garden in the south of Rotterdam is a five-minute bike ride from my apartment. When I acquired the garden a little over a year ago, I wanted to mostly grow organic food (which I now produce prodigiously), introduce some regenerative agriculture experiments (that are ongoing and expanding), and meet some of my neighbors (who are caring and incredibly generous). Surprisingly (at least for me), it has also become a place for grounding grief—for giving grief the space that it needs.

There is always something happening in my garden, and also, compared to the daily onslaught of news announcing the latest global catastrophe, very little at all. In the garden, time stretches and slows down into an unhurried, tender, intimate attunement that unfolds in bodies, breath, rhythms, reciprocal acts of care, and forms of listening. I am attentive to what grows and flourishes from what I have sown and I recognize what emerges of its own accord. I am also witness to what is decaying and dying away. Death and decay are all around me. Many of my fellow gardeners (mainly older women) are also attuned to these cycles of life. As the summer season slowly comes to an end, I observe my neighbors wandering around the garden's complex and nearby park, searching for decaying plant matter; dredging the nearby canal, foraging for garden waste in the compost piles, and picking up fallen weeds that they will collect in heaps and transport back to their gardens in order to nourish the soil for the coming seasons. And I think it is partly due to these humble acts of the transference and transmutation of dead and decaying matter and the promiscuous abundance of the garden and this actually real and grounding experience with circular time that has helped catalyze and connect me to specific questions. With questions, but not necessarily in the quest for answers,[19] around death, decay, and for the processing of grief. I do this for my own and my collective sense of grief.

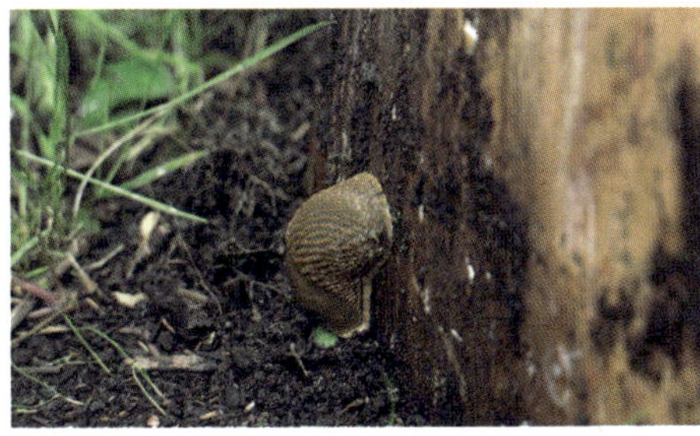

[Practicing]

Let us sit in a circle, each with a bowl of water and a pile of stones. We have collected the stones by walking around our surroundings (a park, a garden, a forest, a city street). Before taking each stone, we make sure to ask first for the stone's permission. Now sitting around the circle, whenever a grief comes to each of us, we pick up a stone, say the grief out loud and then place the stone into the bowl of water. We remember to take time to breathe, pause, and acknowledge each grief entering the circle; not trying to analyze, debate, discuss or resolve any sorrow that is named. Each participant continues speaking of their grief out loud and placing their stones into the bowl until there is nothing more to say. Now each of us takes our bowl somewhere outside and returns the water and the stones to the soil.[20]

[Reading]

In December during one of the year's coldest and darkest days, I organize a reading event around death and decay and collective grief in my garden.[21] I propose two activities: one that looks like reading a book, and one that I now understand as reading an ecology through the act of constructing raised beds.

For the event, we are reading the section "Toilet Teachings" from a chapter in the book *Hospicing Modernity: Facing Humanity's Wrongs and the Implications for Social Activism* by Vanessa Machado de Oliveira.

In her text, Machado de Oliveira writes that because modernity imposes distancing and separability from our shit it has taken away our metabolic literacy about reading dead and decaying matter. Modernity controls death and decay by pushing it away and removing it from sight. She refers to the shit that comes from our bodies and the other 'shit' that is not so easy to decompose: plastics, toxic waste, and other pollutants. We flush shit away; flushing it through pristine, white, clean, shiny toilets; the other shit gets put into shipping containers and sent away to remote and out of site locations. But there is no 'away'. We are entangled with everything else; with the birds, the soil, the squirrels, the trees, the poisonous sludge, contaminated water, the earth gutted by copper mining, and the carcasses of the expendable and exploitable. We are implicated as well. These things are all part of the same metabolism, the pleasant and amiable,

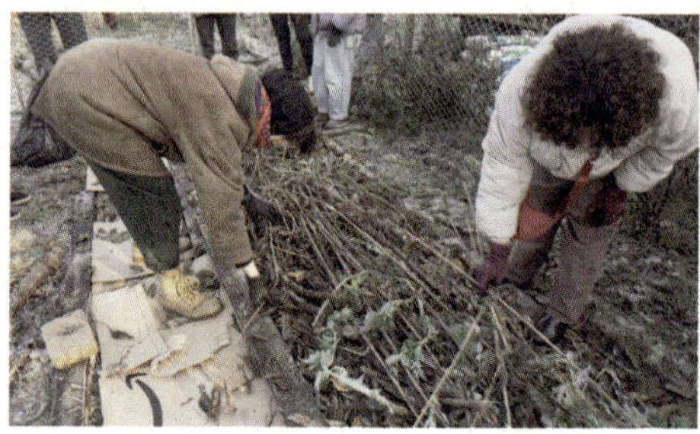

20. Since 2022 I have been fortunate to be part of a study group who meets online monthly. The study group is composed of educators, researchers, facilitators, health practitioners, a journalist, among others, whose members are scattered throughout Canada, The United States, The Netherlands, Italy, and India. In the sessions, two study group members co-facilitate a session where they invite the group to think through texts and practices around hope and hopelessness, living in uncertainty and complexity, entanglement, and ways of holding grief collectively. During one of the sessions, one of our group members proposed an adaptation to a collective grief practice by grief activist Francis Weller. See: Francis Weller, *The Wild Edge of Sorrow: Rituals of Renewal and the Sacred Work of Grief* (Berkeley: North Atlantic Books, 2015), 163.

as well as that which generates visceral fear and disgust.[22] Reading is the ability to see and recognize waste as part of a life cycle where waste returned to the land becomes soil and food before becoming shit once again. This literacy to read decay and waste welcomes death as part of this living cycle while also allowing us to decipher which waste causes sickness and which provides nutrients for new life. Machado de Oliveira, therefore, advocates for regaining our connection with both nature and life's processes. She reminds us that death is part of life's metabolisms and to understand ourselves as a living metabolism through learning how to 'read' decay and to decipher which provides nourishment and which poisons land and bodies.[23]

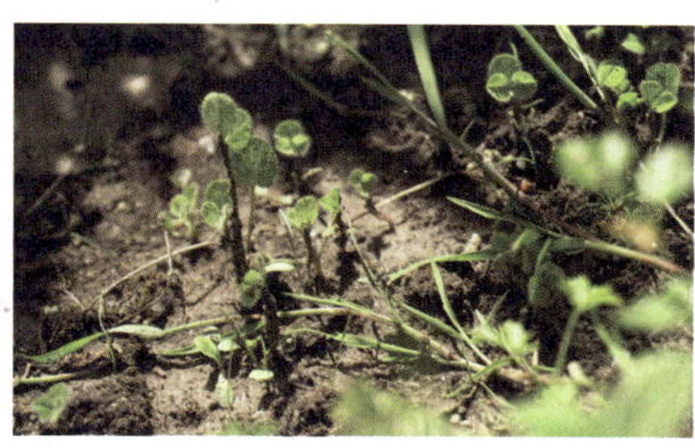

We begin the day with a collective action where our group wanders through the garden and its surrounding neighborhood, 'reading' for any dead and decaying organic matter suitable for making a garden bed. We gather desiccated leaves around my garden, and from the main garden entrance. We excise the slimy remains of artichoke leaves from one of the other garden beds. We break brittle stems off of barren pepper plants, hack and uproot towering sunflower husks, and collect the branches strewn from recent storms. With this accumulated material, we construct the raised bed—piling soil over leaves over rotting organic matter over branches over salvaged cardboard. Then we leave it to rest until the following spring.[24]

Once the bed is completed, we move ourselves into the garden hut to read the text from *Hospicing Modernity*. One of the participants starts a fire that produces a lot of smoke but sufficiently warms the hut enough so that we can read in comfort. The warmth from a smoky fire, with cookies, empanadas, cornbread, and other delectables fuel our reading and infuse it with pleasure. The group works on a collaborative quilt, transmuting the words we read into images of shit, decay, and visualizations of metabolic entanglements. The toilet in the hut has been turned off to prevent pipe damage from the intense cold. The small greenhouse in the back becomes our temporary toilet instead, where

21. I organized this event together with student initiatives Reading Rhythms Club and SPIN collective. Reading Rhythms Club experiments with forms of embodied, situated reading. SPIN collective works on climate and social justice issues as well as being stewards of a rooftop garden at the Willem de Kooning Academy.

22. Vanessa Machado de Oliveira, *Hospicing Modernity: Facing Humanity's Wrongs and the Implications for Social Activism* (Berkeley: North Atlantic Books, 2021), 121-122.

23. Ibid 222-228.

24. The garden bed is now replete with succulent beets, spinach, kale, fennel, spring onions, and leeks, colorful nasturtium and calendula flowers accompanied by the continuous buzzing of bees.

the readers take turns making trips in order to relieve themselves of their liquid waste that they know, from reading the text, will be used to fertilize the soil.

[Loving]

A sunny early Monday morning in the garden. Tucked away under sagging grape vines, laden with swollen, ripening fruit. Between pauses and shed tears, deep breaths, and gulps of water, I carefully blend you, my mother's ashes, together with fresh soil, then release handful after handful of the fresh mixture into newly dug holes awaiting the echinacea, monarda, yarrow, tulip, and dahlia plants, near the front of the garden. As the morning progresses and the garden awakens, some of my neighbors pass by on the way towards their own gardens. H peeks over the hedge to admire the new flowers and then offers me a hazelnut to plant into the soil. T stops by to say hello, smiling widely. Lovingly.

"What would it mean to approach loving the earth? [...] To look at soil and see more than dirt," writes Lola Olufemi.[25]

25. Lola Olufemi, *Experiments in Imagining Otherwise* (London: Hajar Press, 2021), 119.

All images taken by Michelle Teran in her garden, April 2022-December 2023.

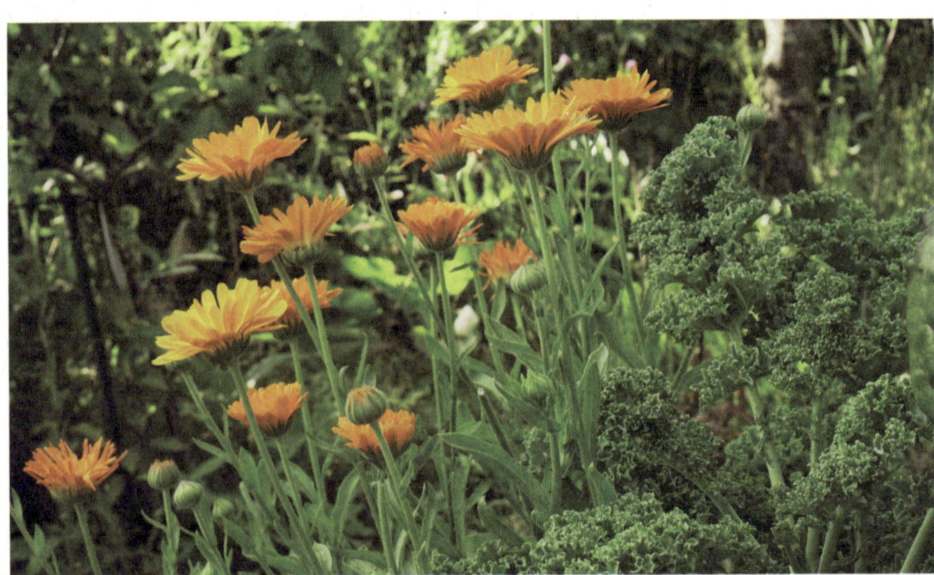

[Learning]

This is not an ending but an invocation for learning.

When I go to my garden, I feel this underlying sadness that brings me to tears. We are feeling a systemic collapse with its death and mass extinction, through our bodies.

When I am in the garden, I dream of it as a ground for learning that allows for learning with grief. How do we learn to grieve? We are learning with

the sowing of grief, to all things living and that which is dying away
a grief that is so immense that it can only be done in community
with others, human, nonhuman, and more-than-human
the pause within the gap and the capacity to stay within the discomfort of the overwhelming and the unfathomable

what lies under the surface
what is not readily seen or understood or analyzed or solved
decay as nutrition, food, and shit
lifeless matter that is not lifeless
flesh that decomposes, leaving bones that will disintegrate, become soil
a way of keeping time that recognizes the circularity of change, and
the thickness of mutual co-dependence and entanglement
the embodied, the relational
the affective ways of knowing and being in relation
grief as with-ness, breathing with
intergenerational learning, soil memory
decline coupled with growth when you least expect it
the potential rippling effects of small, humble acts
difference that is not separability, complexity in abundance
giving support when support is called for
energy in sadness, energy in joy
living well, dying well
a change that is constant.

Welcome Everyone

These conversations are based on two years of teaching at primary schools in three neighbourhoods in Rotterdam: Carnisse, Hillesluis, and Tarwewijk.

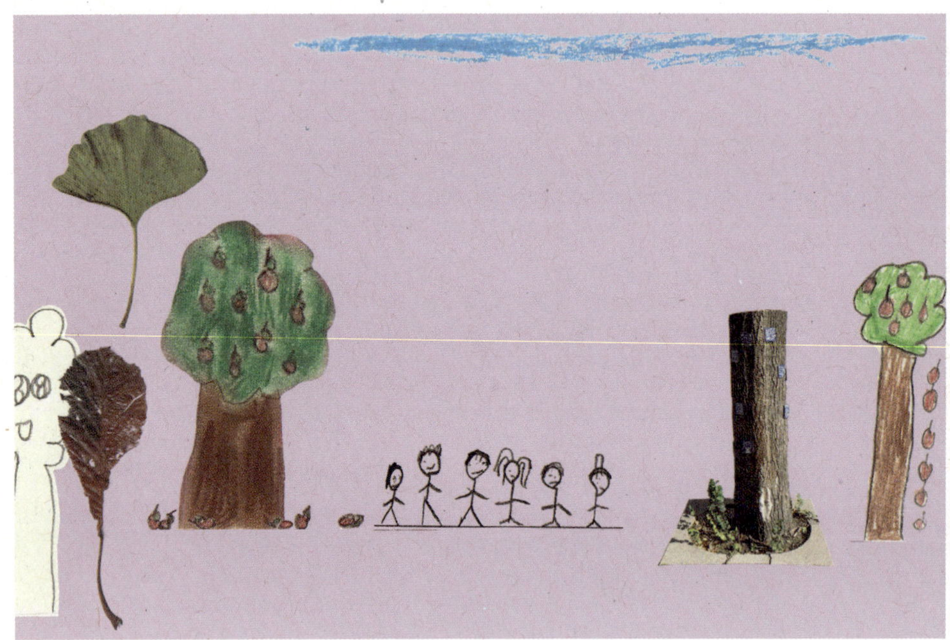

Screenshot of the page representing Tarwewijk, including a photo of a tree in front of the school that was cut down. With blue signs, children turned the remaining trunk into a monument. All screenshots are of the website https://www.uitpluizers.hotglue.me, which was made in collaboration with children. The website allows children to share observations in their garden and neighborhood with children in different areas of the city.

You're allowed to walk everywhere. But there are a few rules for everyone. You can't pick the flowers because the bees and butterflies need them. You can only pick something when there are many of the same flower. Watch out for the fence, because it is sharp and sometimes it cuts a coat. Also watch out for poisonous plants, like nettles and berries with poison. The birds can eat those berries. You can hear the woodpeckers, but we never see them because they live a bit further in the park. Hedgehogs live here too. We have nev-

er seen them because they come when the people have left. But they are here. Sometimes we find a dead animal, like a wood pigeon or a mole. That's sad, but it is also part of nature. That's why we make a grave for the dead animals. Even if it's a worm. By the way, you are allowed to pick a flower for the grave. There is no toilet here, but if you have to go really badly, you can go to the compost. There are people living around the garden, so you shouldn't be too loud. Some of the neighbours scream sometimes, but we know they mean well. Sometimes they just need to scream to feel better. So you don't have to get scared or get angry at them. Oh, if you see red strawberries or raspberries you can eat them. There are many children coming to this garden, so please make sure everyone can taste them.

Greetings from the children in the garden.

"Wow, miss, look, I found a piece of wood and it's soft on the inside!"

"It looks like a sponge! What do you think it's called?"

"I don't know. I call it the white stem. Can I put it here? I want to keep it."

"Of course. We can make a museum with it."

"Yes, a garden museum."

"I also have something for the museum!! Look at these pink berries on this plant. It looks like a pink Pokémon ball. Miss, can we use the app that can recognise plants? We can find out what it's called."

"Here it is. You can make a photo of it."

"Coralberry?? That's a funny name!"

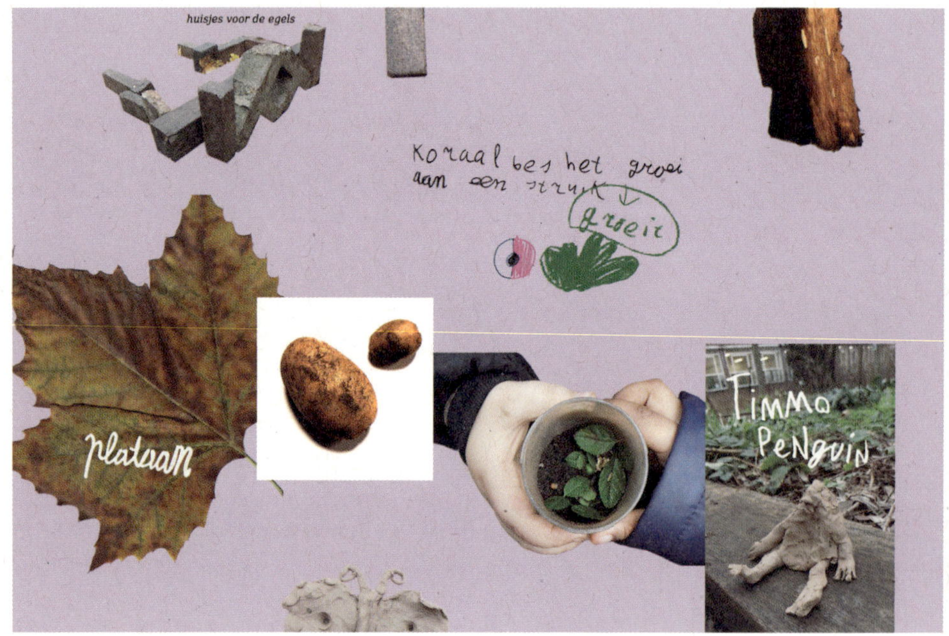

Screenshot of the page representing Carnisse. The caption beside the drawing of the pink circle says *"coralberry, it grows on a bush."*

"Before we go to the garden, there is something I would like to talk about with you. Last week, Zakaria got very angry when we were in the garden. Do you remember, Zakaria?"

"Yes, I was throwing sticks and I screamed at the other children. I get angry sometimes. But then you have to leave me alone. Otherwise I get even more angry and I start screaming and throwing."

"If you get angry, do you think you are able to tell us to leave you alone?"

"Sometimes I can. And if I can't, walk away and I come back when I feel better."

"Then we will keep that in mind from now on. Who else gets angry some times?"

All hands go in the air.

"That makes sense. We all feel angry sometimes, but we don't respond the same way when we're angry. It is important to know from each other what we can do to help."

"I want to smash something with a stick. But I am never allowed to do so."

"From now on, we will have a corner in the garden where you're allowed to smash something."

"But then other children should not go there, because we can hurt them!"

"Can we make a sign? Corner to smash with a stick. One child at the time."

"That sounds like a good plan."

"I just want to give everyone an angry look. But you should not respond to that, because it will make me more angry!"

"When I am angry, I want to draw."

"I always have a stuffed animal with me. When I feel good, it has a smiley face. When I'm angry, I turn it inside out and then it looks sad. When I'm angry, you should make jokes. That makes me feel good again."

"Can we go to the garden now? I want to make angry corners!"

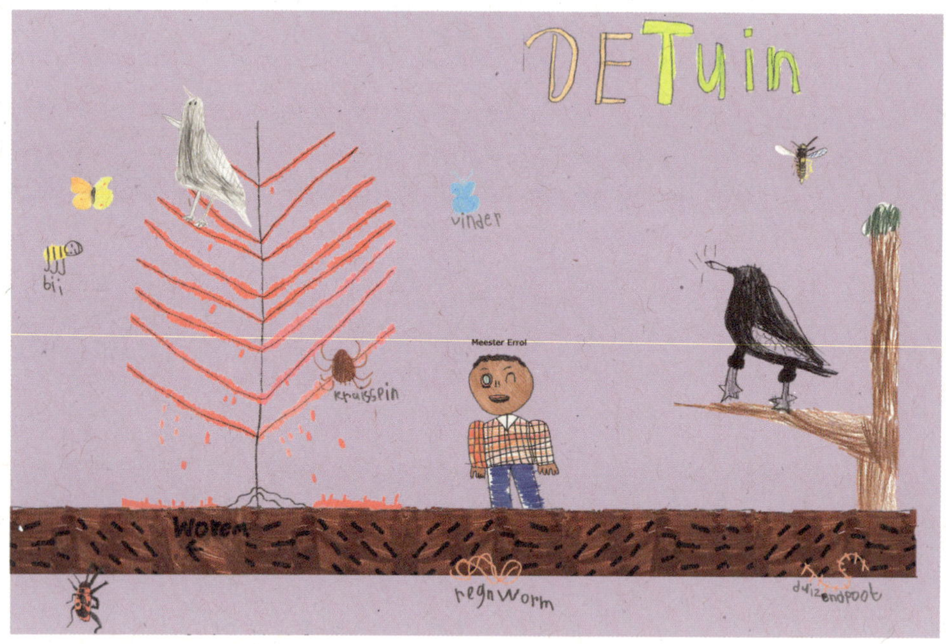

Screenshot of the page representing Hillesluis.

"Miss, do you want to come to our school breakfast tomorrow?"

"I would love to, but I have to teach at another school."

"Really? Do they also have a garden?"

"Yes, they do, but every garden is very different. We have hedgehogs in one of the gardens."

My internet is real bad.

"Hedgehogs?? I want to see one! Can we visit that garden?"

"That's a great idea. It is complicated to organise, but I will give it a try."

"In the meantime, we can make drawings and photos of our garden. You can take it to the other school and show it to the children."

"Or a website! So I can show our garden to my sister!"

"I want to make a website for other children!"

"Me too!"

"Me too!"

"Can other children make photos and drawings of their school garden for you, then?

"Yeeeeeeeeees!"

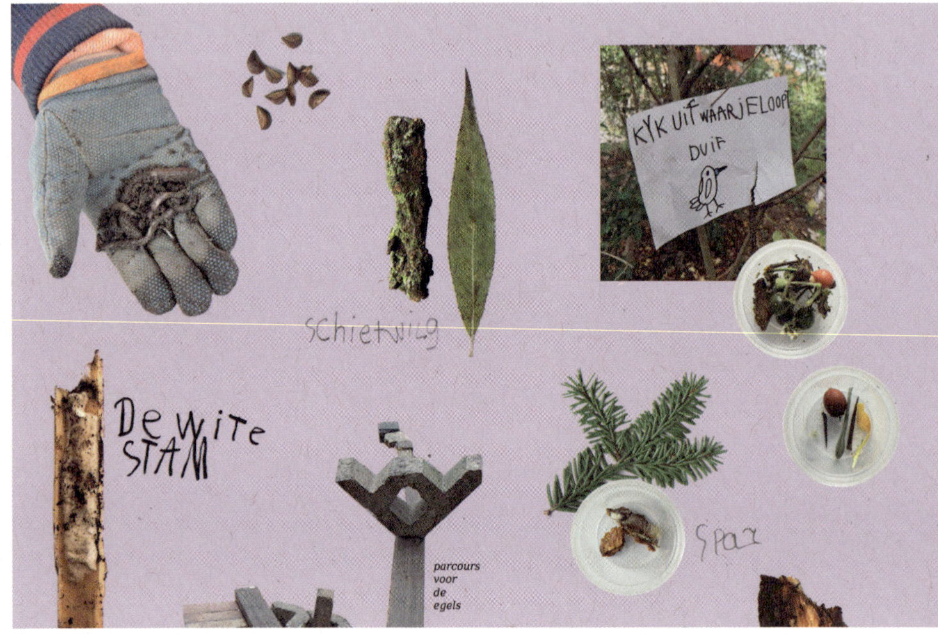

Screenshot of the page representing Carnisse.

“Listen, everyone! You too, miss! Marvin is in the angry corner. We all have to leave him alone and we can’t make fun of him.”

Everyone curiously looks at the angry corner. They realise immediately that it’s better not to look. They continue what they were doing. Five minutes later, Marvin comes back. As soon as he comes back, other children ask if he wants to join them. He nods with a big smile on his face.

"Yamina, Amir, look! A wood pigeon!!”

“Yuck! How did he die? Is there any

Booze gives you hot flashes in menopause.

blood?"

"I don't know. Maybe on the other side. I'll turn him around."

"Not with your hands, otherwise you'll get sick. Get a stick."

"There is no blood on the other side either. I don't know how he died. I don't think it was a cat"

"Maybe he ate plastic."

"Or maybe he was just old."

"Can we bury him?"

"Yes! And we have to give him a name."

"And a note with the date."

"I will wear red clothes. That's what my family does at funerals. We are Muslim, so I think all Muslims wear red at funerals."

"We don't, but we are Muslim too."

"Can we call him Swa?"

"That's Surinamese! My dad always says that. It means friend."

"Swa is our friend, right?"

The children look at the dead pigeon while nodding.

"Let's ask if we can bury him. And if everyone thinks it's a pretty name."

"I will stay with Swa. I don't want the cats to eat him."

Shall we take
a 10 minute break
to attend to
our bodily
needs?

Extend ing Con versa tions

In fall 2023, the Promiscuous Care Study Group organized the interdisciplinary public seminar series Promiscuous Infrastructures to further explore how to invent and enact caring infrastructures and pedagogies of care. The series involved screenings and conversations held at the Willem de Kooning Academy and at TENT Platform for Contemporary Art in collaboration with Reading Room Rotterdam. We were grateful for the opportunity to share the work and ideas of Czar Kristoff P. and Jacquill Basdew, Yoeri Guépin, Edwin Mingard, Lola Olufemi, Laurence Rassel and Selma Bellal with our wider communities. The Extending Conversations section of this book includes edited documentation of the guests' conversations and presentations, each of which is introduced by its host/moderator from the study group.

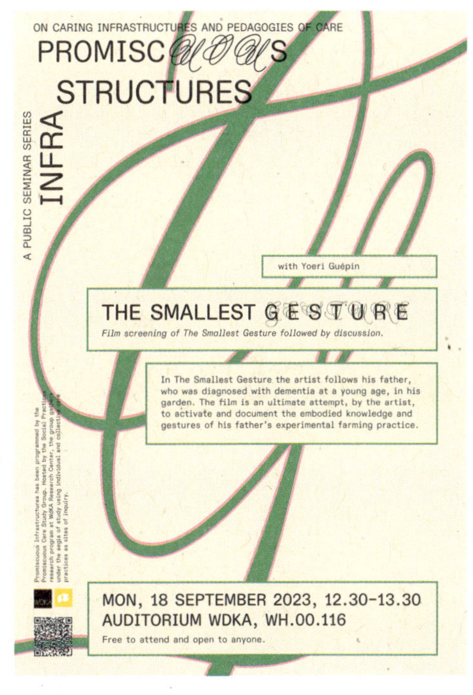

Posters designed by Julia Wilhelm.

ON CARING INFRASTRUCTURES AND PEDAGOGIES OF CARE

PROMISCUOUS INFRASTRUCTURES

A PUBLIC SEMINAR SERIES

THE MEAL IS LANGUAGE

A conversation for the delusional, for the imaginative, the ones in this world but not of this world.

You are cordially invited to attend *the meal is language* planned for *sept 20*. It will be wonderful to have *insert your name* among us! On *sept 20*, the *promiscuous care study group* and *reading room rotterdam* will host *insert your name* and *lola olufemi* and ____ and ____ and ____ and ____ along *yusser al obaidi's sofreh daimeh* at our lovely location *tent*. We are looking for your presence to make it memorable!

with Lola Olufemi,
Reading Room Rotterdam,
and Yusser al Obaidi

Promiscuous Infrastructures has been programmed by the Promiscuous Care Study Group in collaboration with Reading Room Rotterdam and TENT. Hosted by the Social Practices research program at WdKA Research Center, the group gathers under the aegis of study using individual and collective care practices as sites of inquiry.

WED, 20 SEPTEMBER, 18.00–20.00
TENT, WITTE DE WITHSTRAAT 50
Limited availability. Registration required via the TENT Website.

ON CARING INFRASTRUCTURES AND PEDAGOGIES OF CARE

PROMISCUOUS INFRASTRUCTURES

A PUBLIC SEMINAR SERIES

with Edwin Mingard

PRAXIS: AN ETHICS OF CO-CREATION

A screening of a selection of Edwin Mingard's collaboratively made film works, followed by discussion.

Mingard's films are a network of stories told from the margins of society, where collaboraters (undocumented, homeless, or otherwise) are invited to create rich cinematic translations of their daily thoughts and experiences. In this short screening and discussion, we will learn about some of the careful ethics which informs the technichal considerations.

Promiscuous Infrastructures has been programmed by the Promiscuous Care Study Group. Hosted by the Social Practices research program at WdKA Research Center, the group gathers under the aegis of study using individual and collective care practices as sites of inquiry.

THU, 05 OCTOBER 2023, 12.00–13.00
AUDITORIUM WDKA, WH.00.116
Free to attend and open to anyone.

ON CARING INFRASTRUCTURES AND PEDAGOGIES OF CARE

PROMISCUOUS INFRASTRUCTURES

A PUBLIC SEMINAR SERIES

with Laurence Rassel and Selma Bellal

DECOMPARTMENTALIZE TO PREVENT ISOLATION, OR HOW CONFLICT CAN SERVE TO RECREATE TIES

This conversation is devoted to care infrastructure and the potential for systemic change within art and design education, research, and administration. Laurence Rassel and Selma Bellal will share insights from their experience collectively reshaping artistic research, pedagogy, and educational policy at erg (école de recherche graphique) in Brussels.

Promiscuous Infrastructures has been programmed by the Promiscuous Care Study Group. Hosted by the Social Practices research program at WdKA Research Center, the group gathers under the aegis of study using individual and collective care practices as sites of inquiry.

WDKA

FRI, 13 OCTOBER 2023, 12.30–13.30
WDKA, WH.03.155

Free to attend and open to anyone.

ON CARING INFRASTRUCTURES AND PEDAGOGIES OF CARE

PROMISCUOUS INFRASTRUCTURES

A PUBLIC SEMINAR SERIES

with Jim van Geel, Jacquill Basdew & Czar Kristoff

IT DOESN'T STOP AT IMAGES

A generational conversation on queerness, joy and visibility.

This conversation gravitates around the reclaim of queer joy and visibility through generational care. The guest speakers will discuss these topics in relation to the reproduction of a visual collective imaginary around queer experiences throughout the last decades.

Promiscuous Infrastructures has been programmed by the Promiscuous Care Study Group. Hosted by the Social Practices research program at WdKA Research Center, the group gathers under the aegis of study using individual and collective care practices as sites of inquiry.

WDKA

THU, 02 NOVEMBER 2023, 14.30–16.30
RESEARCH STATION WDKA, WH.00.316

Free to attend and open to anyone.

Cooking with Microbes: Changing the Microbiome of Extractive Capitalism

Yoeri Guépin graduated from the Dutch Art Institute in 2013. He is currently a resident at the Jan Van Eyck Academy in Maastricht. In 2023 he was nominated for the Dolf Henkes prize and had a solo exhibition at A Tale of A Tub, Rotterdam.

The following pages are a contribution from Yoeri Guépin, a visual artist and gardener based in the Netherlands. In September 2023, Yoeri made a presentation of his work at the Willem de Kooning Academy to a mix of staff and students as part of the Promiscuous Infrastructures seminar series. The talk was held in a cold, echoey and institutional lecture hall with a poorly calibrated projector. In contrast to this setting, Yoeri gave an informal, but generous, introduction to his broader practice, refusing the hostile choreography of the room by sitting on a table among the audience to talk. He then presented two audio-visual works made respectively with his father and grandmother; two generations of biodynamic farmers. Although different in approach and scope, each work orbits around the subjects of gardening and growing, health, temporality, ecology, knowledge transfer and intergenerational care. Infused with love

A bunch of tomatoes, basil and sunflowers.

and tinged with loss, these works struggle to both illuminate and protect their subjects.

The following pages gather together ephemera from Guépin's recent body of work; stills and 'recipes'; that resist forgetting: There is a text for a workshop to change the microbiome of capitalism, images of Michelle Teran following one of Yoeri's biodynamic (nettle) 'preparation' recipes on the cusp of winter, a recipe for another preparation (yarrow) from the artist's grandmother, and stills from a recent film in which Yoeri's grandmother discusses biodynamic principles as she makes another biodynamic 'preparation'.

Prior to this collaboration, I have known Yoeri for a number of years and always followed his work with interest. His practice was mentioned during multiple conversations in the Promiscuous Care Study Group; ranging from one about food sovereignty to another around outdoor schooling. I think this is because his work has long been deeply and promiscuously caring in its attitude and outlook. As an artist, trained chef and longtime gardener I have witnessed Yoeri nurture multispecies life within his practice: plants, fungi, animals, insects, microbes, soil, seeds and the human bodies that he cooked for.

In Yoeri's practice there is little or no separation between the 'social' and 'ecological'. Whether he is articulating the vernacular garden as a living repository of cultural memory, or revealing the entanglements between neurodiversity and biodiversity, he gently but insistently erodes the boundaries between 'nature' and 'culture' (and the human and nonhuman).

In his work Yoeri also doesn't shy away from the troublesome; uncomfortable colonial histories, embodied chemical legacies, grief, loss or uncertainty. Rather, by using his own garden, hands and relations he reveals the lived intimacy of, and to, these complexities.

Kari Robertson, December 2023

What goes on in the microcosm of the soil seems to follow an archetypical plot. Soil is populated with a trillion tiny microorganisms, including soil bacteria, which can be roughly divided into three camps: The "good", the "bad" and the "opportunists." Good bacteria develop symbiotic partnerships with plants (the mutualists) or break down pesticides and pollutants and are nutrient repositories (the decomposers). Bad bacteria can cause rot and disease (the pathogens). The rest of the bacteria (roughly 80%) choose the side that is dominant.

As a result of chemical fertilizers and pesticides, industrial agriculture under capitalism has created the ideal conditions for the domination of pathogenic bacteria in agriculture soils, which require more sanitization with pesticides in a downwards spiral of treating one evil with another.

It's a small step from the transformation of soil under capitalism, to thinking about ourselves and our microbiome which operates according to the same principles. What does regeneration mean if we apply the principle of soil to ourselves? How can we regenerate the soil and equally create healthy environments for ourselves and our environment?

In the workshop we first examine and analyze different soil conditions. The next step is to learn how to use free available materials and improvised technologies to cook a nourishing meal for bacteria that regenerate the soil. Together we will build, brew, and mix ingredients that create conditions for balanced and biodiverse soil ecosystems.

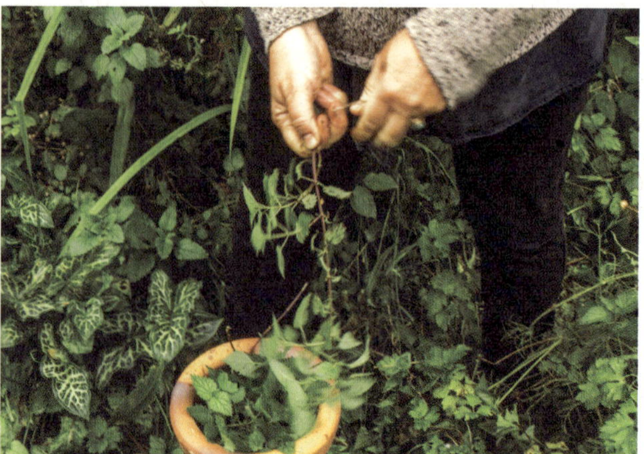

Documentation of Michelle Teran performing preparation recipe from Wilfriede Driehuyzen Guépin's notebook in her garden, South Rotterdam, October 2023.

All photographs by Eli Hooper.

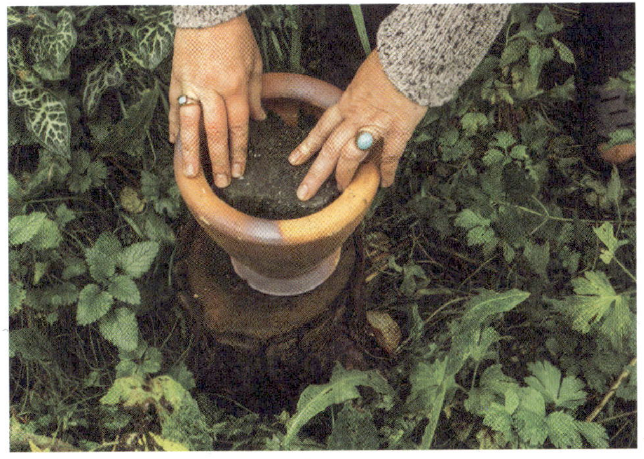

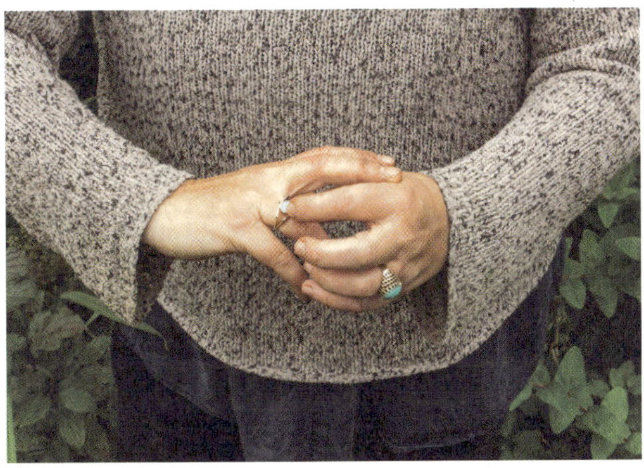

RECIPE

INGREDIENTS:
- 4 handfuls of aged compost or vermicompost (bacteria inoculation)
- 3 spoons of unsulphured molasses (food for bacteria)
- 3 handfuls decomposed wood or forest soil (fungal inoculation)
- 6 spoons of oat flour (food for fungus)
- 6 teaspoons of organic liquid* comfrey, nettles or seaweed (fertilizer and microbe food)
- 1 bucket of non-chloritized water, rainwater is preferred (alternatively, "fill a bucket with tap water and let the water sit for a day or stir it for at least half an hour, the chlorine will evaporate eventually).

MATERIALS:
- A bucket
- A branch or stick
- A broom or large brush

METHOD:
Mix all the ingredients in the bucket of water and start stirring in a vortex from the center with a stick or hand. This process aerating allows micro-organisms to grow at a fast rate (they breathe too). You can change directions occasionally and recite poetry, sing songs, or meditate during the stirring process for maximum results. After an hour the tea will look darker (the darker the better). The tea is now densely packed with life sustaining microorganisms and ready to use. Use the tea immediately. With a broom or a brush, splash the tea on the leaves, stem and fruits of the plants.

*Chop nettles, comfrey or seaweed and submerge in water in a large jar, bottle or closed bucket. Shake or stir it every two weeks. The plant material will dissolve and make a dark awfully smelling liquid that makes an excellent fertilizer. Nettles contain high amounts of nitrogen and comfrey, and seaweed is high in potassium. Use diluted on plants in a ratio of 10% with water. It keeps forever in a cool dark space. Nitrogen stimulates leaf growth, potassium stimulates fruiting.

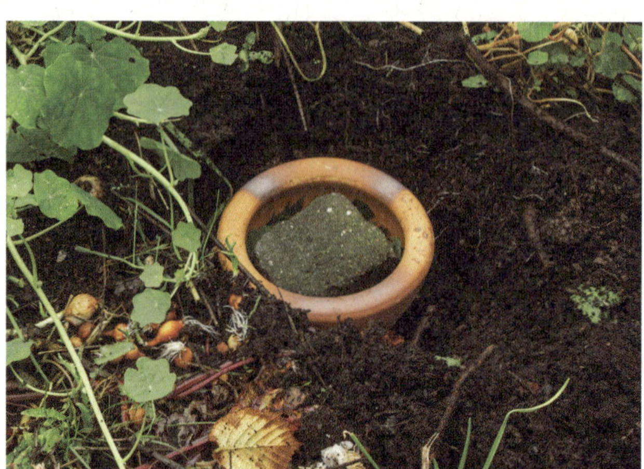

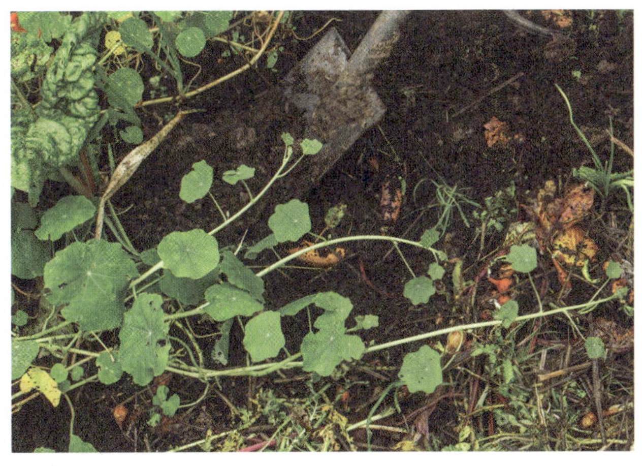

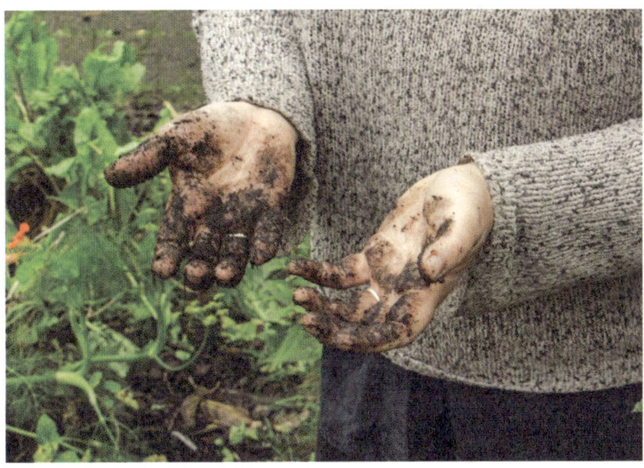

INSTRUCTIONS FOR YARROW PREPARATION*

502 Yarrow (belongs to Venus)

You don't see the working of Venus; listening is Venus-like. Its gesture is the letter A. Receiving. The image of the Opal Scale is also a receiving state. Venus has protein building properties. The first change starts in the stomach, goes to all parts and its residue goes to the udders and bladder. The end point of Venus' action is the bladder. The bladder of a male deer is connected to the environment. Its antlers are sensing the environment, rather than hearing. It sheds its antlers in the autumn. The deer is a particularly sensitive animal (in occultism). Astral and ethereal power radiates through its eyes. The male deer can absorb cosmic forces because it is directed outwards. Female deer have this in the calf and it is directed inwards.

Blossoms of the yarrow are harvested; this can be done to prevent fruit formation. Fresh or dried. Drink tea made from the leaves. Take the bladder of a red, male deer. Cram it as full as possible with the yarrow blossoms. Tie up and hang in the sun until autumn. Bury shallowly in autumn and use in the following summer.

Yarrow preparation has a beneficial effect on potassium processes; vitamin K in plants promotes the strength of the stem, veins and culm. If there is a lack, a crop will quickly collapse. The plants must be able to absorb the K that is there and process it correctly. K keeps the protein forces in the plant in the terrestrial range. It prevents these proteins from evaporating in plants, animals and humans. Venus forces work on protein that is carried by the blood to various organs. Protein is constantly prepared to become a heart substance, then a kidney substance, etc; organs are built up. The protein stream is carried upwards, imbued with ethereal and astral forces, then the process reaches a climax and turns into a digestive process. Ethereal and Astral forces are then released, radiating out through the eye. The Venus effect comes to an end in the udders. The last protein breakdown substances are formed here and collected in the bladder, then excreted. Deer bladder: it is an animal that is particularly receptive to cosmic forces that are in the immediate vicinity of the earth. The deer sheds its antlers in February, and the new ones are ready between July and August. During that time, he stays with the deer calf until the rutting season, October. Achillea millefolium (yarrow), are taken as a remedy for all ailments resulting from insufficiently functioning protein processes.

This plant grows everywhere where there is almost no nutrition in the soil, on rubble heaps, railway lines, along the sides of the road. Preferably all plant preparations are harvested on the land itself. Yarrow radiates good processes.

*Translated page from my grandmother's notebook that she kept during the foundational year of the School for Biodynamic Agriculture, Warmond, 1947-1948.

Stills excerpted from *As Above So Below* video artwork by Yoeri Guépin. The artist's grandmother Wilfriede Driehuyzen Guépin discusses the principles of biodynamic farming practices, and shares pages from her notebook, 2023.

As Above So Below, 2023 Video, 07:51. Made in collaboration with the artist's grandmother Wilfriede Driehuyzen Guépin. Stills courtesy of Yoeri Guépin.

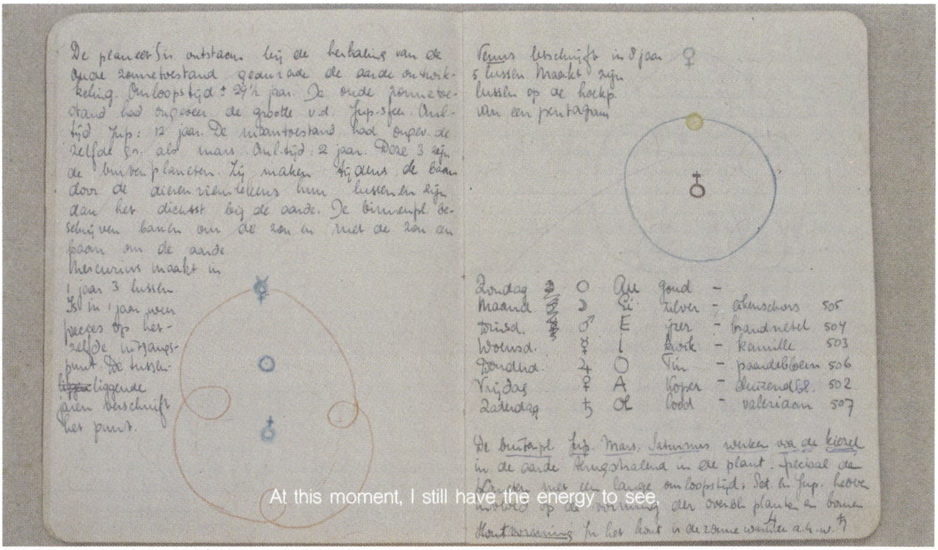

At this moment, I still have the energy to see,

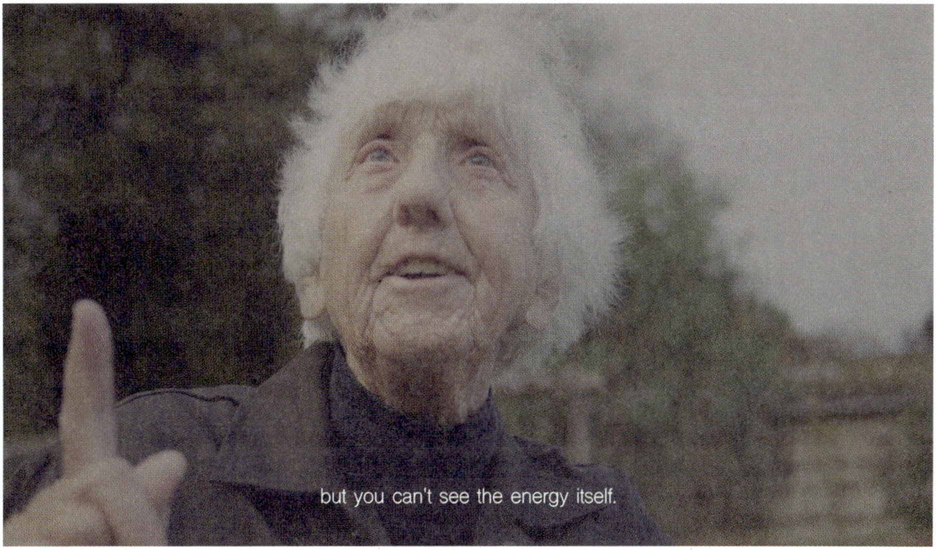

but you can't see the energy itself.

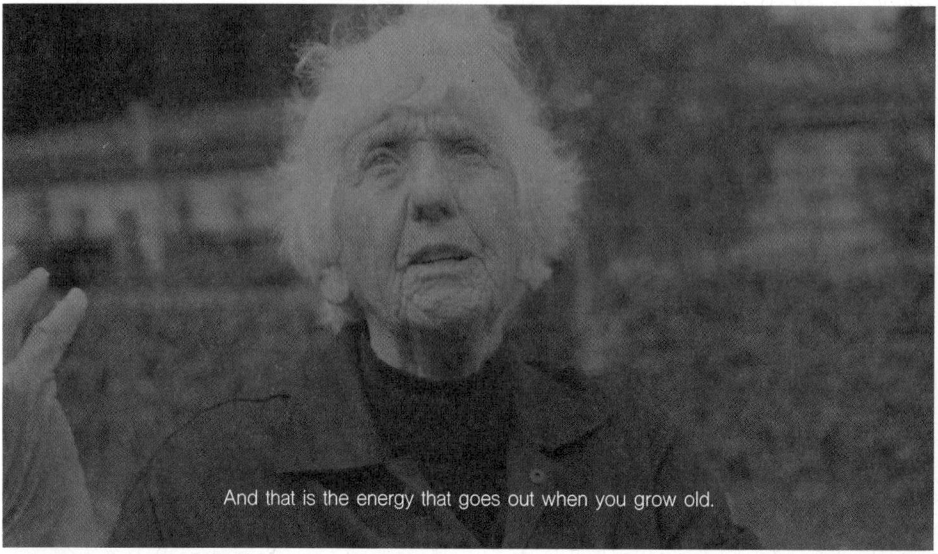

And that is the energy that goes out when you grow old.

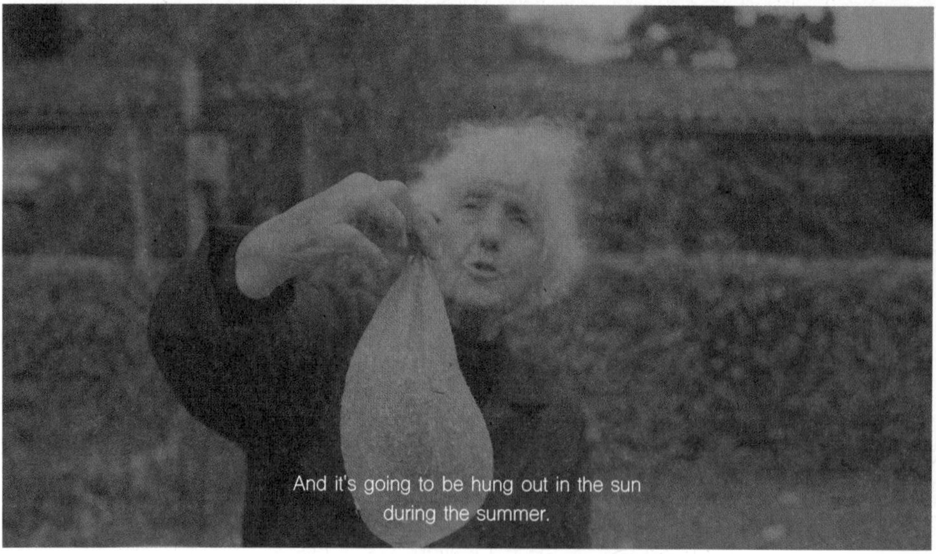

And it's going to be hung out in the sun
during the summer.

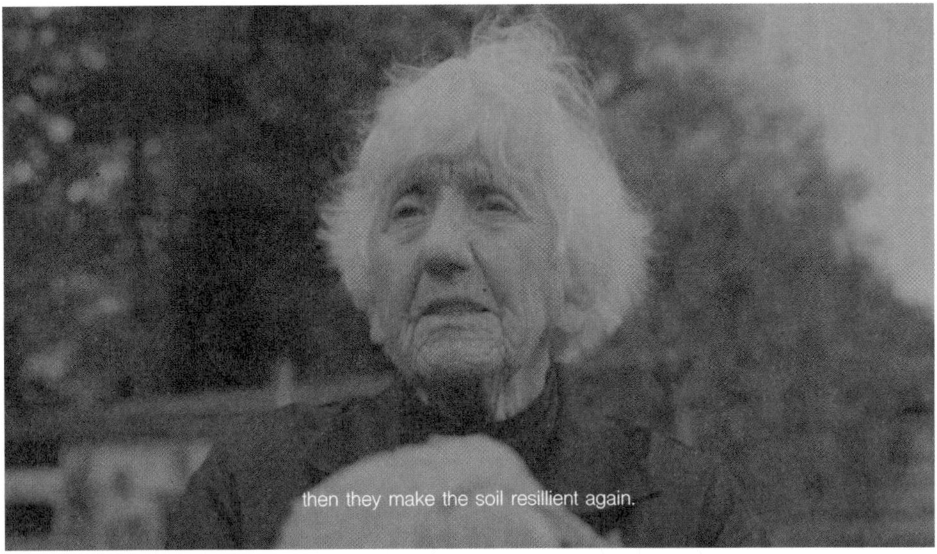

then they make the soil resillient again.

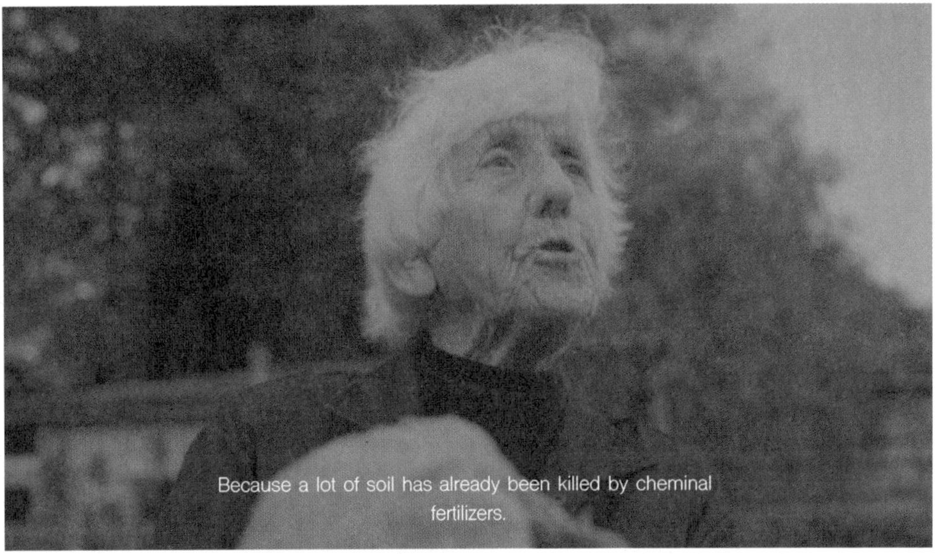

Because a lot of soil has already been killed by cheminal fertilizers.

Praxis: Ethics of Collaboration

Edwin Mingard is a social filmmaker whose cinematic platform places support and collaboration at the heart of its praxis. His films are a network of stories told from the margins of society where collaborators (undocumented, or otherwise), are invited to create rich cinematic translations of their daily lives and experiences. His practice uniquely provides long-term committed support, equipment, training and guidance, to generate spaces for people to share their stories through the lens of their own uniquely authored films.

I contacted Edwin in Spring 2022 after hearing about his screening, 'H is for Hostile Environment', *at the Rio Cinema in Dalston, London. The premise of the film was a collaborative venture made in collaboration with Dr Keren Weitzberg and 26 participants, whose right of abode was affected by the UK's border regime. During the period of the COVID pandemic, Edwin and Dr Weitzberg worked carefully with the group of individuals to develop, produce and direct a 1-minute short film of their choosing. Each minute was carefully crafted through the participants' voices, which shared the impact of the government's hostile immigration policy upon their lives. Through song, dance, poetry, fiction and documentary, the work can be seen as a spectrum in which to view the real-life effects of such policies upon the lives of everyday people.*

Ownership through collaboration is practised strongly by Edwin, and in the course of the making of the film, it was decided that each participant should own the rights to their segment of the film. The ecology of ownership and shared authorship is a meaningful thread interwoven into every stage of the making process, from initial conception to creation, and the distribution of the final work.

Edwin's continuous energy in co-creating projects with people presents him as one of the very few standalone artists whose work ethically works to nurture the visibility of a wide spectrum of groups. His practice of ethical consideration and co-creation becomes a form which informs his practice in compassionately generative and unique ways.

Therefore, inviting Edwin to the Willem de Kooning Academy (WdKA) on

A lot of people are burning out.

behalf of the Social Practices team and the Promiscuous Care Study Group felt necessary. Finally, in the Autumn of 2023, we were able to secure funding to screen a selection of his films. In addition, Edwin felt it important to create something meaningful for our students, so a workshop was developed and delivered to the student cohort. On Thursday 5th October 2023, we learned about an effective range of his ethical and technical processes, and how these processes influence and shape the genre-breaking and collaborative nature of Mingard's work.

The following is a uniquely developed series of exercises by Mingard for the WdKA, enabling our students to think critically through their collaborative projects. What follows is a version of the live workshop which has been transcribed for a wider reading audience.

Seecum Cheung, Social Practices lecturer

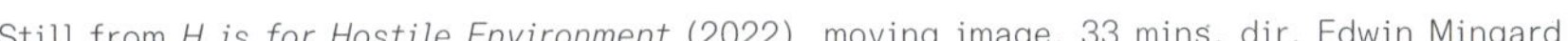

Still from *H is for Hostile Environment* (2022), moving image, 33 mins, dir. Edwin Mingard

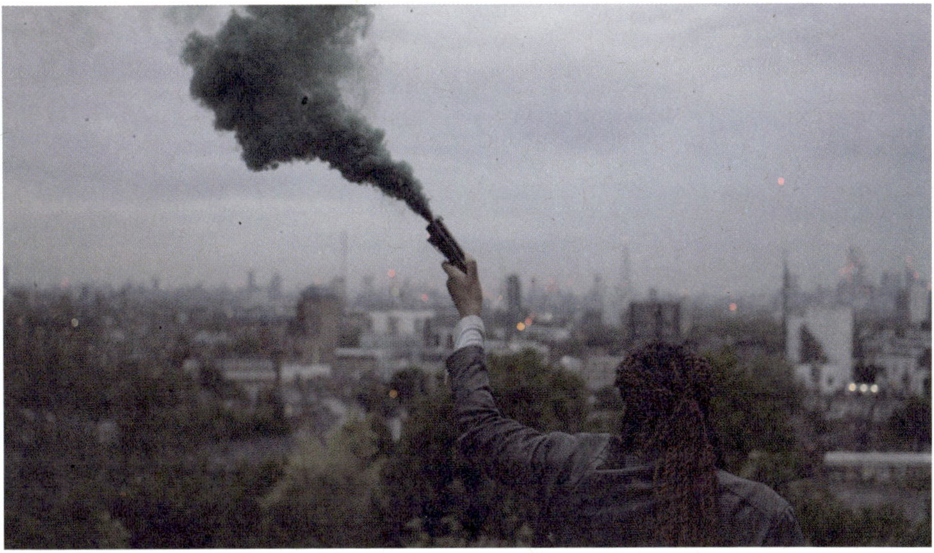

Stills from *An Intermission* (2020), moving image, 22 mins, dir. Edwin Mingard

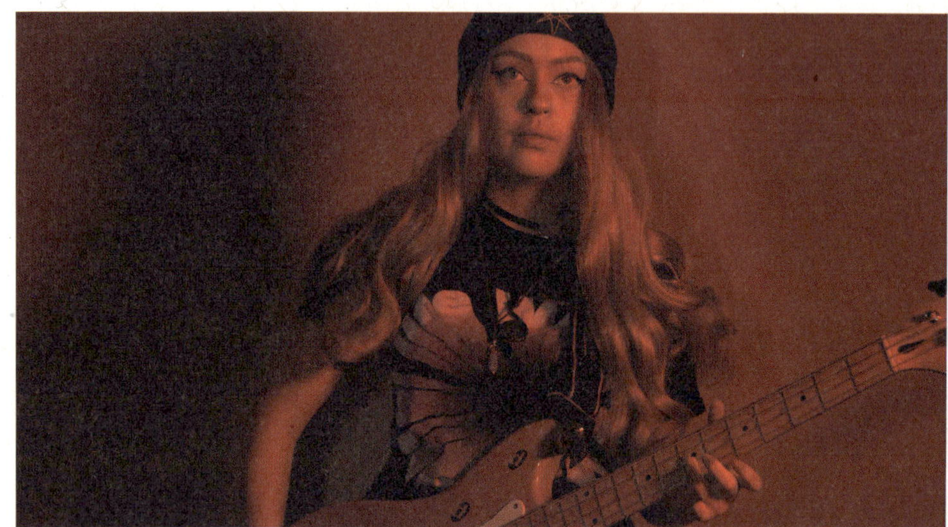

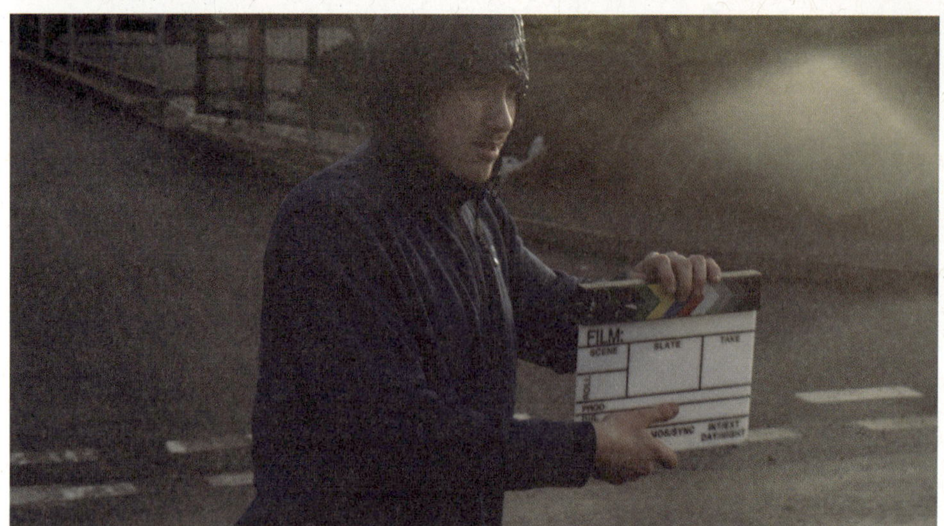

Intro

This text is a primer and provocation to see how you, as the reader, might generate methods of collaboration with other people within your own projects. This text is far from exhaustive: the subject of collaboration has spawned a whole literature across many years and disciplines. The text was developed with a group of WdKA students in mind, who took part in a workshop in October 2023, where we explored collaboration in their own projects alongside members of the WdKA faculty. This text benefits from their collective participation and insights.

Who are you?

You might self-identify as an artist, or something else. I've assumed that you are a key instigator of a creative project, there from day one and with a high degree of agency, although the people you're working with may be key actors within a wider context with which the creative project takes place. I have assumed that you'd like to collaborate with others in the development of your work.

Who are your collaborators?

Who are the people with whom you'll make this work? I have assumed that your collaborators may not see themselves as 'professional artists',[1] although you have been careful to make space for collaborators who do see themselves in this way. I have assumed they're voluntary participants in a creative project (and so have the right to be called artists if they wish), and that your partnership has value to you both.

Who am I?

I am an artist who has developed a collaborative practice through working in specific contexts. I am not writing to teach you how to be me, or to make my work; I'm writing in the hope that it will help you to be better than me, to find new ways of working that draw on what's written here and take it further in your own direction.

I'm not going to discuss content at all, except for using my previous work as practical examples. I'm going to leave the content, this central part, to you—it's your work. I'm going to talk about the conceptual underpinnings, ethics, and practical strategies of co-created work. To overstretch a metaphor, it will form the foundations and basic structure of a building that you'll turn into a home.

1. There are many routes into the arts, and no qualification is necessary—this is important to remember when you're working with people who may not consider themselves artists, or who are taking part in a visible 'arts project' for the first time.

The Five Phases

I have broken the process of making work down into five distinct phases. Anyone, however, who has ever undertaken a creative project knows that these phases are artificial and virtually impossible to disentangle from each other. The idea is that each phase, even if artificial, demands a different way of thinking and therefore a different way of collaborating.

These 5 phases are as follows:

1. Collaboratively conceptualizing work
2. Practical making
3. Documentation of process and work
4. Curatorial editing / Post-production
5. Exhibition & Dissemination

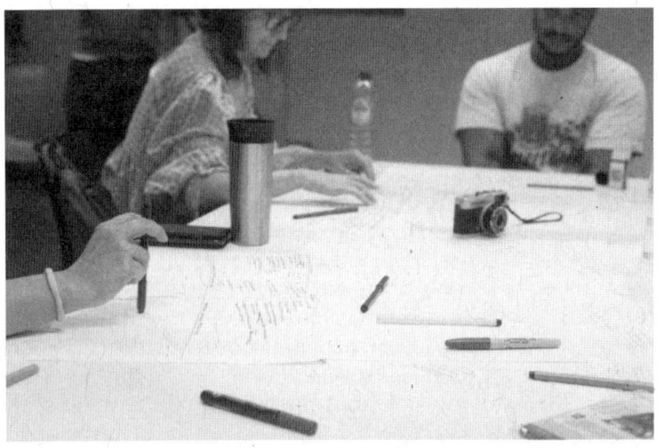

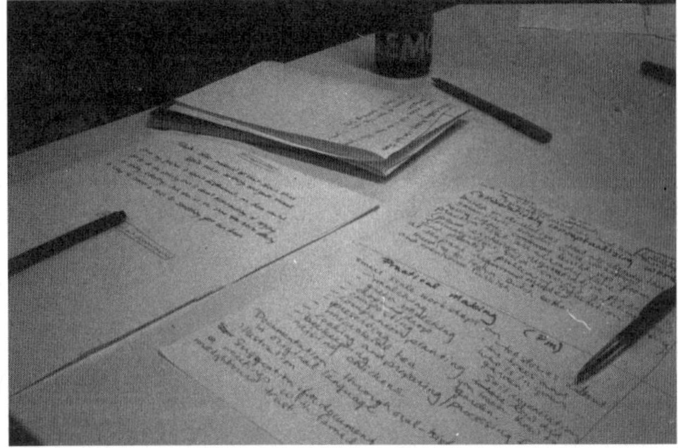

Images from the workshop *Praxis: Ethics of Collaboration* with artist-filmmaker Edwin Mingard. The photos are taken by workshop participants, Bachelor students at the Willem de Kooning Academy.

In the next exercise I will detail a few broader issues in collaborative work. In the following five sections, I will offer prompts for you to critically reflect upon, to help you further develop collaborative working methods for the five phases of your project.

Exercise A:
The table below is a simple matrix with just some of the many potential risks and benefits for artists and participants in collaborative work. Consider what you agree or disagree with. Feel free to add more risks and/or benefits of your own that I've missed out on.

For artists instigating a project:

Benefits	**Risks**
• Work that speaks from multiple perspectives on one topic • Synthesise entirely new perspectives through dialogue and co-creation • Develop new practical and aesthetic techniques through co-creation • Learn from the experiences of others • Meet interesting people and make new friends with different life experiences • Challenge our own assumptions • The above will help us make better work, refining and amplifying what we want to say • Enjoyment and fun—a process that could be quite insular is made social	• Can be a more costly way to make work, including financial and time commitment • Involves ceding control of a project to some degree • Can have an emotional or psychological toll • Can increase the amount of time spent planning, organizing and administrating rather than creating • Risk of harming others if you don't do your job well • Need to simultaneously balance good quality work and high quality experience for collaborators • Can involve work in dangerous or unsafe environments • Long and costly development periods affect quality of life • Need to be available for collaborators at unsociable hours—no 'off switch'

For those collaborating in the project:

Benefits	**Risks**
• Learn new practical or intellectual/creative skills • Vocalize experiences or concerns to an audience • Supportive space for self-reflection • Synthesise entirely new perspectives through dialogue and co-creation • Develop new practical and aesthetic techniques through co-creation • Learn from the experiences of others • Meet interesting people and make new friends with different life experiences • Challenge our own assumptions • Be seen and understood by peers • Feel more connected to a place or community • Be seen and understood by those who may have more social capital/clout • Fun/enjoyment • Route to employment or new career	• Placing trust in an artist who may have more social capital/social power than you • Being exploited as 'material' for someone else's work • Losing public control of your own narrative • Time commitment required for something that isn't your job/potential waste of time • Balancing demands of participation against other demands (work, caring responsibilities, time to socialize or pursue own development) • Risk of traumatic or re-traumatising experience • Inadequate or unprofessional support • Power inequality in decision making process • Being confused, lost or alienated by an opaque process

Whether or not potential benefits or risks relate to your project depends on many things—its duration, scale, content or location for example. Note too that these risks and benefits are not equivalent. Some are minor. Others are big enough to mean someone will definitely want to either be part of a project or avoid participation altogether. Some go way beyond the confines of the project and may have an effect, positive or negative, for years to come.

You cannot promise long-term benefits to collaborators and should not try. Where they do occur, these benefits are usually co-created (ie. they're not simply down to you), and rely on a great

It's the demonstration of care and not the explanation of care.

number of factors outside your control. But you can set the stage to make them more likely to happen.

Long-term harm must be taken extremely seriously. The nature of the work is that many potential harms are psychological or social. As well as practical strategies for mitigation, it is important to set the conditions for open dialogue and reporting, so that potential harm is stymied at the earliest opportunity. For some harms this can be as simple as continually checking in with each other; for others, it might be as complicated as an oversight group comprising social workers, psychologists, and lived experience advocates.

1. Collaboratively conceptualizing work

The conceptualizing of work is an important moment for collaboration because key decisions that will shape the rest of the project are made here. As the earliest point, it is also where power imbalances have the potential to be greatest. You, as a continually practicing artist, are aware of many things potential participants may not be, such as:

- The potential practical details of the work—budget, timescale, any partners or funders
- Potential benefits of participating vs. the time investment necessary
- Artistic mediums that are an option
- What will count as a 'successful' project
- Control over who's part of the project, the working structure etc.

Many of these issues and more might still be in play, so the importance of having collaborators involved is heightened still further.

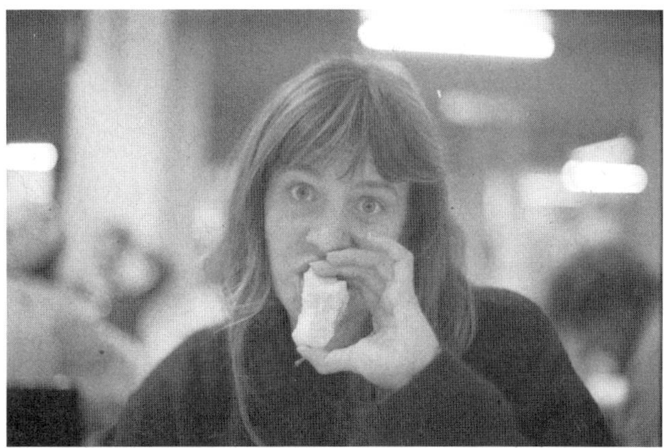

Exercise B:
What strategies could you employ to maximize the potential benefits to everyone involved, and minimize the risks of participation in the conceptualizing phase of the work?

Pick one risk or benefit from each box in the matrix in 'Exercise A' that you think might be relevant to your own project's development phase, and work through how you might enhance each potential benefit and mitigate each potential risk.

The exercise is useful because as an instigator of a project, it is critical to consider how to achieve the maximum benefit for yourself and your collaborators, up to and including, whether the project should take place at all. It's also useful because it throws your own informational weaknesses into perspective. You will gain a better insight into potential costs and benefits to your collaborators if you ask them, and this is precisely the point.

Some examples:

- Might participants benefit from having practical demonstrations of different materials that could be used in making the work?
- How could you structure your development sessions together to fit around everyone's other time commitments?
- How can you be, and be seen to be, a reliable partner?
- How might you share your knowledge and understanding of the art context within which the final work will show, so that decisions around that can be made together?
- How might funding be shared equitably and recognise the time and expertise everyone gives to the project?
- How do you make space for everyone to make mistakes?
- How might participants be part of making these decisions?

These particular examples were a few of the questions I asked when developing 'An Intermission' (2020), an artist's film that employed collaborative working methods throughout.

2. Practical making

For many people, the practical doing or making stage of a project is where it all happens. It can be exciting and empowering but also scary. The nature of many projects (and often their funding or timeline) means this may be a moment that cannot just be repeated if it does not go according to plan. It is the moment you hold hands and jump off the ledge together. You'll potentially be asking a lot of each other, whether this comes in the form of time, physical labor,

Thank you, and thanks for your openness, generosity, and I mean, to me, it also builds intimacy so you can probably imagine I'm into that.

or emotional investment. And you all have a lot to lose. What if the results are embarrassing, or too much to handle, or boring, or just a bit shit?

The irony is that if anyone believes it *might* be a bit shit and so doesn't invest in the making, it probably will be. The porous nature of stages is made real: the place to stop this happening is in development. The reverse dynamic (a great development phase that is not followed through into production) is also a risk.

Early on in my career, I was part of a couple of projects which had caring development phases, then when production happened there was a kind of "this can't go wrong so we have to bring in the professionals" approach, and participants were sidelined in a project they had developed. I was part of another project, years

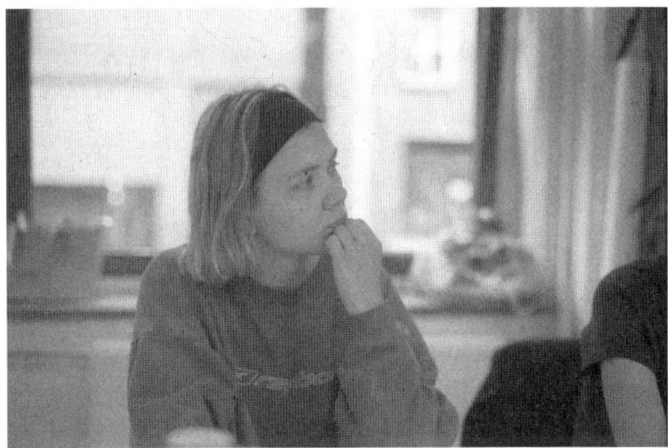

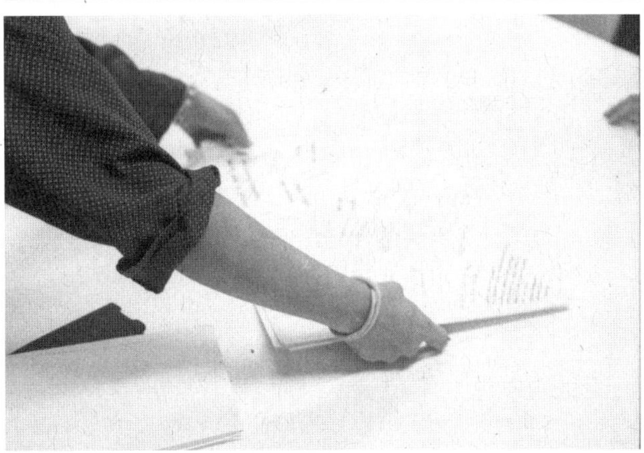

later, where the only employed member of staff living locally (and so with deep contextual experience) was given a cheaper computer than the other employed staff, ostensibly because they were working part-time—another inequality that was a decision, not inevitable. The cheaper computer made their work harder to do and made them appear less 'productive', and at least as importantly, the social signal that their input merited cheaper equipment and fewer hours had disastrous consequences for this key contributor's commitment to the project. There are important things to get right during the making phase that re-emphasises the trust and collaboration you have built in the development phase. Getting this wrong undermines that trust, which is more damaging than not having trust in the first place.

Exercise C:
What strategies could you employ to maximize the potential benefits to everyone involved, and minimize the risks of participation in the making phase of the work?

Pick one risk or benefit from each box in the matrix we looked at in 'Exercise A' that you think might be relevant to your own project's production phase, and work through how you might enhance each potential benefit and mitigate each potential risk.

Some examples:

- How might participants be true collaborators in the making process?
- How might this happen when working alongside any outsiders brought in for their technical skills?
- How should everyone be remunerated, or their time valued, in other equitable ways?
- Is the same level of trust being placed in everyone? Is that recognised?
- Do inequities in terms of responsibilities, control, and equipment provided for a task mirror pre-existing social inequalities? How might this be avoided?

3. Documentation of process and work

As you progress through making the work, you might want to document your time together. You're interested in the process as well as the outcome. This documentation can serve many functions and take many forms. The documentation itself can be a work (or even *the* work) in its own right—this is more true in collaboratively made work than any other medium. Just as you're experimenting with how the work is made and the social relationships that underpin its making, documentation is a time to experiment with who records whom, how, for what purpose and which audience.

I'm showing these contradictions.

Exercise D:
How might the documentation process serve different people's needs and interests? Thinking about your own project, make a list.
Here are some examples from previous projects I've been a part of:

- A reminder of a fun time spent together
- Raising people's confidence at a future time, by reminding them of previous personal success
- Evidence in support of future jobs or opportunities
- Making the collaborative process visible to an audience
- A chance to practice with a camera or microphone that isn't part of making the central work
- Showing an artist's process and working methods
- Sharing knowledge and advocating for collaborative work
- Building group bonds and identity as the project progresses
- Reporting to funders or supporters of a project
- Providing contextual information for the audience of the main work

Now consider these questions in relation to your project:

- Who is present and able to make the documentation?
- Might documentation methods happen in another more creative or engaging way?
- Can they be altered to make the act of documenting more accessible?
- Are there any risks to documenting for the individuals involved? Social or political factors like discrimination, migration status or repressive state policies might mean there are material risks to documenting.
- Are there any safeguarding issues to documenting? Are there individuals or groups who should be notified about who is documenting whom?

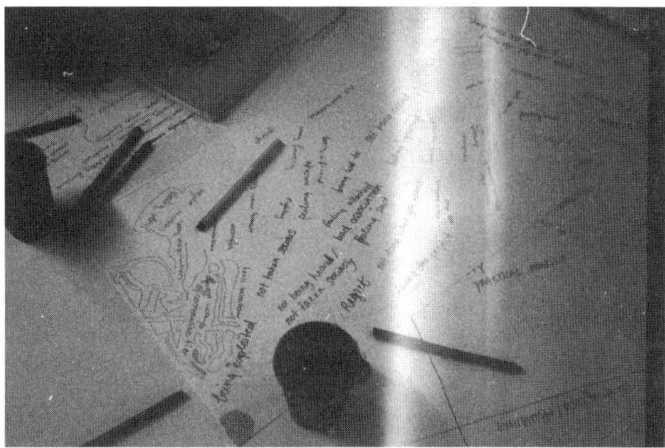

- How can people feedback to request that a specific image or recording where they're present isn't included in the documentation?
- Who has access to the documentation material? How might this be shared or democratized?

As a brief rule of thumb, once everyone involved has agreed that an image or recording can be public, I would aim to make sure every member of the group has a copy to share how they wish. There may be valid reasons why this is not possible, but again pay close attention to whose interest is being served. Maybe the funder doesn't want images shared until an exhibition opens, but your collaborators want to post photos on social media. Think carefully about what the final decision communicates, who made it, and the implications for the project's aims.

4. Curatorial editing/Post-production

There's an old film adage (sometimes attributed to Robert Bresson), that a film is born three times: in the script, in the production, and again in the edit. Whether you're making a film, a performance, an exhibition, or anything else, the same will apply. There are artists whose entire careers have been built on demonstrating that narrative, indeed any meaning at all is created not in the making but in the edit. There is a much bigger army of editors and curators who know this to be true because of first-hand experience.

The role is as powerful as a screenwriter or director, to keep stretching the film analogy. Yet whilst you can probably reel off a list of your favorite film directors, authors, playwrights or screenwriters, unless you work in film, chances are you cannot name a single editor let alone speak meaningfully about their work. It's a hugely influential role that is perhaps even more powerful in its invisibility.

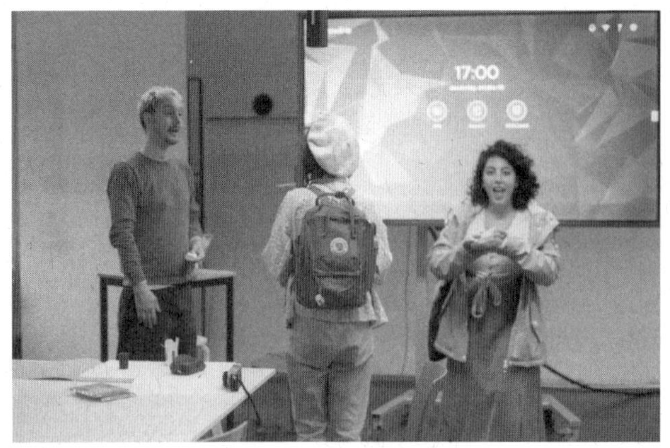

I have been sitting a lot with grief.

If you were working as a solo artist, a good editor would perform the role of fresh eyes as well as a confidante. They see things in the work that the person making it did not; they understand the intention and process, and spot moments that speak to the intention that may have eluded the people present in the moment itself. An expression that reveals how someone was really feeling; a juxtaposition of two elements that reveals a greater truth about both. The task in collaborative work is this: *how can the editing process be truly creative; stay true to the intentions of the wider piece; and be participatory?*

A film director will keep scenes in their film that should be cut because they're emotionally attached to them—and this director will be a paid professional with perhaps lots of experience. How is someone who may be working on a funded art project for the first time supposed to cut the element they were most involved with because it will make more sense to an audience that way? Should they even cut the element?

Exercise E:

Think through the reasons someone involved in a project might want control over the edit. Think about why you might want control over the editing of your work—there's probably a lot of overlap. From previous experience, people can be:

- Concerned about how they sound or appear
- Worried about their work, or things they say or do, being taken out of context
- Concerned a process they've never been through before is being 'done to them'
- Curious about the editing process
- Wanting to control personal visibility, whether making themselves more or less prominent
- Engaged in the process of making work and wanting to be involved in every aspect

What other reasons can you think of? Think about times when you've been recorded in some way by someone who worked in a different field from you. What were your concerns?

Finally, and most importantly of all: How might you marry the material reasons people wish to be involved in the editing process with their participation in that process as a creative act? These two motivations can sometimes be in conflict, and overcoming this is key.

5. Exhibition & Dissemination

Collaboratively made work has historically often underplayed the power of exhibition and dissemination. This has resulted in a dearth of examples of the way exhibition can be a part of the collaborative process when compared to, say, production. Sharing the results of your work can take many forms and provides a wide range of ways to achieve shared ambitions for the project.

Exercise E:
Make a list of everyone's ambitions for the exhibition and dissemination of the work. If you're doing this as a planning exercise before you have a team, try to think of the possible reasons the whole group might like to share work but be prepared to re-run the exercise once everyone is in place and adjust your plans. Think about why you want each to happen.

Form	Reason
Holding an exhibition	Getting your work seen
	Celebrating with everyone involved
News coverage	Taking part in wider public discourse
	Changing opinion about a particular issue
Social media sharing	Professional networking
	Sharing an achievement with family and friends

- What are the outcomes everyone wants? Label these 'List A'.
- What are the outcomes a smaller group or an individual wants? Label these 'List B'.
- Go through 'List B' and work out which would stop, or seriously harm, anything in 'List A' if they were to happen. Relabel these 'List C'.
- Looking at 'List C', are there any that could be achieved another way that isn't in conflict with 'List A'? If so, change their description and add them to 'List B'.
- Is there anything in 'List C' chosen by anyone where that was their only, or strongest, preference?

Patriarchy and what patriarchy does to me on so many levels.

Have a discussion as a group and see if there is any way you can accommodate this wish. Would the rest of the group be willing to give up something from 'List A' to make it achievable?

You now have a list of all the potential public outputs of the work that are achievable together. The list may be too long and unwieldy to carry out, and perhaps you'll change your minds as a group as you work through it, but it's a solid starting point.

You will find that decisions get harder the more specific you are with outcomes. Perhaps everyone wants an exhibition, but some people want it to be in the area where the project took place so that everyone can come, whilst others want it to be where decision-makers about a particular issue will be, to raise awareness, and you only have the budget for one of these to happen.

It Doesn't Stop at Images

A Preface for An Ongoing Conversation on Generational Queer Joy, Care, and Visibility

During the Summer of 2023, I asked a few collaborators to join me for a conversation about generational queer joy, care and visibility. I invited them to browse through hundreds of images sourced for my project It Doesn't Stop at Images *at IHLIA Heritage. The intention was to engage in a conversation with words that departed from images and experienced. That conversation never happened due to an intense Storm Ciarán which shut down train travels and prevented our guests from reaching WdKA.*

The following pages are the results of reenacting that possible conversation, that never happened, via digital meetings and email exchanges.

Pablo Lerma

The institution will always keep you busy, which keeps you away from the actual work.

Czar Kristoff P.

All images used in this visual essay are from Pablo Lerma's research project *It Doesn't Stop at Images. It Doesn't Stop at Images* is a research-based project using printed matter—magazines and daily publications—archived at the IHLIA (Internationaal Homo/Lesbisch Informatiecentrum en Archief) Heritage depot in Amsterdam. Pablo Lerma, 2021.

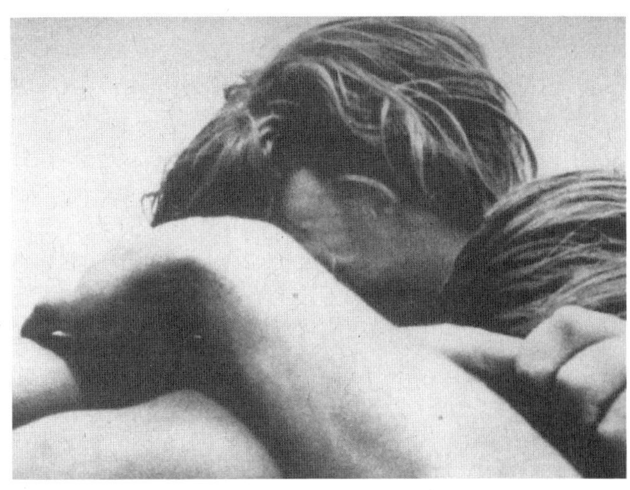

In my culture, touch is highly practiced when an infant is born, through carrying, feeding, cleaning and protecting them until the child reaches that stage that they learn how to groom, feed themselves, etc. Then, for some reason it disappears when the child finally becomes a teenager, a stage where their body is changing.

My parents separated when I was four years old so that means my journey to touch as a language is quite different from others. It abruptly stopped. This particular moment in my life is the beginning of my intimacy conflicts. Intimacy conflicts[1] occur when the symptoms of PTSD prevent the establishment or maintenance of trusting interpersonal relations. Anger toward a loved one often is accompanied by anxiety about the attachment, as these feelings are elicited in the same circumstances. Purposeful distanciation allows the individual to control the degree of emotional attachment by partially numbing feelings and by not permitting personal disclosure that would lead to the formation of friendship or deeper levels of caring for others.

This behavior has affected me when it comes to establishing relationships in the past, whether when I am looking for friendship, a romantic or sexual partner. There are many layers of walls that the other person has to go through in order to figure out what I really feel or think. And I can't imagine what it is like to be on the other side but I am sure it can be exhausting.

In the past few years, through the help of friends, family and books, I allowed myself to trust people once again. As well as accepting every rejection as a form of new beginnings.

1. Barbara Whitmer, *The Violence Mythos* (Albany: SUNY Press, 1997), 48.

Songs to sing:
Touch By Touch, Joy.
Sometimes When We Touch, Dan Hill.
Touch My Body, Mariah Carey.
Touch My Hand, David Archuleta.
Touch Me, The Doors.
Everytime We Touch, Maggie Reilly.

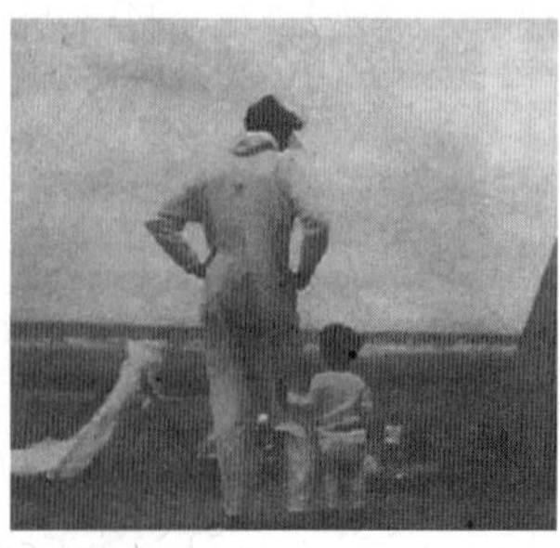

A friend once told me that healing begins once I have forgiven the people who hurt me and most importantly, forgiven myself.

In the past years, I started revisiting my past traumas through my practice, in the hope to dissect and articulate them. However, regardless of whether I read books or constantly make projects, it is as if the pain is still the same.

According to Lois Tonkins' theory of growing around grief,[2] painful feelings remain present, but through new experiences, meeting others and the pursuit of new activities, enjoyment can be achieved.

When I was a child, my best friend drowned by the river near our house. I was supposed to join their boat ride one afternoon but for some reason I stayed at home. I vividly remember all the details of that day, the cries, the wet blanket wrapped around my friend's body, the humidity, the sound of the trees, the dust on the road, the sound of the television when I arrived home, and the food we ate that evening. For many years I carried that memory with me. That is why it was only later in life I learned how to swim.

As an adult, I take refuge when I am near any bodies of water, my particular favorite are rivers or lakes as they are calm most of the time. I think my recent memories with friends did really help in redefining the word water, that just like memory, it is capable of reshaping itself.

2. Lois Tonkin TTC, "Growing around Grief—Another Way of Looking at Grief and Recovery," *Bereavement Care* 15, no. 1 (1996): 10, DOI: 10.1080/02682629608657376.

What are your needs for us to meet in terms related to our questions of safety?

Songs to sing:
Waterfalls, TLC.
Part Of Your World, The Little Mermaid.
Shape Of My Heart, Backstreet Boys.

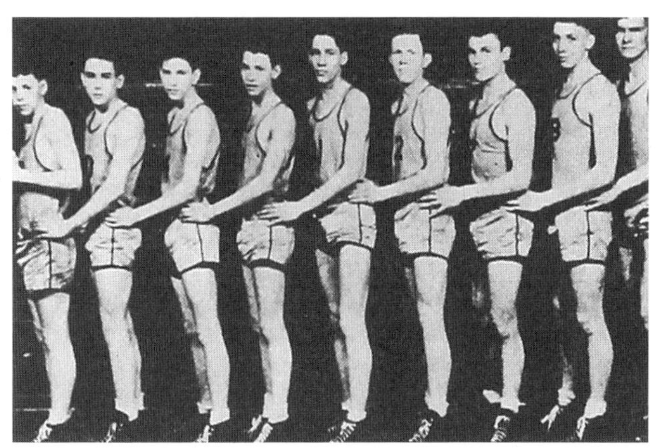

Ever since it was introduced by the Americans during their colonization, basketball has become a big part of the Filipino male identity.[3] These days, uniforms are worn on a daily basis, only the shirt or the shorts, never together, sometimes during their shift as a tricycle driver, street vendor or a jeepney driver. Sometimes it is also worn at home as the fabric material is breathable, conducive with humid weather. The basketball uniforms are also a way for male bodies to identify themselves—which team they play, which place they are from, as well as which surname they carry. Basketball uniforms can be compared to a knight's armor, it is a display of pride, power and identity, within and outside of the courts.

Few months ago, I attended a workshop facilitated by Gabriel Fontana and Maria Molteni at Ultradependent Public School[4] in BAK Utrecht. They asked each participant about our relationship with sports. It was my first time to be confronted with this question. Paraphrasing my answer, "I do not think I have a good relationship with sports, more likely because I also do not have a good relationship with my body while growing up. To be a *bakla* (queer is the closest English translation) kid in a conservative Catholic town, shame really warped my mind, my heart and my body."

I think biking helped me navigate that mindset. I was able to be in control of my body once again, as well as to let go of that control. Through biking I allowed my body to fall, to be wounded, to cry, to even accept the possibility of death, as well as to become my own

3. Rafe Bartholomew, *Pacific Rims* (New York: Penguin Random House, 2011).

4. See BAK's Ultradependent Public School, https://www.bakonline.org/program-item/ultradependent-public-school-2/.

navigator, to be my own cheerleader, to keep going, to pedal faster every time there are dogs chasing me. But recently, I also learned that it is okay to bike slowly and pause when needed. Through these pauses I was able to review the spaces I used to be afraid of, including basketball courts. I am more amused now than scared of it. Basketball courts these days are designed to be multifunctional. It can be used as a volleyball court, temporary school, cultural space, shelter during typhoons, and vaccination centers during the COVID-19 pandemic. It has morphed from a very masculine architecture into a more inclusive architecture.

5. In the 90s, due to extreme poverty, people would steal rail tracks and sell them in exchange for money. https://en.wikipedia.org/wiki/PNR_South_Main_Line.

Songs to sing:
Basketbol, Viva Hot Babes.
Space Jam, Quad City DJs.
Bicycle Race, Queen.

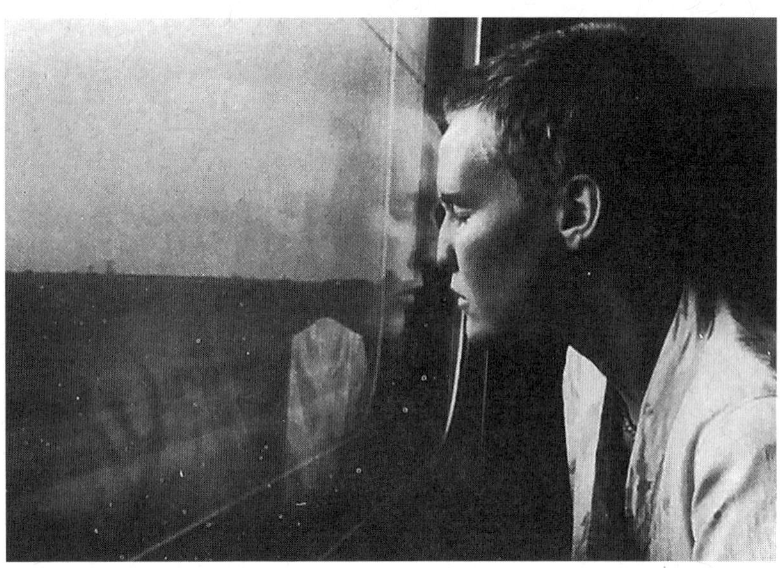

My early memory of taking a train took place in the early 2000s. It was when my older cousins and I traveled to our hometown from Manila with no accompanying adult. The 10-12 hour train ride felt like an excursion to me until it stopped at approximately 40 KM before our destination, with only leftover food and water in hand. We waited for hours hoping the train would be fixed, not knowing that there was a big gap in the railtrack. As an adult, I always revisit this memory everytime I take the train, especially when I am in the Netherlands.

yeah, we were able to get our booster this week.

Mobility is a rare privilege especially to those who are from a brown working class family. I am only able to have access to it due to the generosity of my relatives who are migrant workers and friends and allies who are cultural workers in the EU. Through these travels I was able to see a broader perspective of the world as well as rediscover my deepest memories and feelings that have been silent due to the everyday noises I hear in my country, the Philippines. Noises produced by its people, by the culture, by the machines—the agony of my country from centuries of oppression and extraction by its colonizers are translated through the constant singing of melodies about longing;[6] blasting Western music and local EDM in tricycles, grocery stores, even within funeral homes; motorists showing off their modified mufflers, etc.

6. A Filipino, Roberto Legaspi del Rosario, invented and holds the patent on the karaoke machine. https://en.wikipedia.org/wiki/Roberto_del_Rosario.

Being in the train has allowed me to reflect on the "noises" I have created through the years as a semi-discrete *bakla*. One of my reflections is that maybe my academic and career achievements were unconsciously built to become a smoke screen of the real me, that maybe through these credentials I could be worthy of love and respect from my family and community. Some sort of filler to the missing train tracks. Or maybe it is a form of making a set of new train tracks.

Songs to sing:
This Train Don't Stop There Anymore, Elton John.
Ticket To Ride, The Beatles.
Voyage Voyage, Desireless.

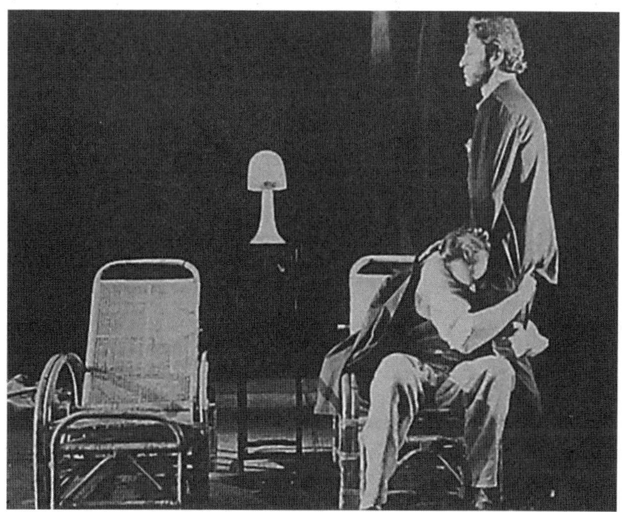

The images of arrival and departure are often identical and interchangeable. Most of the time I get confused and wonder if identifying them is still important.

Articulating my desires has always been a challenge growing up. Maybe because the household who raised me were never really expressive except when the adults burst into rage. I never learned the importance of expressing appreciation or love until the later part of my life through my friends and past lovers.

Weeks before my father passed away, he asked me about my attraction towards men. I answered and he replied that if that's what I really want, he can do nothing about it. It was our last conversation. I revisit this memory from time to time, most especially at times when my heart is heavy and/or confused. In some way this memory serves as punctuation to our relationship and also serves as an entry point to potential relationships I will build.

Songs To Sing:
Hello, Adele.
Hey QT, QT.
Finally, Cece Peniston.
Happy Together, The Turtles.
Angel Baby, Troye Sivan.
Top Of The World, The Carpenters.
Lumayo Ka Man Sa Akin, Rodel Naval.
Wala Na Bang Pag-ibig, Jaya.
Ray Of Light, Madonna.
Hiram, Zsa Zsa Padilla.
Believe, Cher.

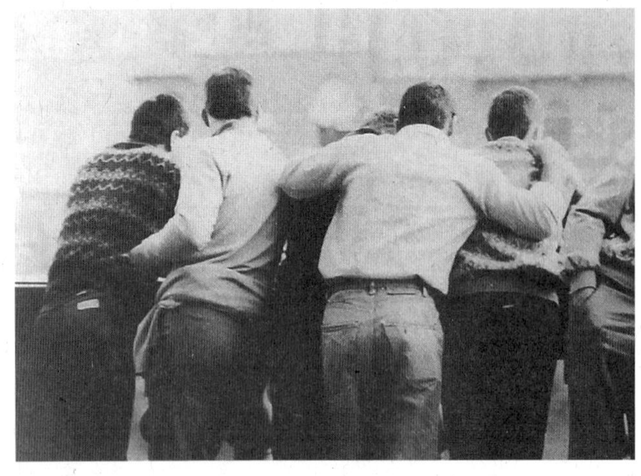

I always feared that I would be alone, that I wouldn't have a family.

My gaze towards men and my definition of beauty is definitely shaped by my consumption of Western media growing up as well as by the culture I was raised in. Gaze is a byproduct of colonialism and imperialism.[7] In my early 20s during the beginning of my photography practice, I met a group of skateboarders called *Sanib* and documented our journey together. While I did enjoy looking at their bodies (only to some!) either slamming the ground or resting while peeking (most of the time) at the small window of my camera, the rage and frustration when they cannot land a trick, the celebratory unison taps of the board when someone lands a trick, the joy and excitement when they see a planter box or stairs (non skaters will never understand!) and the stories that unfolded during after game drinking sessions, have made me re-evaluate a lot of things, how I see body, desire, beauty even my *kabaklaan* (queerness is the closest English translation). I do not think that the project I did with my friend Zeus Bascon called *Sunset Garden*[8] will be realized if my path with *Sanib* did not happen.

7. Ciara Mae Gonzales Tirona, "The Impact of Colonial Beauty Standards in the Ethnic Identity and Mental Health of Filipino Americans," Master of Social Work diss., (San Francisco State University, 2023). https://scholarworks.calstate.edu/downloads/z890s1602.

8. sunset garden. hotglue.me

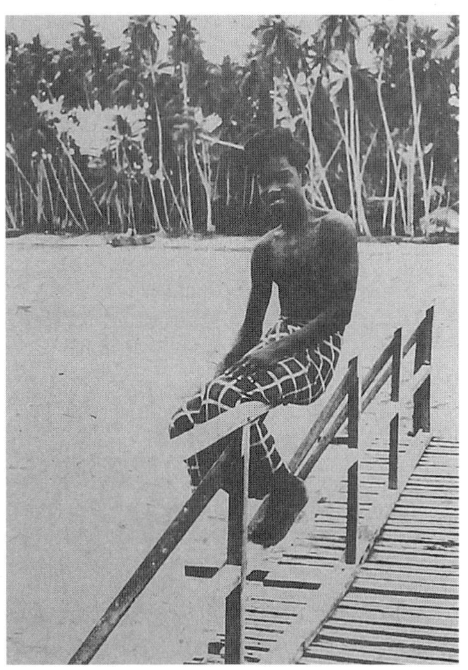

In the Philippines, once people found out that you are a *bakla*, they would automatically label you as effeminate and submissive. This means your "ideal partner" should be a masculine man, who is athletic, with a deep voice, a provider and a dominant. This concept is highly rooted in the Western ideology of binaries and gender roles. Being raised in a community where the elder *bakla* have accepted this construct has influenced how I envisioned my future. However, there is one *parlorista*[9] in my hometown who "broke" this stereotype: Argon, a flamboyant gay man who has blond hair and brown highlights, wears excessive jewelry and cologne, who is happily married to a lady and blessed with a daughter. Years later, a popular Filipino *bakla* celebrity, Ogie Diaz has also told the press that he has a female partner, to whom he has five children. Other people might see both of these situations as a form of self erasure as Argon and Ogie have allowed themselves to perform the roles that are expected from them but for me personally, the grayness of Argon and Ogie's situation is valid. Regardless of my exposure to their story, I do not think it is the path I wanted to take but I am super grateful that it gave me an opportunity to understand that there are many forms of *bakla*—it made me understand that it doesn't have an absolute form and so is every *bakla*'s journey, it is always uncertain.

9. A low-income male homosexual who behaves in a feminine manner and stereotypically works in a beauty parlor.

Additional Texts to Read:

Robert Diaz, "The Limits of Bakla and Gay: Feminist Readings of My Husband's Lover, Vice Ganda, and Charice Pempengco," *The University of Chicago Press Journals* 40, no. 3 (Spring 2015): 721-745. https://doi.org/10.1086/679526.

J. Neil C. Garcia, *Philippine Gay Culture* (Hong Kong: Hong Kong University Press, 1996). https://hkupress.hku.hk/image/catalog/pdf-preview/9789622099852.pdf

J. Neil C. Garcia, "Male Homosexuality In The Philippines: A Short History," *International Institute for Asian Studies* (2020). https://www.iias.asia/sites/default/files/2020-11/IIAS_NL35_13.pdf.

Don Jaucian, *Brief Histories* (Manila: Everything's Fine, 2022).

Carlo Tadiar, *Kolboy: Denial, Disgust, and the Production of Value in Male Sex Work in the Philippines* (Quezon City: UP Press, 2021). https://press.up.edu.ph/store/books/view_item/764.

Lee Yarcia, Tesa de Vela, and Michael Tan, "Queer Identity and Gender-Related Rights in Post-Colonial Philippines," *Australian Journal of Asian Law* 20, no. 1 (November 17, 2019): 265-275. Available at SSRN: https://ssrn.com/abstract=3488543.

Films to See:

The Blossoming Of Maximo Oliveros, Auraeous Solito, 2005.
Die Beautiful, Jun Robles Lana, 2016.
Contestant #4, Celeste Lapita and Kaj Palanca, 2016.
Zombadings and the Curse of the Zombadings, Jade Castro, 2011.
Markova: Comfort Gay, Gil Portes, 2001.
Kalel, 15, Jun Robles Lana, 2019.
Lingua Franco, Isabel Sandoval, 2019.

Jacquill Basdew

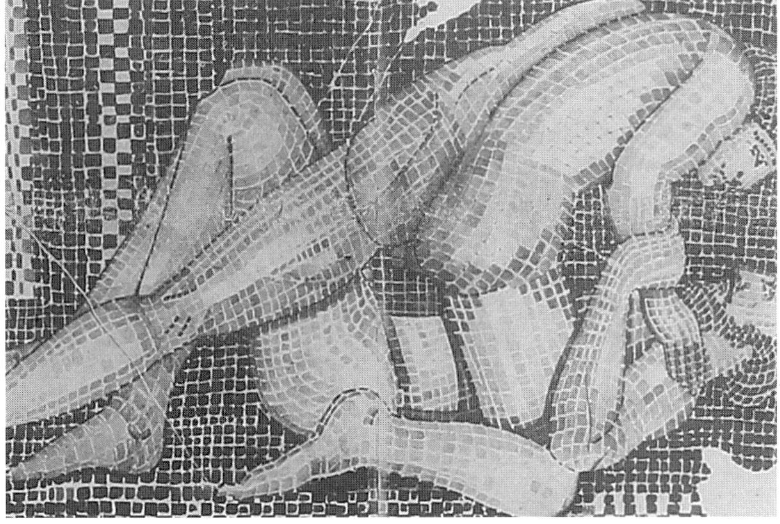

I liked that you said that there were so many images to choose from. And when I'm presented with something like that I really try to..., and this might sound abstract, but turn off the brain or the mind, and really tap into a feeling and try to feel which images speak to me, and why. And this image that we now see here is one that actually reminded me of my childhood, in a way, because there's many things that you could see within this image. Of course, now, as an adult, I see two men holding each other. But there's many different ways that that could be interpreted. So what are they doing? Are they wrestling? Are they fighting? Are they making love to each other? The image to me is very fluid and open to interpretation. And I think it's also a very interesting way to maybe present these kinds of images to a larger audience who might not see what's actually being said. So there's a hidden message within it. And that's what speaks to me a lot. The layeredness of this image.

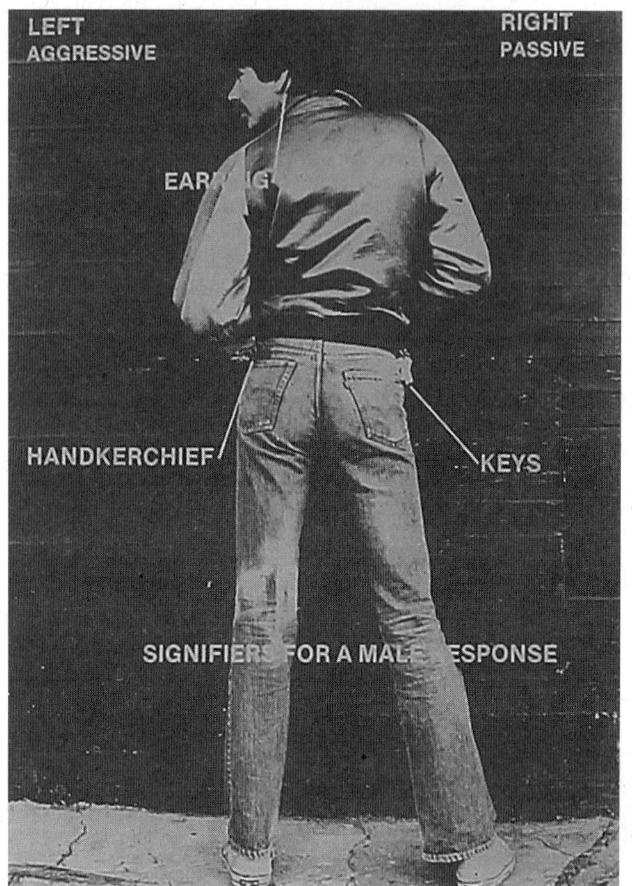

I've loved this image ever since I saw it in OBA (Openbare Bibliotheek Amsterdam). That's where I first saw it during your exhibition. And me, you know, being a young queer, I was unfamiliar with these kinds of codes and especially because I haven't studied... I haven't gone to school to study more about queer history or ways of communicating with each other. I was very pleasantly surprised to learn more about these hidden ways of communicating with each other and made me wonder, okay, "if this is how we used to communicate, is this still the same way we're communicating nowadays?" And how could these methods of communicating, how can they be used for maybe sharing other messages than what they were originally intended for? Is there also space to rewrite that story and give it a new meaning? So that's what it triggered.

Now I'm back in the spiral of YEAH, contracts are not going to be renewed. This is my check in.

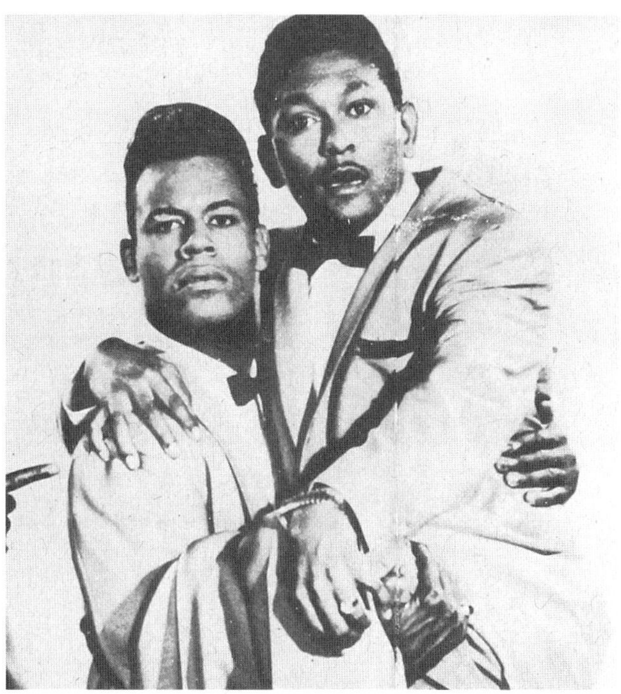

So the next image, this also relates to the first image, is that what does this mean? Right? And the reason why I have selected this image is because I see a reflection of myself. I see men of color. I see them dressed up in suits, it made me think of the film *Looking for Langston* by Isaac Julian in which we saw these men dressed up in very beautiful suits, going to meet each other in secret. Knowing what they came for when they met each other, but the outer world not knowing what was going on, and simply thinking "these are men in suits." And kind of placing them in their own construct of the mind in which they think what their stories are.

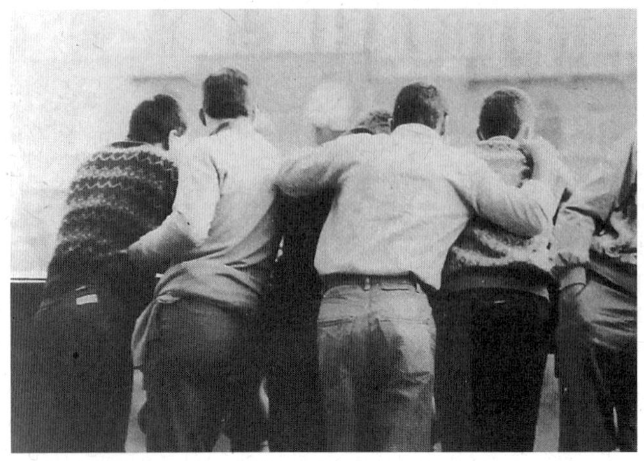

Well, I think this image, well the reason why I was drawn to it is because it responds to my longing for collectiveness in the here and now. Right? In a world in which we see so much division. This image was very soft to me. And when there's a particular kind of softness that I really appreciate. And that is when it's between men, whether they are into each other or it's a friendship or a familiar bond. It just gave me a really good feeling, this image. And it could, again, be whatever. We don't know what's going on here. But just seeing men being together, in a soft way, is what draws me to this image. Yeah, I found this image so incredibly interesting, because it presented me with a huge question mark. And made me wonder why is this picture in here? Because I didn't know anything about the background. And that then again, also informed me about the kind of bigger question that I felt that I had to ask myself or that we should ask ourselves, why we often try to draw conclusions based on the things we see on the surface? Because, okay, I'm not able to tell who this person is, where he lives, where he's from. I can guess. But what I cannot guess at all is, if he is queer, or maybe... I don't know anything about this image. It could be anything. And because it can be anything it really spoke to me. Because everything could be anything, if you allow it to be.

The amount of people who are required to work sick.

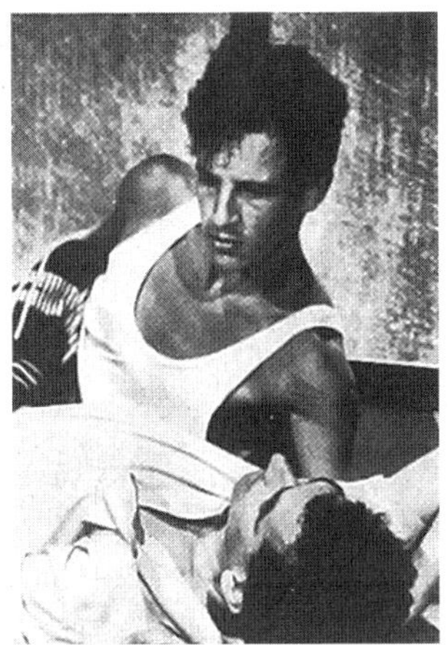

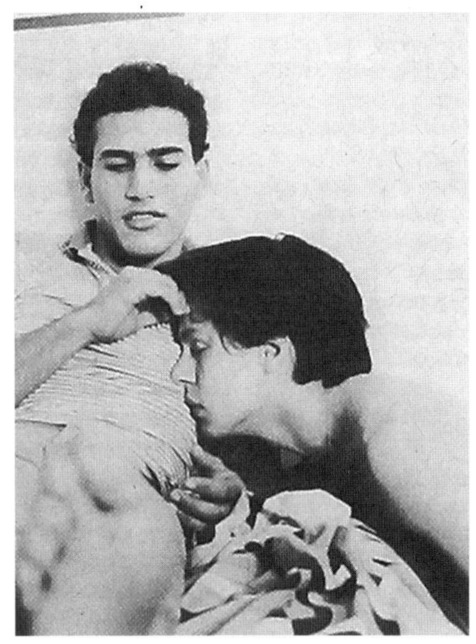

Again, I was really drawn, there's something about images in which we see the softer sides of men or the intimate sides of men. Because often when we look at popular media, and they depict queer, gay relations, it tends to lean towards some more sexual tone. Whereas I feel the need for more intimate, softer tones, which really focus on our shared humanity. Because we know that in the past and still (now) they waged a war against gays that they weren't human and that they were only homosexuals with an emphasis on the sexual aspect. That these men were just interested in each other, for fucking each other, when there's so much more going on. Men loving men is more than just sex. It's about the intimate aspect. It's about feeling seen, heard, supported, secure, protected. And that's what I saw in this image. I saw humanity. I see that I'm constantly being drawn to the same kind of recurring theme. Right. And that is, I think, that's also what I started out with, when I said that I didn't want to think but I want it to feel when going through these images. And I think it's just an internal longing that lives, that is present. And that's the feeling of wanting to be with another man, but just being me in my full, unapologetic, vulnerable human form. And not kind of being forced to walk in the footsteps of what society expects of men being with men. What that should look like. And again, I saw this again, just being with someone you want to be with, and hopefully also love.

Decompartmentalize to Prevent Isolation *or* How Conflict Can Serve to Recreate Ties

Laurence Rassel and Selma Bellal work together at erg–un lieu de recherche, an art academy in the heart of Brussels. Before becoming director at erg, Laurence led the Fundacio Antoni Tàpies in Barcelona (2008-2015), and she was a founding member of the non-profit organization Constant (1997-2008), which operated across the arts, media, society, and technology. Selma Bellal is a political scientist, researcher, and educator. Selma works side-by-side with Laurence, colleagues, and students at erg, toward the collective transformation of erg's pedagogical and administrative structure, and its approach to art education and research. Selma is especially interested in transformative justice practices that can shift our understandings of equality and progress. Upon our invitation, Laurence and Selma offered to discuss the ways in which conflict emerges within their transformative practices, how it influences and shapes infrastructure and psycho-social dynamics. Given our familiarity with conflict-ridden transformations, we felt we could learn a lot from them. And we did.

Our fall seminar session involved a tandem talk by Laurence and Selma and a question and answer session between them and those who attended (WdKA-Piet Zwart Institute students and staff, Promiscuous Care Study Group representatives). What follows is an edited and abridged version of their presentation.

Vivian Sky Rehberg

Vivian Sky Rehberg: Today we are here under the aegis of how conflict can help to recreate ties. Laurence, you've said before that you used to be quite uncomfortable with conflict. What has changed?

Laurence Rassel: That's thanks to Selma. Sometimes I think of Selma as I fall asleep and I tell myself "conflict is nice, conflict is nice, and we can learn from it ..."

Selma Bellal: I'm a political scientist. I teach social sciences and political sciences at erg, and I was also in charge of quality coordination for two years. And at erg it's an obligation to evaluate quality. But we see that more as an opportunity to develop social and human concerns rather than bureaucratic and procedural ones. Some of the things that we will present today are related to this quality process. And are linked to sustainability, but sustainability seen in relation to the human as the core of the institution's concerns more than anything else. Maybe we can put things into practice at erg because of only having 600 students, six times fewer than here at WdKA, and a small building. We are together, we know each other, we share values. It's a context in which keeping the human at the center is easier.

LR: Now I will speak as "director." It's funny when Selma says "small" school, because it's kind of heavy for me to have 600 human beings connected to all of us and each other. erg is an art school with thirteen orientations; like drawing, video, and so on. It's not part of the university system, which means in terms of interaction or decision, as director I can take responsibility. I have a contract with the board, and I'm paid by the Ministry of Education. Rules are set by the legal system. We have some flexibility in terms of interpretations of the rules or in terms of how we behave and the contents of the programs. I'm saying this because sometimes when we talk about what we do, it looks easy. It's not. It looks like a moral judgment of how you should work. It's not. We share the experiences we have in the circumstances we have. We are an art school in higher education, we are not a bunch of activists, it's not a cooperative. We obey the rules that get people a diploma or get them paid. When erg was founded in the 1970s it was created to be as interdisciplinary and as experimental as possible, with theory and practice interrelated. The legal and political circumstances allowed for the creation of a new school different from what already existed.

So, we are haunted by ghosts, and Jean Oury also acknowledged ghosts in the framework of Institutional Psychotherapy. Maybe you have ghosts you don't know of yet, or in the future there will be zombies. We try to be friends with ghosts and to not ignore them. It's important to know what we inherit somehow. It can be a myth, but it can also be a base for establishing what we think. To be coherent with erg's mission we are careful about doing what we say. And we are careful about being coherent with pedagogy, with what we teach. How we run the school, I hope, is coherent with the pedagogy and with the mission of an art school. It makes sense within that school to take time to teach art and to discuss working conditions. Those conditions can be legal, financial, related to sustainability conditions, and the conflicts that we encounter. It can be heavy and it's not without consequences. We take time within pedagogy to discuss how we do what we are doing. When changes occur within the legal frameworks, we assemble, we flyer, we deliberate, we announce changes within the physical building, within the time we have, within the budget. We try to take care of the fact that people come to the school to teach and learn. That is at the center. Conflicts are good, but how can we ensure that conflicts still enable us to maintain pedagogical relationships?

In this regard, Selma has helped me learn from conflict. We created transversal collective projects and practices with the students in connection with the teachers and administrative team. We show this entanglement and complexity on our website (designed by your colleague/teacher Michael Murtaugh), we are never alone. We must

Hey you have a different zoom background! I see two orange sweaters.

think all the time about our interconnection with those who are collecting the trash, who are cooking, who are teaching, who have access, about the rules of the system we are in and that defines us. We inherit from art history the tendency of separating art practice from the political, social, environmental, gender, contexts. So, we always put conflicting people back into a context. We are in this constellation, with multiple spaces of listening and dialogue in the school, one of which is the classroom.

SB: Our purpose with mapping where and how communication takes place at erg was to avoid one-way streets in interpersonal relationships and to reveal connections between us.

LR: Selma made a map of all the areas where we are in dialogue. Because the school is part of the public legal system and that has its own administration, we don't try to substitute ourselves for that. One example is the legal obligation to have a Student Council, which is really important because it has a voice and acts across different domains than, for example the Pedagogical Council, where you have representation from teachers, the administration, the students, the unions, and from the government. We don't want to overload students, but they are also part of the recruitment processes for new teachers, and when they have time they participate in administrative teams too. We have the legal obligation to provide inclusive education and accompany people with learning difficulties or medical issues. At erg, there's a group of neurodivergent students who have built up their own support system in conversation with the person responsible for implementing inclusive education. They gather regularly. We don't enter into their private worlds, and everything we discuss is confidential. The city of Brussels also has resources for students who face discrimination and harassment. In addition, we are working on a complaint framework at erg. It's important to know where the first line of help is available for students and staff. When students encounter individual social situations, you need people and systems you can trust.

SB: Regarding conflict: a year ago we conceived of a Transformative Justice Council, as a place for living and disobeying together. The council offers mediations and reparations that promote collective conflict management by devising non-punitive responses to conflict.

It's for responses to conflicts that do not involve serious misconduct and acts that undermine health, dignity, rights, freedom, the honor or safety of the individuals. It's for dealing with conflicts around compliance with school study regulations. We seek non-punitive responses that attempt to repair the damage caused. And we have two different procedures, one for misconduct, and one for serious misconduct. This council tries to promote awareness about different dimensions raised by conflicts, racism, microaggressions, sexism, homophobia, etc. There are also conflicts around the collective management of work-spaces, equipment, safety, cleanliness, and sometimes problems due the use of alcohol or drugs in the space of our school.

We also had some conflict last year around the collective framework we constructed around non-violent performances, for example. So, we faced the question of playing with the limits in art practices, and the fact that you cannot do whatever you want at school and when you are with and in a collective that contains a lot of different people's fragilities. The principle of transformative justice is that the person implicated is not invited to return with their head down but must collectively support and explain the reparation process in which they're involved. We believe that conflict is not an aggression, after Sarah Schulman, and that conflict is a necessity and an opportunity to do justice together and avoid polarization.[1] And to also avoid the temptation to take justice into one's own hands, because that kind of situation displays or reconstructs violence, which is not acceptable for us. We think that we really have a collective responsibility when there is conflict.

So, we attempt to collectively transform our practices and to put our value into practice. And to do so, we also decide on requests to justify transgressions of certain rules. So, we try to permit some transgression, but they must be official, they must be requested, and not be done impulsively and without dialogue. In doing so, we try to promote the appropriation of rules consistent with the pedagogical project and to consider the singularity of artistic approaches without neglecting societal responsibilities.

The Transformative Justice Council is animated, as are the majority of the spaces at erg, by teachers, students, administrative and management staff, because we try to represent different experiences of and different points of view on the rules. We invest in the council as volunteers and restrict it to conflicts between students. For conflicts between teachers, and between students and staff, there is a mediation process we employ that relates to legal workplace procedures in Belgium.

LR: We've been trying to create a safer space. I tell the students when they enter the school, "erg is not a

1. See Sarah Schulman, *Conflict is Not Abuse: Overstating Harm, Community Responsibility, and the Duty of Repair* (Vancouver: Arsenal Pulp Press, 2016).

I am also quite stressed about the future.

safe space." We know we are not outside society. We decided to train (on a voluntary basis) some students, teachers, and administrators to be the first points of contact whenever there is an aggression. In situations like this, students tend to talk to a teacher or to a friend who needs to know how to react to this kind of testimony. I try to be the director and stay out of that, in case I need to be the third person or the authority at one point. Selma was doing this with our colleagues, listening to the student, listening to the teacher, to see if a mediation is possible or see if a formal complaint is necessary. We also trained with a lawyer so the management team knows what we legally can do and what our obligations are. There is a difference between what the law states and recognizes as transgressive or illegal, and the council's mandate. Of course, whether to trust the law is another question. We know it's complex, because human relationships are. We don't say "this is how it is," we look for opportunities to think with conflicting parties.

SB: We are always trying to understand why a situation happens at erg and what happens between the individuals involved. How can we work to avoid the reproduction of the situation? We are always trying to take every situation as something that questions collective dynamics. We also really believe that punitive responses dehumanize the other and make the problem individual when they are systemic, which is not helpful. These are not individual problems.

LR: Punitive responses also dehumanize me as a director. For example, one student built a fire for an artwork and another student used the alarm system for an artwork, and those acts created risks to life. And so, what do I do? I punished them. But we don't learn anything from that, and I don't want to repeat this situation, this performance of authority that asks how we arrive at the point where there is an act of transgression. We don't learn answers to questions like, "why don't you think of the people who are cleaning?" "Why don't you think of the people who have autism in school?" So now, instead, we say: "Stop. Let's see what we can learn."

SB: And to be sure, we need room to say that we've done wrong. Excuses are political, but so are the lack of them. We really try to roll the idea of political responsibility and the non-reproduction of violence together.

The Meal is Language *and This is a Dinner Party*

INVITATION

You are cordially invited to attend ____*The_Meal_is_Language*____ planned for ____*SEPT_20_2023*___ . It will be wonderful to have ____*INSERT_YOUR_NAME*____ among us! *The_Promiscuous_Care_Study_Group_and_Reading_Room_Rotterdam*____ will host ___*INSERT_YOUR_NAME*__ and _*Lola_Olufemi*_ and _______ and _________ and__________ and_________ along ____*Yusser_al_Obaidi's_Sofreh_Daimeh* at our lovely location____*TENT_Rotterdam*___ . We are seeking your presence to make it memorable!

This is a gathering for the delusional, for the imaginative, the ones in this world but not of this world. Taking inspiration from Lola Olufemi's work, we will open up a space for thinking otherwise. Otherwise as in, the political horizon awaits, as in the firm embrace of the unknowable, as in refusing the structures that confine while thinking of other ways of existing. Join us and sit down in conversation as we ask ourselves: What else is possible when we start to imagine another world?

We met each other at the Sofreh Daimeh, a spatial poem by Yusser al Obaidi; a metaphorical yet real space of hosting otherwise. Here, surrounding the plastic sofreh, we hosted a collective conversation—a metaphorical meal of words, if you will. The documentation of this conversation opened with a dialogue between sections from Lola Olufemi's Experiments in Imagining Otherwise, *and from notes from Yusser al Obaidi's unpublished* Dear Barzakhiya *(excerpts of which are published as the text* Let Us Meet in the Margins [Barzakh] *also contained within this publication). After the event's brief conversation between Lola Olufemi and Yusser al Obaidi, the space opened up for attendees to join as guests at the sofreh, hungry with questions.*

For the sake of brevity, we have only transcribed the initial conversation between Lola Olufemi and Yusser al Obaidi. Please come hungry with questions and full of wishes. We hope you can catch up and join the conversation too. We're looking to exchange strategies to cook up an other future.

Yusser al Obaidi

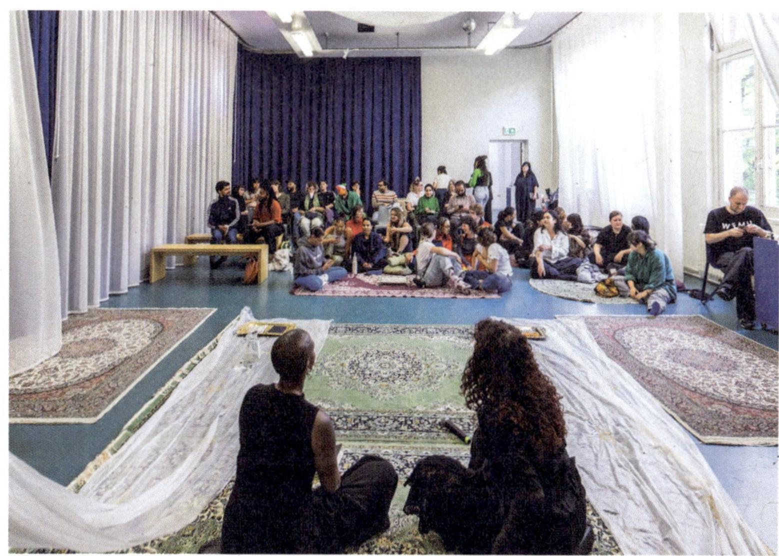

All photographs are by Steven Maybury.

Yusser al Obaidi: Hello. Hi. Hi everyone. Welcome to *The Meal is Language*. For those who don't know me, I'm Yusser al Obaidi. I'm an artist, designer and writer who seeks to acknowledge and enable the radical potential of intimate relational spaces. And my main central concern is how can we affirm other ways of being/knowing. Next to me, we have the most amazing Lola Olufemi. Lola Olufemi is a black feminist writer and Stuart Hall Foundation researcher from London. Her work focuses on the uses of the feminist imagination and its relationship to cultural production, political demands, and futurity. She is author of *Experiments in Imagining Otherwise*, and *Feminism Interrupted, Disrupting Power*, and a member of bare minimum, an interdisciplinary anti-work arts collective. Today will be mainly focusing on *Experiments in Imagining Otherwise*. In a bit, we'll be having a conversation between our texts. We'll invite you to join afterwards. Maybe you can say something about the format that we'll be using.

Lola Olufemi: Hi, everyone. I'm Lola. I just wanted to say when we were conceiving of this event, we wanted it to feel like an offering and an invitation and a kind of gathering rather than just us speaking to you. And so, I suggested we use the Long Table format, by Lois Weaver,[1] who's a feminist artist, amongst other things. And basically, the format of the Long Table is an invitation for knowledge, exchange, and collaboration and dialogue. And how it works is that two people begin the conversation. And language is the meal. We will ask you to join us on our 'fictional table', which is these two green rugs here.

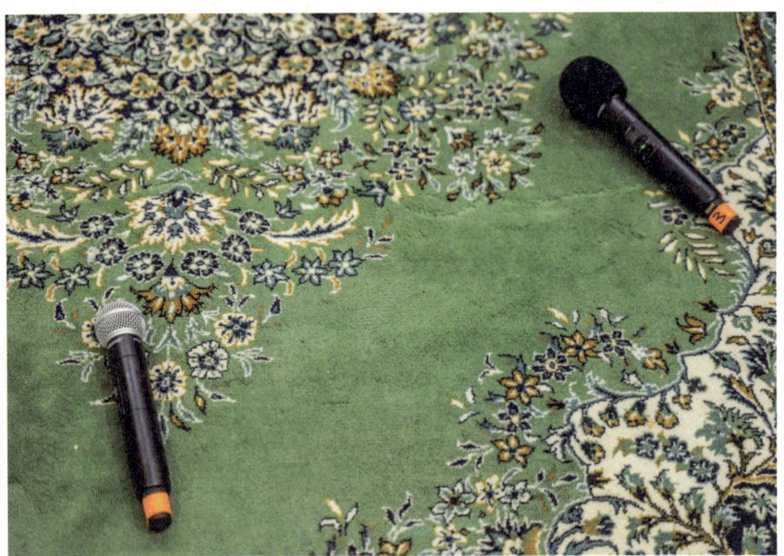

The external terrible news and insecurity is not good for my general anxiety, which tends to be very high.

1. "Lois Weaver," Split Britches, accessed December 10, 2023, https://www.split-britches.com/lois.

2. Lola Olufemi, *Experiments in Imagining Otherwise* (London: Hajar Press, 2021), 126.

3. Yusser al Obaidi, unpublished notes from the ongoing research project "Dear Barzakhiya" excerpts of which are published in the essay entitled "Let Us Meet in the Margins [Barzakh]" also contained within this publication.

At any point, anybody in the room can come and sit on the rug and join the conversation. You can ask questions, leave comments. At any point, you can leave the table. Hopefully it's a way for us to get to know you, and to hear the things that you want to share. Please don't be scared because the concept does not work if you do not participate.

YO: Okay, we can start the dialogue.

LO (reading from Lola Olufemi, Experiments in Imagining Otherwise): Somebody screams HOLD THE LINE, and the vibrations ricochet off any available surface. There is a space between the page & the words on the page. There is a space between looking at the words on the page & hearing the words read aloud. We need to find a name for that space. When we find that name, we will realize that nothing is, as yet, decided.[2]

YO (reading from Yusser al Obaidi, Dear Barzakhiya): I think this is why I was attracted to the idea of the *barzakh* and why I feel myself so deeply to be a *Barzakhiya*. It's about inhabiting the difference. Making it cozy to be in difference. Having spaces where paradoxicality is actually a form of knowledge. Like in the *barzakh*, where all the unmanifested potential lies. Where metaphors and myths and dreams hang out together. And where we go when we imagine those. The realm we access then. I think my aim is to invite us there. That's what I'm trying to do with my work, to let you enter into the world that exists between the lines. The extratextual reality that is accessed. That is felt. That is actually so hard to talk about. I think it's really hard for me to know how to have a conversation about this actually. And it feels dangerous. Because I don't want to slip into it forever. I also want to talk about reality. The reality of struggle.[3]

LO: Some call that an escape from the misery of the day,
'utopia'
becomes a retreat, or another map for the future
but I want the full story suspended in impossibility
dripping with conjured things,
information *in media res*
And in place of data there would only be stuff to
make more of that good stuff,
no maps—no coordinates, or roots, only a
pattern of intensity that responds to the skin on
our fingertips, a pattern that changes every 10 minutes.
I want facts to curdle. That's a spoiled substance
we could use.
I want knowledge you can sit a while in,

knowledge that won't expel you for pontificating
knowledge that knows there is no certitude
in a political economy that wants you dead or worked to
death or alive but not really here, or banished, or picking
off scraps, or preoccupied with the violence done
unto you—so hurt you find it hard to breathe whilst drowning
in a bed of your tears, so alienated you look at yourself
and say 'who is that?'—or sectioned, or having a heart
attack, aged forty-six, or flesh blown to smithereens, or
living in the shadow of an assassinated martyr, or earning
your breakfast, lunch and dinner, or going hungry so your
kids eat, or rotting in a flat somewhere, or trapped by
something as arbitrary as a border. Sorry, *if the fantastic
seems appealing*. We're alive there.[4]

4. Olufemi (n 2) 124.

5. Al Obaidi (n 3).

6. Olufemi (n 2) 34.

YO: I think poetry is a method. A way of writing. But also a way of being that I need to be and stay close to. I would like to free poetics from the discipline of poetry. To claim poetics without claiming poet. I have never felt comfortable or confident with the label poet. I think there are poetic ways of seeing which transcend the functions of our eyes, that require us whole, present, in the world in order to conjure up an arrangement of words in the same way that you would pick and create a flower arrangement. I say you here, but I realize not everyone picks their flowers with the same care. You need to be a flower lover for that. And so you need to be a lover to be poetic too. You need to stir and be able to be stirred. Something needs to move in you in order for you to move. Liberating sense in one way and reconfining it in another. Doing that again and again to uncover more and more meaning and beauty and tiny layers (maybe in the form of flakes?) of the world. Creating endless new confinements creates endless configurations in which liberation accumulates. There is so much to be liberated from. There are so many barriers, earthly hijabs which separate us from connecting. Truly connecting is what دِين is about. Working towards that is political. The love for liberation is poetic. Poetics is the love for liberation.[5]

LO: Revolutionary movements require a teleological pool from which to draw. The imagination is that teleological pool: it not only creates liberatory drives; it sustains, justifies and legitimizes them. It undoes entire epistemes and clears a space for us to create something new. Though this 'newness', or the demand for *something else*, can never be fully realized in the realm of the discursive, it exists in other registers: it can be felt, heard, touched, tasted. The structural limits of this world restrict our ability to articulate all that the imagination is capable of conceiving. Do not forget this.[6]

To those of us who relate to contamination or post contamination or however you want to say it.

YO: Through poetics you give a taste, not an answer nor an argument. It is a self aware performative enactment. A way of seeing and being and becoming. It is not presenting itself as a being itself. It is a logic which unleashes another logic. A trajectory towards a trajectory. Call it whatever you want. Pluriverse is but one concept that we don't need to make dominant.[7]

> LO: The feminist imagination carves out a site of agency that forms the impetus for action. It has many purposes, but in this regard, it enables resistant acts to take place by dismantling hegemonic notions of what is permissible under current conditions. The imagination is central to the cultural production of revolutionary movements; its primary role is to signal *what could be*. *What could be* is a linguistic stand-in for a set of political, social and cultural demands, strategic aims, revolutionary longings. As such, it resists singular definition: It is an unwieldy phenomenon, and its currency is chaos. It is an unwieldy phenomenon, and its currency is chaos.[8]

YO: This is not a secular rational closed system of sensing that I am trying to argue for and put forward here. You do not have to be convinced, but come join me here in the building if you'd like? Come join me here in sensing, in being receptive anyways? Come join me here in imagining? Let's be *Barzakhiyaat* together? This is not an empty framework, but neither is it a singular one. Come, build here with—alongside us?[9]

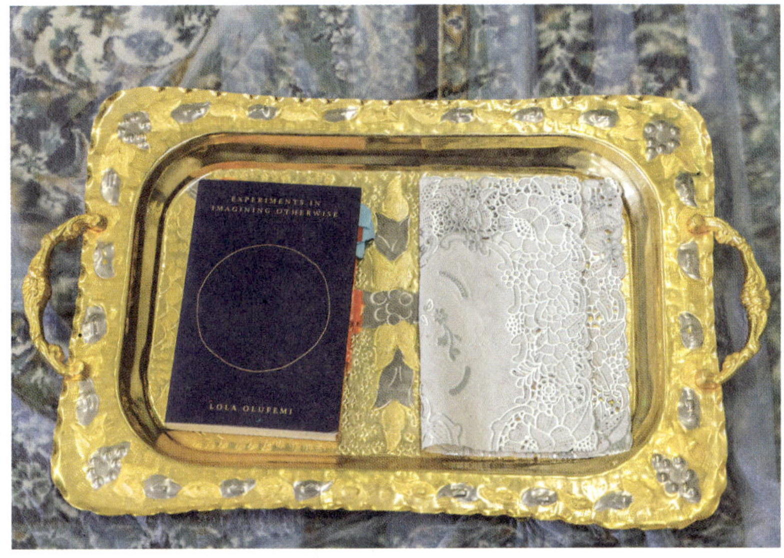

7. Al Obaidi (n 3).

8. Olufemi (n 2) 35.

9. Al Obaidi (n 3).

LO: Thank you. I was thinking, when you were reading, about Glissant's *Poetics of Relation*, and thinking about, I guess, the importance of interdependence in both of our works. I think in both things we've just read, there's this thread running through that's concerned with connectivity, with the ability to see and be with each other, meaningfully. I wondered what you thought about interdependence because I think about it as this way for us to be able to collectively express a set of wishes, desires, wants, or needs that do justice to the lives that we want to live, and also help us express our political demands as a collective voice. So yeah, what do you think about that?

YO: I think it shows that writing itself is also interdependent. Writing is not an act that you do on your own. You're continually in conversation with other texts. That's what I like about doing this experiment together. I think that interdependence becomes clearer in struggle. You really need it. That's the strength of more disenfranchised communities. It is really evident there, how much you need each other, how much you depend on each other. When you climb the [financial] ladder, you start to have this false idea that you're an individual, that there is no interdependence, or you don't need it as much, just because you're using your money to buy off interdependence.

LO: I hear you on that. One of the things that neoliberalism has managed to do really well, obviously, is fracture, alienate, to concentrate wealth, and really privatize and securitize the

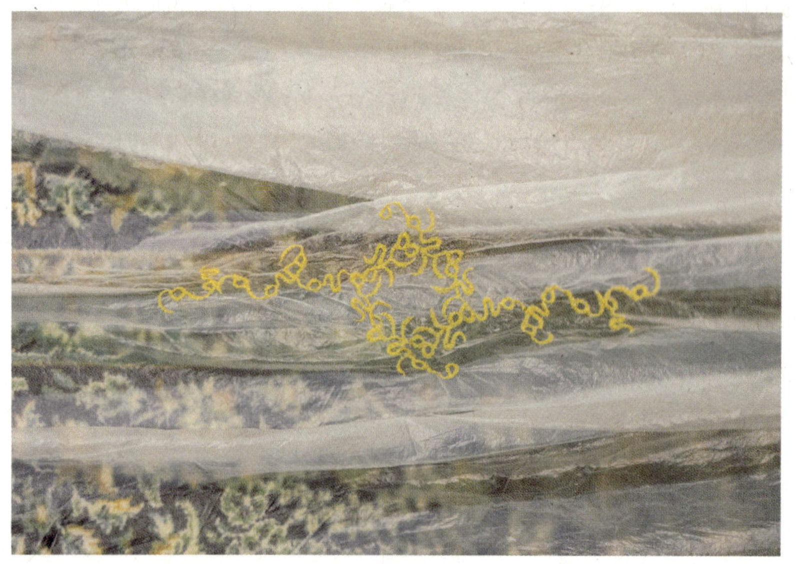

The biggest fear is to be incapacitated and without any support network.

ways that we relate to one another. And I was thinking about our conversation yesterday and what you were saying about difference and different texts meeting. Even our conceptualizations of the imagination–you are drawing from Islamic epistemologies, I am thinking about a Marxist framework or a materialist framework for imagining. Those two do meet in the realm of we're trying to give language to or trying to name through poetics, all the forcefield of relation. Basically, all these are currents and charges that fly through the air between individuals, in moments of political aspiration, or in moments of intimacy or in moments of care, both public and private. And I think that's also one of the great things that I love about the imagination as a concept that is inexhaustible. And so there are several layers to it, but also several ways that it might be articulated, expressed, engaged with and accessed. I think we both have an interest in cultural objects as one of those means of accessing. Right? I wondered if you wanted to talk a bit more about the place of objects or the place of sharing in your work or even the space that we're in now.

YO: Yeah. The space that we're sitting in now is an artwork that I created called سفرة دايمة [Sofreh Daimeh]. سفرة دايمة is a saying in Arabic, which means "may the سفرة [sofreh] persist." In Arabic, a سفرة is the spread of food as well as the cloth on which the food is presented. It's like a tablecloth, but you don't need a table for it. I think of this phrase as a poem that I'm inviting you to enter. When you're invited to have a meal at someone's house, after you finish the meal, you say: "سفرة دايمة." دايمة [daimeh] here means "may it always be so", and is related to the word دايمة [daimen] which means "always". Both words come from the root دوم [d-w-m]. So "سفرة دايمة" would mean "may you be able to continue hosting people in this manner with this abundance, may this live on and be forever." I think it says something about hospitality and the communities that we're from. That when people come over, you have this huge spread of food, no matter how little money you have. And the fact that abundance also exists within these communities. While, in the Dutch context, you're asked to leave as soon as it's time for dinner. The other interesting thing about the سفرة, especially this plastic سفرة, is that you can put it out in rows as long as the whole room. It's not like a table where there's a set dimension where there are only so many people you can invite to the table. It's ongoing. It's like this super thin plastic and you just roll it out. Even if you go outside, the whole world becomes the table. That's really interesting for me. And so I embroidered the plastic with gold threads with the letters دوم [d-w-m], with the root of the word دايمة [daimeh]. Arabic works with a root system. So it's دوم [d-w-m], which is embroidered as a pattern on this plastic سفرة.

LO: I think what you are describing is a kind of love ethic that has collaboration baked into it. Before we got out here, you asked me a really good question about being a materialist, or being a Marxist Communist and taking up the imagination, which has been theorized as this subjective, non-rational process and the tension between those two things. It makes me think of this idea that Moten and Harney expressed that forms of collaboration heighten your receptiveness to each other. For me, the imagination is one way of heightening forms of receptiveness to one another, but also trying to find a way to think about the present moment that we find ourselves and all the discourses that surround us about stasis and immobility. This feeling that we are stuck or that the present is kind of like drawn out. And the imagination for me, in trying to theorize that kind of materialist approach, is about trying to intervene in that discourse to say there are multiple alternatives. In order to think through the starkness of this present moment, we have to rethink time. We have to rethink the ways that we relate to each other. We must rethink history and forms of chronology and the stories that we tell each other about the movement of peoples or the movement of history, you know? That's something that always remains a tension as well. In my work, I'm trying to argue that the imagination is this substance, it can be made real. And if it can be made real, then it can be scaled up. Or if it's felt in a roomful of people, then it might be able to be accessed. I wondered what you thought about that.

YO: I'm wondering, the idea of mobilization/immobilization, how does that function with imagination? Because I feel like imagination, or the realm of imagination, it could go both ways, right? You can get stuck in there, you can fall into it. But it could also be something that you draw from. I wonder how you see that difference?

LO: I think in my work, and definitely in my writing, I turn away from the kind of escapist utopian understanding of the imagination, precisely because I'm trying to draw out a practical purpose. Or I'm trying to draw out a sense that the imagination is connected to necessary forms of action for the sake of our lives, for the sake of a different set of material conditions. And for me, my interest in it began because I was often in organizing spaces, or I was in rooms where I felt something that I couldn't quite articulate. Or when I was trying to write about it, I was kind of grasping at something. When we would

There are always pockets of hope that help make sense and meaning of it.

come together, and we would decide, “Okay, we're going to do this action, or we're going to make this decision,” that it felt like a kind of potentiality was somewhere in the air, moving through people. I could look at people that otherwise really annoyed me, and in that space be like, “Okay, no, you understand. You see me as a political actor, and I'm seeing you as a political actor at this moment. And we're going to work towards a common goal.” And I got that same feeling when I went into the archive and was looking at the material forms of anti-racist and feminist organizing groups, and reading that material and thinking, "Oh, this feels familiar, it feels like someone I know wrote it or it feels like I could write it or it feels like somebody in my family wrote it." And what's that? What's that kind of temporal blowback or loop that I'm feeling, even though I'm 20 years removed from this thing? And I guess I wanted to, in my work, take that seriously. To say that our affective landscapes and the structures that we give to feeling are really important because we act precisely because we feel. If you feel permissible, you with your body, then you with your relation make other things more permissible. And where I felt it was really undertheorized, I thought: okay, what's often seen as feminine or feminist, to think about feeling and affect and movement, is actually crucial to defeating this idea that nothing can be done.

YO: What I'm hearing is that it's about using imagination as a faculty or using imagination as something that is real. Not

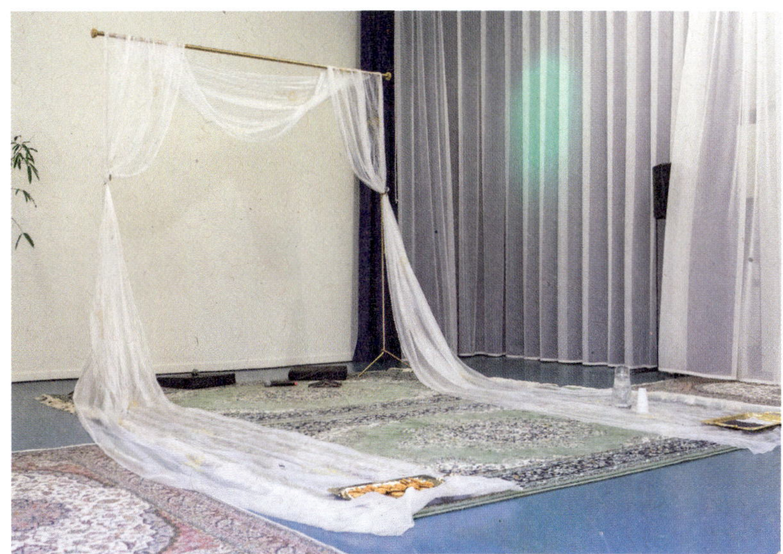

as fantasy, but as a faculty, an understanding and getting to knowledge through that. And getting to a knowledge that is more than just textual. A knowledge that is in the air.

LO: Yes. The working definition I use of the imagination is a process that brings that which does not previously exist into being. And it's purposefully vague and broad because so many people have theorized the cognitive realm of the imagination, or the creative realm of the imagination, or the political realm, blah, blah. And for me, it's all about movement and flexibility and contingency, which is why I think it comes most naturally to me to think through imagination using language. Because I think that with language you can represent that flexibility, or that contingency. Or you can say this, and you can capture this thing exactly. And you can leave yourself a note and then pick it back up. You can admit to your reader, "I'm not really quite sure, but this is how it feels." You can make it into fiction, you can put it in a story and play around with it there. And I think in my book *Experiments in Imagining Otherwise*, that's what I was really doing. I had all these textual fragments and experiments but I wanted them all to be anchored by a story in which I took up the concerns of my research which are revolution or temporality. There's a story in the book where one of the characters is just being plopped in different major historical events. And she doesn't really know what to do. And she's seeing how that kind of unfolds. I feel that language has a kind of texture.

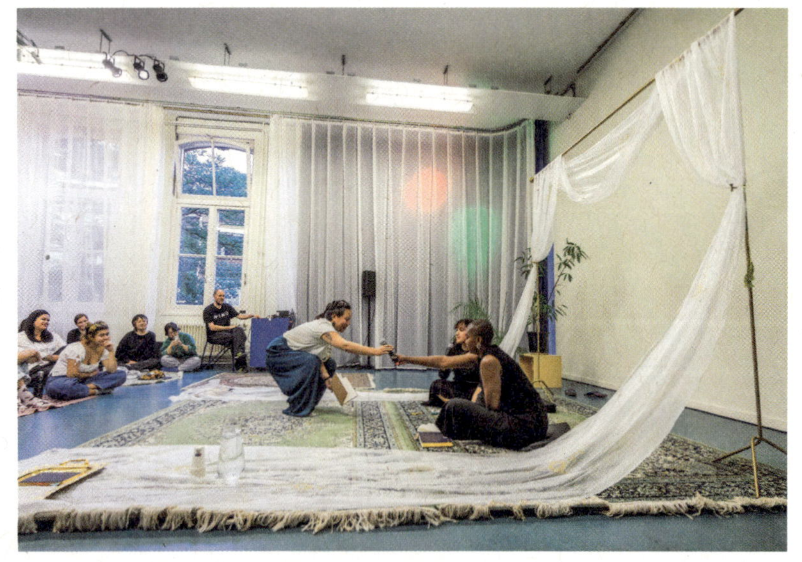

It's just the strangeness of distance and not knowing what to do.

It adds a new texture to the way that we move through the world. And so that's why I think I go there.

YO: I'm also thinking back to the definition of imagination that I use. It's not just a definition, but it's a way of seeing rooted in an Islamic framework. Specifically the one by Ibn Arabi, who's an Andalusian mystic, a Sufi mystic. His Islamic definition of 'imagination' is that imagination is a faculty, but also a realm. There's also a realm of imagination. And that's the *barzakh* that I've been talking about. This realm of imagination contains all possibilities. It's a realm that differentiates the spiritual [unmanifest] and the materialized [manifest]. At the same time, by differentiating, it's uniting them. It becomes this space of paradoxes and metaphors. For me, it's so powerful to think about difference and the space of difference as the space of imagination. Thinking of it as a space of difference but at the same time unity, of this space of paradoxes. Because it's through the lens of imagination, through the process of imagining, that you can understand how paradoxes are so very real. It's this pool that you can draw from. It's this space containing everything that exists but is not yet manifested. All potentiality lies in this realm. There is a collective framework that takes this into account, that sees this realm of imagination as something that's part of reality, and not a fantasy. Not just reserved to theory writers who don't relate to this world. It does relate to this world. And it's how we create. We need this realm of imagination to create alternatives, and to imagine an otherwise.

LO: And, I think discourse is really important. What we say about a particular moment, defines the structure of feeling of that moment. And so, in creating new interventions, we're not necessarily trying to use the imagination to come up with different forms of language. I think that one of the roles is to attempt to denaturalize what is otherwise an incredibly alienating experience of life. Like the requirement for you to sell your labor for a wage, that there are so many wars, that deportations are processed all around us. All the misery of our current political conditions. Often, they are naturalized and normal so that it's really nothing for you to see suffering, or to turn your back, or to not assume responsibility for the other people around you. Because you feel so alienated by forms of difference, or because you've been taught that under a specific form of government or social order that those people have nothing to do with you. Just to bring it back to a kind of microcosm, I'm always thinking about my home city of London, in the very carceral landscape that I exist in. I'm constantly seeing people get stopped and searched, illegally, all the time. And I'm part of all these kinds of Copwatch formations, grassroots autonomous formations, that are trying to get people to know their rights in terms of the police, but also de-arrest people. But I'm constantly struck by how many people turn their backs when they see that happening or don't intervene. And it's not only because they don't know what to do. It's more because they think of that person who is being harassed or being stalked or being detained as somehow different from them, rather than completely interdependent. Rather than this person's life depends on mine and mine depends on that person. And that is what would make you assume a kind of responsibility that would force you to intervene, right? It would force you to say, "I can't abide by forms of suffering or forms of violence," and that would galvanize you to go on and do other sorts of things. The way I think about the imagination is so often expressed in those kinds of small moments and thinking about all of the steps that go before the thought or the feeling. What are those forces that create the conditions for a particular feeling to emerge? Or a particular thought to emerge? And how do you change that? How do you go about introducing potentiality into an otherwise very squalid landscape?

YO: You're also touching upon what I think are the myths that we have around us. The myths that we believe in, that people believe in, that are stopping us from seeing this very real interdependence. There's a lot of these ideas about what it means to exist and what it means to be. What our entity is. Just the whole idea of seeing yourself as an I, and not seeing that interdependence when you're walking by. That is also formed by a form of myth that we are inhabiting. I think that's also where the power lies in imagination; in creating these new—maybe myths is not the right word—these new stories to inhabit. Stories that offer us or push us to create a new world, different worlds. Maybe not even new. Maybe the world that we want to inhabit has been there already.

LO: It makes me think about how different people engage with *Experiments in Imagining Otherwise*. Often, I get questions about, "Oh, your work is really optimistic." And I don't really think that's true. I guess I don't really believe in optimism. I believe in political determination. Saidiya Hartman said this thing about optimism and hope being too facile to deal with the seriousness of the given. And I think about that a lot. I guess what I should say is the way that hope and discourses of optimism are operationalized by states and by liberal

Thanks everybody for sharing.

democracies. Meaning, they are telling you in the face of all manner of violence to have hope in the state or in the flag or in the prison or in these means of protection. And I feel the imagination is so tied into forms of political determination because it orientates you against that. And I think as a concept, it's a bit stronger, because determination can be tested, it can be tried. You can still despair and be determined, but I don't know whether you can be an optimist and despair.

YO: Or you can be an optimist and read the news.

LO: Or I think optimism often points you back to [the] liberal universal. So, the idea of 'human' or the idea of kindness as a political virtue. Sometimes you need something stronger. I think you need to be much more strategic, especially in different landscapes where the state is literally at war with people. Kindness, hope, they don't really do much in that.

YO: It feels wrong to tell people to still have hope, especially to people that have lost so much. What are you doing then? You're not actually looking at their reality. And that's where determination, political determination, does something. Okay, things are shit but we can still do something. Whereas hope; it feels immobile. It is immobilizing in a way. It feels like something that you do on your own, you hope. But it could also be something you do collectively?

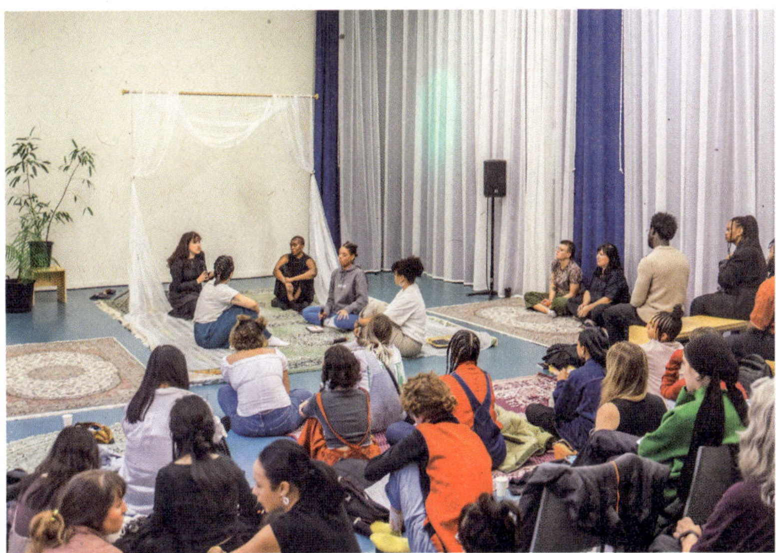

LO: I guess that's how I theorize so much of the imagination in my work, as collective and as access through creative means but also through dialogue and collaboration. One can have an individual conceptualization of what the imagination is but it can't be sparked unless you're with others, in the presence of others. It's in being witnessed, in talking, in disagreeing, in agreeing, in sharing, laughter, love, all these things. That spark of imagination is released into the air, for want of a better phrase. I think it's very hard to imagine a liberated future alone, because you need other people to say, "Well, haven't you thought about how x y z work?" What's the machinery of x y z? You need that. Those relationships.

YO: *Having said that, maybe someone wants to join the conversation?*

Take care. Bye bye.

Writing prompts from an experimental writing workshop by Lola Olufemi for 3rd year Bachelor students in the Social Practices Cultural Diversity study programme at the Willem de Kooning Academy, Thursday, 21st September 2023.

Lola Olufemi's Writing Prompts:

Make a list of all the things that suppress, exhaust, tire, alienate or suppress you. Find a way to write back at that list.

Write a story about entering a place where freedom is using the collective we.

Using poetry or a manifesto, write about the future. Write what it looks like, smells like, sounds like. Write about how people are organizing.

How is
your energy?

How is
your breathing?

Gratitude

We give gratitude to those who cook the food, serve our meals, clean the toilets, sweep the floors and turn on the lights, fix our computers, turn the soil and water the plants, tend to sick children and vulnerable bodies, lend an attentive ear to grievances and pain, clean and fix the streets, make the beds, wash the clothes, run the trains and buses, teach and mentor, do the laundry, protest, organize, strike, fill out excel spreadsheets, write, read, and send endless emails. We offer our thanks to those who came before, whose names are unknown and unsung but were pivotal in their attentiveness, to those whose histories and labor laid divergent pathways, to those who held silence and space in anticipation of the yet-to-be, to those who bore witness, and to those who listened, extended grace, wisdom, and patience, and to all the countless hours of unseen labor that contributed to the making of this book.

Bibliography

Act Up. *ACT UP Oral History Project*. 2002-2015. https://actuporal history.org/.
Adele. *Hello*. 2015.
Adnan, Etel. *Of Cities and Women*. Sausalito CA: The Post-Apollo Press, 1993.
Adusei-Poku, Nana, Iris Schutten, Roger Teeuwen, and Peter Troxler. "Social Design as a Political Act: Position Paper Social Practices WdKA." *Beyond Social*. 2017. https://beyond-social.org/wiki/index.php/Social_Design_as_a_Political_Act.
Ahenakew, Cash. *Towards Scarring: Our Collective Soul Wound*. Guelph: Musagetes, 2019.
Ahmed, Sara. *The Promise of Happiness*. Durham NC: Duke University Press, 2010.
———. *Living a Feminist Life*. Durham NC: Duke University Press, 2017.
Akomolafe, Bayo. *These Wilds Beyond Our Fences: Letters to My Daughter On Humanity's Search For Home*. Berkeley: North Atlantic Books, 2017.
Alexander, Jacqui. *Pedagogies of Crossing*. Durham NC: Duke University Press, 2006.
Archuleta, David. *Touch My Hand*. 2008.
Artomity, no. 10, (Autumn 2018).
———, no. 12, (Spring 2019).
———, no. 13, (Summer 2018).
———, no. 14, (Autumn 2019).
Ashwin, Paul. *Transforming University Education: A Manifesto*. London: Bloomsbury Academic, 2020.
Backstreet Boys. *Shape Of My Heart*. 2000.
BAK, Ultradependent Public School. https://www.bakonline.org/program-item/ultradependent-public-school-2/.
Banerjee, Samiran, and Marcel G. A. van der Heijden. "Soil Microbiomes and One Health." *Nat Rev Microbiol* 21 (2023). https://doi.org/10.1038/s41579-022-00779-w.
Bartholomew, Rafe. *Pacific Rims*. New York: Penguin Random House, 2011.
Bashier, Salman H. *Ibn al-'Arabi's Barzakh*. Albany NY: State University of New York Press, 2004.
The Beatles. *Ticket To Ride*. 1965.
Bednarek, Steffi. "Climate Change, Fragmentation and Collective Trauma. Bridging the Divided Stories We Live By." *Future Foundation*. https://futuref.org/climate_change_fragmentation_and_collective_trauma_en.

bergman, carla, and Nick Montgomery. *Joyful Militancy: Building Thriving Resistance in Toxic Times*. Oakland: AK Press, 2017.

Bhattacharyya, Gargi. *We, The Heartbroken*. London: Hajar Press, 2023.

Bibi Sheik, Zuleika. *Liminagraphy: Lessons in Life-affirming Research Practices for Collective Liberation*. 2021. Erasmus University Rotterdam. PhD dissertation.

Biss, Eula. *On Immunity: An Inoculation*. Minneapolis MN: Graywolf Press, 2015.

Bossé, Laurence, Suzanne Pagé, Claire Staebler, and Philip Tinari, eds. *Bentu: Chinese Artists in a Time of Turbulence and Transformation*. Paris: Editions Hazan/Foundation Louis Vuitton, 2016. Exhibition catalogue.

Boulanger, Agathe, Signe Frederiksen, and Jules Lagrange. *Ce que Laurence Rassel Nous Fait Faire*. Paris: Paraguay Press, 2020.

Braidotti, Rosi. “On Putting the Active Back into Activism.” *New Formations: A Journal of Culture/Theory/Politics*, Special Issue: ‘Deleuzian Politics?’, no. 68, (2009).

brown, adrienne maree. *Emergent Strategy*. Chico CA: AK Press, 2017.

Butler, Octavia E. *Parable of the Sower*. New York: Grand Central Publishing, 1993.

The Care Collective. “COVID-19 Pandemic: A Crisis of Care.” *Verso*. March 26, 2020. https://www.versobooks.com/en-gb/blogs/news/4617-covid-19-pandemic-a-crisis-of-care#_edn1.

———. *The Care Manifesto: The Politics of Interdependence*. London: Verso, 2020.

Carey, Mariah. *Touch My Body*. 2008.

The Carpenters. *Top Of The World*. 1972.

cassandra johnson, michelle. *Finding Refuge: Heart Work for Healing Collective Grief*. Boulder: Shambhala Publications, Inc., 2021.

Castro, Jade. *Zombadings and the Curse of the Zombadings*. 2011.

Castro-Gómez, Santiago. *Zero-Point Hubris*. Lanham MD: Rowman & Littlefield Publishers, 2021.

Centers for Disease Control and Prevention. *Antimicrobial-Resistant Aspergillus*. Accessed December 27, 2022. https://www.cdc.gov/fungal/diseases/aspergillosis/antifungal-resistant.html.

Césaire, Aimé. *Lyric and Dramatic Poetry, 1946-82*. Translated by Clayton Eshleman and Annette Smith. Charlottesville: University Press of Virginia, 1990.

Cher. *Believe*. 1998.

Chittick, William C. *Imaginal Worlds: Ibn al-'Arabi and the Problem of Religious Diversity*. Albany NY: State University of New York Press, 1994.

Chong, Heman, and Melissa Lim. *The Sole Proprietor and Other Stories*. Guangzhou: Vitamin Creative Space, 2007.

Cmiel, Kenneth, and John Durham Peters. *Promiscuous Knowledge:*

Information, Image, and Other Truth Games in History. Chicago: University of Chicago Press, 2020.

Cowden, Stephen, and Gurnam Singh. *Acts of Knowing: Critical Pedagogy In, Against, and Beyond the University*. London: Bloomsbury Academic, 2013.

Cox, Nicole, and Sylvia Federici. *Counter-planning from the Kitchen: Wages for Housework, A Perspective on Capital and the Left*. New York: Wages for Housework Committee and Falling Wall Press, 1975.

Cree, Laura Murray. *Ai Weiwei—Under Construction*. Sydney: University of New South Wales Press, 2009.

Crump, Sage, Mia Herndon, and adrienne maree brown. “Radical Grievance with Malkia Devich-Cyril.” *The Emergent Strategy Podcast*. June 2022. https://open.spotify.com/episode/1AjW8v05FwDVuqC0Z6c5XJ.

Dawei, Fei. *Cai Guo-Qiang*. Paris: Publication Fondation Cartier pour l’art contemporain, 2000.

DeLoughrey, Elizabeth M., and George B. Handley. *Postcolonial Ecologies: Literatures of the Environment*. New York: Oxford University Press USA, 2011.

Desireless. *Voyage Voyage*. 1989.

Devich-Cyril, Malkia. "To Give Your Hands To Freedom, First Give Them To Grief." *Holding Change: The Way of Emergent Strategy Facilitation and Mediation*. Edited by adrienne maree brown. Chico: AK Press, 2021.

Diaz, Robert. “The Limits of Bakla and Gay: Feminist Readings of *My Husband’s Lover*, Vice Ganda, and Charice Pempengco.” *The University of Chicago Press Journals* 40, no. 3 (Spring 2015). https://doi.org/10.1086/679526.

The Doors. *Touch Me*. 1969.

Edjabe, Ntone. *FESTAC ’77: 2nd World Black and African Festival of Arts and Culture*. London: Afterall Books and Chimurenga, 2019.

84 Steps. https://www.kunstinstituutmelly.nl/en/experience/29-84-steps.

El-Zein, Amira. *Islam, Arabs, and the Intelligent World of the Jinn*. Syracuse NY: Syracuse University Press, 2009.

Escher, Joris, and Martijn Kielstra. *The Selected Scriptures of Hong Hao*. Amsterdam: Canvas Foundation, 1999.

Fanon, Frantz. *Black Skin, White Masks*. Translated by Charles Lam Markmann. London: Pluto Press, 1986.

Federici, Silvia. *Caliban and the Witch: Women, the Body, and Primitive Accumulation*. London: Penguin Classics, 2021.

Fisher, Mark. “Reflexive Impotence.” *K-punk*. April 11, 2006. https://www.k-punk.abstractdynamics.org/archives/007656.html.

Fleury, Cynthia. *Le soin est un humanisme*. Paris: Gallimard, 2019.

———. “Mot Clé.” *L’humanité*. March 2019. https://www.humanite.fr/mot-cle/cynthia-fleury.

Fleury, Cynthia, and Antoine Fenoglio. *Ce qui ne peut être volé: Charte du Verstohlen*. Paris: Gallimard, 2022.

Fokianaki, iLiana, and Laura Raicovich. "The Role of Ideology in Institutions: iLiana Fokianaki and Laura Raicovich." *E-flux Podcast*. February 2020. https://www.e-flux.com/podcasts/407862/the-role-of-ideology-in-institutions-iliana-fokianaki-and-laura-raicovich.

Fokianaki, iLiana. "The Bureau of Care: Introductory Notes on the Care-less and Care-full." *E-flux*. November 2020. https://www.e-flux.com/journal/113/359463/the-bureau-of-care-introductory-notes-on-the-care-less-and-care-full/.

———. *Bureau of Care*. 2020-present. http://thebureauofcare.org/.

freethought collective. *Spectral Infrastructure*. 2020-2022. https://www.bakonline.org/long-term-project/spectral-infrastructure/.

Fremeaux, Isabelle, and Jay Jordan. *We are 'Nature' Defending Itself: Entangling Art, Activism and Autonomous Zones*. London: Pluto Press/Journal of Aesthetics & Protest, 2021.

Gannon, Kevin M. *Radical Hope: A Teaching Manifesto*. Morgantown WV: West Virginia University Press, 2020.

Garcia, J. Neil C. *Philippine Gay Culture*. Hong Kong: Hong Kong University Press, 1996.

———. "Male Homosexuality In The Philippines: A Short History." *International Institute for Asian Studies* (2020). https://www.iias.asia/sites/default/files/2020-11/IIAS_NL35_13.pdf.

Gesturing Towards Decolonial Futures Collective. "Education 2048 Version 2." *Gesturing Towards Decolonial Futures*. https://decolonialfutures.net/portfolio/education-2048-v2/.

Glissant, Édouard. *Poetics of Relation*. Ann Arbor MI: University of Michigan Press, 1997.

Gonzales Tirona, Ciara Mae. *The Impact of Colonial Beauty Standards in the Ethnic Identity and Mental Health of Filipino Americans*. 2023. San Francisco University. Master dissertation.

Gran Fury. *Street Poster Campaign*. New York City, 1987-1995.

Guo-Qiang, Cai. *Hanging Out in the Museum*. Taipei: Taipei Fine Arts Museum, 2010.

Haraway, Donna. "Situated Knowledges: The Science Question in Feminism and the Privilege of Partial Perspective." *Feminist Studies* 14, no. 3 (Autumn 1988).

———. *Staying with the Trouble: Making Kin in the Chthulucene*. Durham: Duke University Press, 2016.

Hardt, Michael, and Antonio Negri. *Empire*. Cambridge: Harvard University Press, 2000.

Harney, Stefano, and Fred Moten. *The Undercommons: Fugitive Planning & Black Study*. Colchester UK: Minor Compositions, 2013.

2003 Hermes Foundation Missulsang. Seoul: Artsonje Center September 27-May 15, 2003. Exhibition catalogue.

2008 Hermes Foundation Missulsang. Seoul: Artsonje Center 2008. Exhibition catalogue.

Hersey, Tricia. *Rest Is Resistance*. London: Little Brown Spark, 2022.

Hill, Dan. *Sometimes When We Touch*. 1977.

hooks, bell. “CHOOSING THE MARGIN AS A SPACE OF RADICAL OPENNESS.” *Framework: The Journal of Cinema and Media*, no. 36 (1989). http://www.jstor.org/stable/44111660.

Imprint of the Heart: Artistic Journey of Huang Xinbo. Hong Kong: Leisure and Cultural Services Department, 2011. Exhibition catalogue.

Ingold, Tim. *Making: Anthropology, Archaeology, Art and Architecture*. London: Routledge, 2013.

Isabella, Brigitta, and Rieneke de Vries. “We Sell Reality? Who Are ‘We’ and What Do We Mean by ‘Reality’?” *Art for (and within) a Citizen Scene: A Look at Art Primarily Active in the Context of Daily Practices*. Edited by Iris Ferrer, Emily Shin-Jie Lee, reinaart vanhoe, and Julia Wilhelm. Eindhoven: Onomatopee, 2022.

Jaama, Sumia, and Michelle Teran, et al. *In Search of Otherwise: (A)positional Paper Social Practices*. Research Center WdKA. 2022. https://research.wdka.nl/index.php/news-activities/in-search-of-otherwise-apositional-paper-social-practices/.

Jaucian, Don. *Brief Histories*. Manila: Everything’s Fine, 2022.

Jaya. *Wala Na Bang Pag-ibig*. 2000.

John, Elton. *This Train Don't Stop There Anymore*. 2001.

Joy. *Touch By Touch*. 1986.

Kincaid, Jamaica. *My Garden (Book)*. London: Vintage, 1999.

———. “The Disturbances of the Garden.” *The New Yorker* (August 30, 2020).

Klein, Naomi. *The Shock Doctrine: The Rise of Disaster Capitalism*. Picador, 2008.

Kosofsky Sedgwick, Eve. *Touching Feeling: Affect, Pedagogy, Performativity*. Durham NC: Duke University Press, 2004.

Köseoğlu, Çağlar. “Onze Liefde is Terroristisch.” *DIG (De Internet Gids)* (December 12, 2023). https://www.de-internet-gids.nl/artikelen/onze-liefde-is-terroristisch.

Laderman Ukeles, Mierle. *MANIFESTO FOR MAINTENANCE ART, 1969!* https://queensmuseum.org/wp-content/uploads/2016/04/Ukeles-Manifesto-for-Maintenance-Art-1969.pdf.

Lapita, Celeste, and Kaj Palanca. *Contestant #4*, 2016.

Latin 251 Class of Colby College 2022. “Weaving and Writing: Censorship in Arachne.” *Ovid and the Censored Voice*. Edited by Kerill O’Neill. https://web.colby.edu/ovid-censorship/censorship-in-ovids-myths/weaving-and-writing-censorship-in-arachne/.

Le Guin, Ursula K. *The Carrier Bag Theory of Fiction*. 1986. https://www.anarchistfederation.net/ursula-k-le-guin-the-carrier-bag-

theory-of-fiction/#/.
The Little Mermaid. *Part Of Your World*. 1989.
Liwen Deng, Zoénie. *Be Water, My Friend: Non-Oppositional Criticalities of Socially Engaged Art in Urbanising China*. 2020. University of Amsterdam. PhD dissertation.
Liwen Deng, Zoénie, and Elaine W. Ho. "Strolling South: Reflecting on Our Institutionalisations & Otherwise Collectivity." *Art for (and within) a Citizen Scene: A Look at Art Primarily Active in the Context of Daily Practices*. Edited by Iris Ferrer, Emily Shin-Jie Lee, reinaart vanhoe, and Julia Wilhelm. Eindhoven: Onomatopee, 2022.
Lorde, Audre. *When I Dare to Be Powerful: Women so Empowered are Dangerous*. London: Penguin Books, 2020.
———. *Your Silence Will Not Protect You*. London: Silver Press, UK, 2017.
Macfarlane, Robert. *Landmarks*. London: Penguin Books, 2016.
Machado de Oliveira, Vanessa. *Hospicing Modernity: Facing Humanity's Wrongs and the Implications for Social Activism*. Berkeley: North Atlantic Books, 2021.
Macy, Joanna, and Chris Johnstone. *Active Hope: How to Face the Mess We're in with Unexpected Resilience and Creative Power*. Novato, CA: New World Library, 2022.
Madonna. *Ray Of Light*. 1998.
Maldonado-Torres, Nelson. *Against War: Views from the Underside of Modernity*. Durham NC: Duke University Press, 2008.
Martis, Alfrida, and Ali Şahin. *We Have to Change: Advisory Report by the Office for Inclusivity on the State of Equity, Diversity and Inclusivity at WdKA*. Rotterdam: Willem de Kooning Academy, 2022.
Marya, Rupa, and Raj Patel. *Inflamed: Deep Medicine and the Anatomy of Injustice*. London: Penguin Books, 2021.
Maturana, Humberto, and Francisco Varela. *Autopoiesis and Cognition: The Realization of the Living*. Dordrecht NL: D. Reidel Publishing, 1980.
Maule-O'Brien, Skye. *Intimate Pedagogy: Visual Explorations of Race and the Erotic*. 2021. York University. PhD dissertation.
Mbembe, Achille. "Bodies as Borders." *From the European South*, no. 4 (2019).
McKittrick, Katherine. *Sylvia Wynter: On Being Human as Praxis*. Durham NC: Duke University Press, 2015.
Menakem, Resmaa. *My Grandmother's Hands: Racialized Trauma and the Pathway to Mending Our Hearts and Bodies*. London: Penguin UK, 2021.
Michiochi, Ross. "Episode 119: Michelle Cassandra Johnson—Finding Refuge Healing Collective Grief." *Banyen Books Branches of Wisdom*, November 2022. https://open.spotify.com/episode/5dAfZgHyJACfQ1IXs5us5T.

Mignolo, Walter, and Catherine E. Walsh. *On Decoloniality: Concepts, Analytics, Praxis*. Durham NC: Duke University Press, 2018.

Millner, Jacqueline. *Care Project Network*. https://www.careprojectnetwork.com/.

Munroe, Alexandra, and David Joselit. *Cai Guo-Qiang: I Want to Believe*. New York: Guggenheim Museum Publications, 2009.

Naval, Rodel. *Lumayo Ka Man Sa Akin*. 1991.

Nelson, Maggie. *On Freedom: Four Songs of Care and Constraint*. Minneapolis MN: Graywolf Press, 2022.

Olufemi, Lola. *Experiments in Imagining Otherwise*. London: Hajar Press, 2021.

Orientation. Yogyakarta: Cemeti Art Foundation, 1996. Exhibition catalogue.

Oury, Jean, Mauricio Novello, and David Reggio. "Jean Oury: The Hospital is Ill." *Radical Philosophy* 143 (May/June 2007). https://www.radicalphilosophy.com/interview/jean-oury-the-hospital-is-ill.

Ovid. *Metamorphoses: Book IV*. Translated by A. S. Kline. Poetry in Translation, 2020.

Park, Chankyong. *Ghosts, Spies, and Grandmothers: Modernities Against Modernity*. Seoul: Hyunsil Books/Seoul Museum of Art, 2014.

Peniston, Cece. *Finally*. 1991.

Peteet, Julie. "Closure's Temporality: The Cultural Politics of Time and Waiting." *The South Atlantic Quarterly* 117, no. 1 (2018).

Portes, Gil. *Markova: Comfort Gay*. 2001.

Povinelli, Elizabeth. "Geontologies of the Otherwise." *Society for Cultural Anthropology* (January 2014). https://culanth.org/fieldsights/geontologies-of-the-otherwise.

Puig de la Bellacasa, María. "Soil Times: The Pace of Ecological Care." *Solitude Journal* 1 (2017).

———. *Matters of Care: Speculative Ethics in More Than Human Worlds*. Minneapolis MN: University of Minnesota Press, 2017.

QT. *Hey QT*. 2014.

Quad City DJs. *Space Jam*. 1996.

Queen. *Bicycle Race*. 1978.

Reilly, Maggie. *Everytime We Touch*. 1992.

Robcis, Camille. *Disalienation: Politics, Philosophy, and Radical Psychiatry in Postwar France*. Chicago: University of Chicago Press, 2021.

Robles Lana, Jun. *Die Beautiful*. 2016.

———. *Kalel, 15*. 2019.

Rogoff, Irit. "From Criticism to Critique to Criticality." *Transversal Texts* (2003). https://transversal.at/pdf/journal-text/1364/.

———. "Smuggling'—An Embodied Criticality." *European Institute for Progressive Cultural Policies* (2006). https://eipcp.net/dlfiles/rogoff-smuggling.

———. “Infrastructure.” *Former West* keynote lecture. March 20, 2013. bak basis voor actuele kunst. https://formerwest.org/DocumentsConstellationsProspects/Contributions/Infrastructure.
Salih, Yusser. “Kom, behoor ook tot ons huishouden.” *nY tijdschrift voor literatuur, kunst & kritiek, studY*, no. 47 (March 2022).
Sandoval, Isabel. *Lingua Franco*. 2019.
Saraceno, Tomás. “3-Dimensional Digital Archive of Spider/Webs.” *Arachnophilia*. Accessed May 16, 2022. https://arachnophilia.net/scanning-the-web/.
———. “Vibrating with the Web.” *Arachnophilia*. Accessed May 28, 2022. https://arachnophilia.net/sonifying-the-web/.
Sayer, Emma J., John A. Crawford, James Edgerley, et al. “Adaptation to Chronic Drought Modifies Soil Microbial Community Responses to Phytohormones.” *Commun Biol* 4, 516 (2021). https://doi.org/10.1038/s42003-021-02037-w.
Schulman, Sarah. *Conflict is Not Abuse*. Vancouver: Arsenal Pulp Press, 2016.
———. *Let the Record Show: A Political History of ACT UP New York, 1987-1993*. New York: Picador / Farrar, Straus and Giroux, 2021.
Sheller, Mimi. *Citizenship from Below: Erotic Agency and Caribbean Freedom*. Durham NC: Duke University Press, 2012.
Shin-Jie Lee, Emily, and reinaart vanhoe. “A Warm Welcome.” *Art for (and within) a Citizen Scene: A Look at Art Primarily Active in the Context of Daily Practices*. Edited by Iris Ferrer, Emily Shin-Jie Lee, reinaart vanhoe, and Julia Wilhelm. Eindhoven: Onomatopee, 2022.
Sivan, Troye. *Angel Baby*. 2021.
Solito, Auraeous. *The Blossoming Of Maximo Oliveros*. 2005.
Solnit, Rebecca. *Mother of All Questions: Further Feminisms*. London: Granta, 2017.
Stengers, Isabelle. *Another Science Is Possible: A Manifesto for Slow Science*. Cambridge: Polity, 2018.
Tadiar, Carlo. *Kolboy: Denial, Disgust, and the Production of Value in Male Sex Work in the Philippines*. Quezon City: UP Press, 2021.
TLC. *Waterfalls*. 1994.
編集東京都現代美術館 and 東京都現代美術館 (henshū Tōkyō-to and Gendai Bijutsukan). Selected Works from Museum of Contemporary Art, Tokyo. Tokyo: 東京都現代美術館, 1995.
Tonkin TTC, Lois. “Growing Around Grief—Another Way of Looking at Grief and Recovery.” *Bereavement Care* 15, no. 1 (1996). DOI: 10.1080/02682629608657376.
Truman, Sarah E. *Feminist Speculations and the Practice of Research-Creation*. Oxfordshire UK: Routledge, 2021.
Tuck, Eve, and K. Wayne Yang. “Decolonization is Not a Metaphor.” *Decolonization: Indigeneity, Education & Society* 1, no. 1 (2012).
The Turtles. *Happy Together*. 1967.

Vázquez, Rolando. *Vistas of Modernity: Decolonial Aesthesis and the End of the Contemporary*. Amsterdam: Mondriaan Fund, 2020.

Velasco, David. "No Motive." *Weight of The Earth: The Tape Journals of David Wojnarowicz*. Edited by Lisa Darms and David O'Neill. South Pasadena CA: Semiotext(e), 2018.

Viva Hot Babes. *Basketbol*. 2004.

Wahab, Amar. *Colonial Inventions: Landscape, Power and Representation in Nineteenth-Century Trinidad*. Newcastle Upon Tyne UK: Cambridge Scholars Publishing, 2010.

Wall Kimmerer, Robin. *Braiding Sweetgrass: Indigenous Wisdom, Scientific Knowledge and the Teachings of Plants*. London: Penguin Books, 2013.

Walsh, Catherine E. "Decolonial Pedagogies Walking and Asking. Notes to Paulo Freire from AbyaYala." *International Journal of Lifelong Education* 34, no.1 (2015). DOI: 10.1080/02601370.2014.991522.

Weiwei, Ai, and Juliet Bingham. *Sunflower Seeds*. London: Tate Publishing, 2010.

Weiwei Ai, and Hans Ulrich Obrist. *Ai Weiwei Speaks: With Hans Ulrich Obrist*. London: Penguin House, 2011.

Weller, Francis. *The Wild Edge of Sorrow: Rituals of Renewal and the Sacred Work of Grief*. Berkeley: North Atlantic Books, 2015.

Whitmer, Barbara. *The Violence Mythos*. Albany: SUNY Press, 1997.

Wojnarowicz, David. *Close to the Knives: A Memoir of Disintegration*. New York: Knopf Doubleday Publishing Group, 1991.

Wynter, Sylvia. "Unsettling the Coloniality of Being/Power/Truth/Freedom: Towards the Human, After Man, Its Overrepresentation—An Argument." *CR: The New Centennial Review* 3, no. 3 (2003). http://www.jstor.org/stable/41949874.

Yarcia, Lee, Tesa de Vela, and Michael Tan. "Queer Identity and Gender-Related Rights in Post-Colonial Philippines." *Australian Journal of Asian Law* 20, no. 1 (November 17, 2019). https://ssrn.com/abstract=3488543.

Zsa Zsa Padilla. *Hiram*. 2002.

Zwartjes, Arianne. "Autotheory as Rebellion: On Research, Embodiment, and Imagination in Creative Nonfiction." *Michigan Quarterly Review* (July 2019). https://sites.lsa.umich.edu/mqr/2019/07/autotheory-as-rebellion-on-research-embodiment-and-imagination-in-creative-nonfiction/.

Contributors

Carla Arcos is a multidisciplinary artist, graphic designer, and organizer. In recent years, her practice has been committed to facilitating socially engaged spaces in order to foster community through making, reading, cooking, dancing, protesting, studying, and grieving. Much of her work is and has been devoted to SPIN, an artist and justice collective passionate about publishing. Their activities as a collective combine art, design, and activism.

Jacquill Basdew is a multi-talented artist and advocate, embracing inclusivity and empowerment in diverse spheres. Through his transformative artistic practice, *Yazija*, Basdew amplifies voices, including those of the LGBTQ+ community, fostering visibility and acceptance. As an Arts and Culture intermediary, he supports emerging talents, celebrating diversity and bridging gaps in the art world. With evocative writings, Basdew sheds light on unique identities, including queer experiences, fostering understanding and compassion. Passionate about connections and social progress, he inspires a more harmonious society, where every voice, regardless of background, finds its place. Basdew's dedication to promoting inclusivity stands as a testament to his commitment to creating a world where individuality thrives, enriching our collective experience.

Selma Bellal is quality coordinator at erg (école de recherche graphique) in Brussels. Trained in political science, Selma Bellal is interested in transformations of notions of equality and progress, and the mechanisms involved in the social construction of legitimate speech and legitimate violence.

Seecum Cheung is an artist, educator and filmmaker. Her manifold cinematic projects draw an explicit arc progressing from observational documentary toward experiential fiction, blurring the borders of subject, politics, and identity. Each work builds on comprehensive research, expert collaboration, oral history, and personal experience. Attentive consideration, enveloping soundscapes, and evocative editing techniques are some of her empathetic tools to articulate the meaningful agency of individuals. She teaches in Social Practices at Willem de Kooning Academy, Rotterdam NL; a professional director of photography in film; and a member of the ESEA artist collective *Sunday (fka Rising Buns)*. She studied at Piet Zwart Institute in Rotterdam.

Yoeri Guépin (he/him) is a visual artist, researcher and gardener. His projects are collaborative and oriented towards the long term involving experimental forms of care, working with embodied knowledge, intergenerational storytelling and ecosystems at the margins. Guépin holds an MA from the Dutch Art Institute and is currently a resident at the Jan Van Eyck Academy in Maastricht (2023-24). His work has been nominated for the Dolf Henkens Prize (2023) and exhibited at A Tale Of A Tub, TENT, Sharjah Biennale (2023) and Kadist San Francisco (2022).

Marc Herbst is a broadly interdisciplinary researcher, artist, editor/publisher and sometimes activist whose core experiences are built upon work on the *Journal of Aesthetics & Protest* that he co-founded in Los Angeles in 2001. His often collaborative, and often embedded practices are grounded by DIY social practice, and engage with social transformation oriented toward ecological and justice-based horizons. With Michelle Teran he developed a project around conflict resolution and dreaming, “To Sleep Together in Common, Which is Political”. He is currently interested in energy, entanglement and something like surrealism. He is a researcher at the Free University of Bozen-Bolzano in Italy, and also enjoys Leipzig, Germany.

Czar Kristoff P. is an artist, publisher and educator from Laguna, Philippines, interested in (re)construction of space, memory and identity, through concepts of nesting and temporary architecture, for (pedagogical) occupation. Cottage industry publishing—blueprints, xerox, and other low-fidelity printing methods—is his material realm. His work has been exhibited at the Stedelijk Museum, Foam Fotografiemuseum, BAK, Showroom MAMA, De Appel, Nieuwe Instituut (NL), Deutsche Börse Photography Foundation (DE), Jogja National Museum (ID), C3 Artspace (AUS), Bangkok Arts and Culture Center (TH), Vargas Museum and Cultural Center of the Philippines (PH). Kristoff is a recipient of the Foam Talent 2022 (NL), Thirteen Artist Award 2021 (PH) and Ateneo Art Award 2017 (PH). He runs Temporary UnReLearning (URL) Academy, a school with no permanent address, interested in queering the art and cultural production in the Philippines.

Cooking Something Up (Carla Arcos, Yusser al Obaidi, Freeke van der Sterren, Thao Tong, Julia Wilhelm) is a project centered around reproductive labor and care work. They want to politicize and make explicit these forms of labor. Intimacy is part of this process. Placing study within the realm of domestic work, how do you do that? How do you make connections explicit that study has always been within the domestic sphere? The collective organizes weekly dinners together, cooking for each other, and talking where they bring in their embodied and emotional experiences, and think about ways to do research in a way that acknowledges these things. They made a cookbook out of recipes inspired by dinners.

Pablo Lerma is a queer visual artist, publisher and educator in the Social Practices Department at Willem de Kooning Academy. His artistic research is developed at the intersection of image and text with a focus in visual archives and vernacular materials dealing with notions of collective memory, care, parenthood, visibility, representation and queerness. His work takes various forms from photographic installations to publications. He runs the publishing project Meteoro Editions dedicated to the publishing and exposure of vernacular photography, archives and archival practices through publication formats.

Judith Leijdekkers lives and works in Carnisse in Rotterdam South. Her work is on art, social work, gardening and anthropology, and is also related to education. The neighborhood is where she situates herself and her practice. She teaches gardening in schools. Through the garden you can speak about forms of care. You can also make connections between what's in the classroom and what is outside the classroom, and vice versa. She is thinking about gentrification processes, but also how one builds relationships in the neighborhood. She witnesses that certain forms of racism are mirrored by children. She completed the teacher trainer program at Willem de Kooning Academy and is now teaching within the MBO school system, by doing social work.

Carmen José is an illustrator, educator and activist interested in questioning the reproduction of visual stereotypes, with focus on embodied processes. In her work she aims to facilitate spaces for dialogue and coming together. Carmen is thinking about redefining care outside of capitalizing care. She teaches in Illustration and Social Practices at the Willem de Kooning Academy. She is also an illustrator, works with Feministas Rotterdam, and is currently preparing presentations on failure and success in relation to capitalisation and profit. Carmen has worked with neighbors in Growing Space Wielewaal, a condemned neighborhood that will be knocked down and rebuilt with unaffordable housing. In getting to know the neighborhood, in a highly conflicted place, she is aware that international artists are seen as highly problematic, and as a part of gentrification.

Edwin Mingard is a filmmaker and social practitioner whose award-winning films have garnered the support of The Guardian, Joseph Rowntree Foundation, Doc Society and the British Film Institute. His work has toured the festival and art exhibition circuits including IDFA, London Short Film Festival, Chisenhale Gallery and Aesthetica Art Prize. Mingard's work is a cinematic platform which places support and collaboration at the heart of its praxis. His films are a network of stories told from the margins of society, where collaborators (undocumented, homeless, or otherwise) are invited to create rich cinematic translations of their daily thoughts and experiences. By providing long-term committed support, equipment, training and guidance, Mingard generates a space for groups to share the stories of their lives through their own uniquely authored films.

Skye Maule-O'Brien is an educator and creative researcher that often works collaboratively, combining theory, narrative, and visual methods. Her practice of intimate pedagogy, explores intimacy and vulnerability as transformative pedagogical tools to promote social and environmental change. At Willem de Kooning Academy, she leads interdisciplinary pedagogical projects and decolonial shifts in curriculum and research. She comes to the care study group with trepidation, questioning what if I/we don't care or don't care enough? Can we still act with accountability without caring for the other on an individual scale? Or what if we don't have the capacity or resources to do so? Within these limits, she feels resistant to sentimental or harmonious ideals, assumptions, and demands to care. For her, promiscuous care and study is to act in relation. So even when I/we don't care or don't feel there is enough space to care, there is still connectivity and intimate learning happening.

Yusser al Obaidi is a decolonial feminist writer and designer who seeks to acknowledge and enable the radical potential of intimate relational spaces.

She graduated in the RASL Dual Degree Bachelor programme, in graphic design at Willem de Kooning Academy and political philosophy at Erasmus University College. Her practice revolves around intimate forms of publishing and the mobilization of alternative knowledge circulation patterns for writing that sits close to the skin. Her central concern: how can we affirm other ways of being/knowing?

Lola Olufemi is a black feminist writer and CREAM/Stuart Hall Foundation researcher from London. Her work focuses on the uses of the feminist imagination and its relationship to cultural production, political demands and futurity. She is the author of *Experiments in Imagining Otherwise* and *Feminism, Interrupted: Disrupting Power* and a member of 'bare minimum', an interdisciplinary anti-work arts collective.

Laurence Rassel is director of erg (école de recherche graphique) in Brussels. Trained in the visual arts, pedagogy, and the management of arts institutions, from 2008 to 2015 she was Director of Fundació Antoni Tàpies, Barcelona, an institution created in 1984 by the artist Antoni Tàpies to promote the study and knowledge of modern and contemporary art. From 1997 to 2008, Rassel was a member of Constant, a non-profit association and interdisciplinary arts-lab based and active in Brussels in the fields of art, media and technology.

Vivian Sky Rehberg's primary areas of practice have been shaped by lifelong encounters with artists, scholars, and creative practitioners, alongside the interdisciplinary study of modern and contemporary art. VSR has published widely on modern and contemporary art and was a contributing editor and freelance correspondent for Frieze magazine between 2006 and 2019. You'll find her work in the archives of existing and defunct magazines and online platforms (including Artforum, Art Agenda, Mousse, A Prior, e-flux criticism and e-flux journal), and between the covers of artist monographs, exhibition catalogs, and anthologies. She has spent the past two-decades in international higher art education, in combined teaching and leadership roles. She is currently Senior Research Lecturer at the Willem de Kooning Academy-Piet Zwart Institute in Rotterdam, and an associate of the Rotterdam Arts & Sciences Lab and the Research Centre WdKA. VSR has contributed to the visibility of issues in contemporary art and arts education by creating and participating in public programs in art academies, universities, art centers, and museums. VSR's current research focuses on relationships between art, the psyche, education, and wellbeing. This research not only informs the direction of her writing projects, it drives her investment in her roles and acts as an educator, mentor, colleague, and advocate-at-large for the arts and culture.

Reading Room Rotterdam is a nomadic roaming library traveling throughout the city on a cargo bike. The library functions as a gathering agent for communities to entangle with one another and for knowledge to be disseminated. Through public events and the library service, the RRR offers an exchange of mediums of knowledge, be it through shared dinners, workshops, gardens, or text.

Kari Robertson is an artist, educator and researcher. She currently lives and works in The Netherlands where she holds a teaching position in Social Practices at the

Willem de Kooning Academy, Rotterdam and is a research fellow at BAK, Utrecht. Kari works across moving image, sound, text and sculpture. In recent research and works she interrogates 'myths of separability' that emerge from modernity/coloniality, and explores notions of 'toxicity' and 'contamination' within complex natureculture contexts. Recent projects include SLEEP UP/WAKE DEEP commission for Lake Radio Copenhagen 2023 and Material Memory exhibition TENT Rotterdam 2022.

Michelle Teran is an artist, educator and researcher. She has many interests. By way of introduction to the reader and to the Promiscuous Care Study Group, she offers research areas that circulate around critical care and regenerative practices and transformative pedagogy with a focus on the ecologies of care, collective grief, feminist, eco-social, and critical pedagogies. She often thinks about discomfort, disturbance, and emergent practices as ways of thinking and practicing through and across difference. She is a professor (lector) of Social Practices at the WdKA Research Center affiliated with the Willem de Kooning Academy in Rotterdam. Michelle Teran received her philosophiae doctor (Ph.D.) in Artistic Research, Faculty of Fine Art, Music and Design, University of Bergen. She is a member of de Zandweg allotment garden community in Rotterdam South where she grows vegetables, experiments with regenerative agriculture methods, and hosts different educational activities. In 2021, she initiated the Promiscuous Care Study Group.

Renée Turner is an artist and writer. Whether working with others or on her own, her research embraces learning from the quotidian, the layered entanglements of space and place and encounters with others in their varied earthliness. She is a Senior Lecturer at the Willem de Kooning Academy, a researcher at the Rotterdam Arts and Sciences Lab, and a Fellow at V2 Lab for the Unstable Media. Currently pursuing a doctorate at LUCA's Intermedia Research Unit: Deep Histories Fragile Memories, her research proposes closely reading and writing through her small urban allotment garden to highlight histories and knowledge embedded within the soil.[1]

Julia Wilhelm is a cultural worker based in Rotterdam. She is interested in building otherwise infrastructures for coming together, critical pedagogy, and rethinking processes of knowledge creation and circulation. In her ongoing research project *Autoarachnology*, she draws from ecofeminist frameworks to investigate how to navigate neoliberal art world infrastructures in search for strategies of resistance. Her affiliations and stewardships include climate justice collective SPIN; embodied research group Cooking Something Up; Nightly Manifesto, a show on WORM Radio; and Reading Rhythms Club, an alternative reading group. She was coordinator for Ultradependent Public School at BAK.

1. Writing a bio blurb always triggers an existential crisis in me. After three decades of writing them, tweaking and tuning them according to context, each time feels like a confrontation that only worsens as I get older. Part of this struggle stems from imposter syndrome—questioning if I am genuinely these things and, if so, what does that mean? And there is all that other stuff that occupies my time which never makes the cut, like being with friends and family, feeding the cat, doing endless amounts of laundry, cooking, parenting, remembering to send out birthday wishes, being a lover, watering plants, watching Netflix, worrying, laughing, sleeping and waking. It reminds me of Anne Boyer's short text *Not Writing*, from *Garments Against Women*. In it, she lists everything she is *not writing*, like memoirs, poems, blurbs, Facebook status updates and much more. (1) It is the guilt list. Then, in the subsequent chapter, she describes all those activities that constitute not writing, such as *"when not working at paid work working at unpaid work like caring for others."* (2) Since caring is a testimony to our connection with others, something of substance, rather than a footnote to our lives, I hope one day I'll be able to write a bio blurb that preserves all those precious ties that bind.

(1) Anne Boyer, *Garments Against Women* (London: Penguin Books, 2019), 51-52.

(2) Ibid.

index

Colophon

Editors
Michelle Teran, Vivian Sky Rehberg, Renée Turner

Outside Editor
Marc Herbst

Contributors
Carla Arcos, Jacquill Basdew, Selma Bellal, Seecum Cheung, Cooking Something Up (Carla Arcos, Yusser al Obaidi, Freeke van der Sterren, Thao Tong, Julia Wilhelm), Yoeri Guépin, Marc Herbst, Czar Kristoff P., Pablo Lerma, Judith Leijdekkers, Carmen José, Edwin Mingard, Skye Maule-O'Brien, Lola Olufemi, Laurence Rassel, Vivian Sky Rehberg, Reading Room Rotterdam, Kari Robertson, Yusser al Obaidi, Michelle Teran, Renée Turner, Julia Wilhelm

Book Design
Yusser al Obaidi, Julia Wilhelm

Paper Inside
80 gr. Circle Offset White

Copy-editing
Marc Herbst, Michelle Teran

Paper Cover
240 gr. Munken Lynx

Poster and Map Illustrations
Carla Arcos

Print
NPN Drukkers, Breda

Typefaces
Diatype Rounded Semi-Mono, G2 Ciao

Publishers
Journal for Aesthetics & Protest, Leipzig
Marc Herbst and Christine Ulke, co-editors
WdKA Research Center, Rotterdam

This book is the research outcome of the Promiscuous Care Study Group. Initiated by Michelle Teran, members of the study group are Carla Arcos, Seecum Cheung, Pablo Lerma, Judith Leijdekkers, Carmen José, Skye Maule-O'Brien, Vivian Sky Rehberg, Kari Robertson, Yusser al Obaidi, Michelle Teran, Renée Turner, and Julia Wilhelm.

It was published with the support of the WdKA Research Center and the Willem de Kooning Academy Rotterdam.

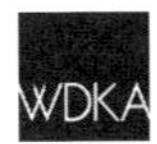

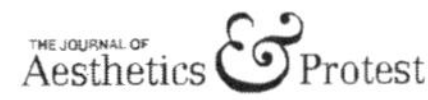

ISBN 979-8-218-36682-7
Rotterdam, 2024. Second print.

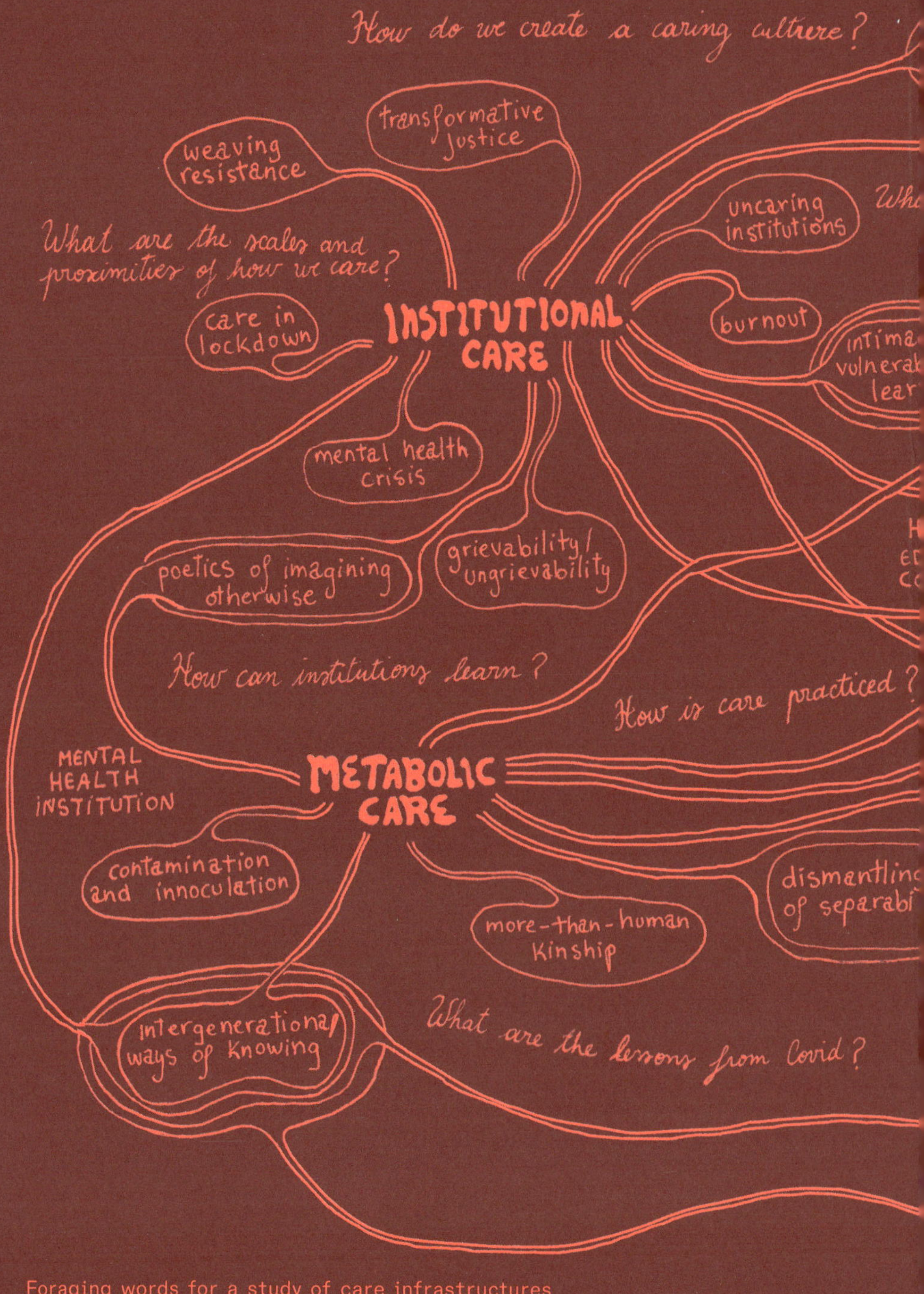

How do we create a caring culture?

transformative justice

weaving resistance

What are the scales and proximities of how we care?

uncaring institutions

burnout

care in lockdown

INSTITUTIONAL CARE

mental health crisis

poetics of imagining otherwise

grievability/ ungrievability

How can institutions learn?

How is care practiced?

MENTAL HEALTH INSTITUTION

METABOLIC CARE

contamination and innoculation

dismantling of separabi

more-than-human kinship

intergenerational ways of knowing

What are the lessons from Covid?